Cloud Computing Simplified: A Practical Guide to Mastering Modern Cloud Technologies

From Fundamentals to Advanced Solutions Across AWS, Azure, and Google Cloud

Lance P. Hancock

Preface

Welcome to *Cloud Computing Simplified: A Practical Guide to Mastering Modern Cloud Technologies*! Whether you're just starting to explore the world of cloud computing or you're looking to deepen your expertise, this book is designed to provide you with a comprehensive, accessible, and hands-on approach to understanding cloud technologies. In the following chapters, we'll demystify cloud computing concepts, explore real-world use cases, and guide you through practical implementations, all while making complex ideas clear and digestible.

Why Cloud Computing?

If you're reading this book, you're likely aware that cloud computing has become a game-changer for businesses of all sizes. In fact, it's hard to imagine a modern organization that doesn't rely on the cloud in some capacity. From launching a website to managing massive datasets or building complex AI-driven systems, cloud technologies have revolutionized the way we work, communicate, and innovate.

What makes cloud computing so compelling? It's about scalability, flexibility, and cost-effectiveness. Rather than spending hefty sums on infrastructure, cloud computing allows companies to leverage shared resources, quickly scale up or down based on demand, and only pay for what they use. In essence, the cloud enables businesses to be agile and responsive, no matter the size or sector.

Who is This Book For?

This book is for anyone interested in understanding the fundamentals and advanced topics of cloud computing. Whether you are:

- A **beginner** looking to understand the foundational concepts of the cloud,
- An **intermediate professional** wanting to dive into hands-on tutorials for popular cloud platforms like AWS, Azure, and Google Cloud,
- An **advanced practitioner** interested in mastering cloud architecture design, automation, or DevOps practices,

- Or a **specialized expert** seeking to apply cloud solutions in fields like healthcare, finance, or retail.

You'll find something for everyone. Each chapter is designed to meet you where you are on your cloud computing journey, with clear explanations, practical examples, and real-world case studies that demonstrate how these technologies are applied across various industries.

What's Inside?

- **Core Cloud Concepts**: We begin with the essentials, helping you build a strong foundation in cloud computing. We'll define key terms, discuss cloud models (IaaS, PaaS, SaaS), and look at deployment models (public, private, hybrid). You'll understand why cloud computing is such a transformative force in the IT world.
- **Hands-on Tutorials**: For those ready to roll up their sleeves, we've included detailed, step-by-step tutorials for popular cloud platforms like **AWS**, **Azure**, and **Google Cloud**. You'll learn how to set up your first cloud instance, deploy applications, manage storage, and configure networks.
- **Cloud Security and Architecture**: As cloud adoption continues to rise, security and architecture are at the forefront of industry conversations. We'll guide you through best practices for securing your cloud environment and designing scalable, reliable systems.
- **Specialized Cloud Use Cases**: We don't just look at generic applications; we dive into specific use cases in industries like **healthcare**, **finance**, and **retail**. How does the cloud power telemedicine? What role does the cloud play in financial services? How are retailers using cloud technologies to enhance customer experience? These chapters will give you a deeper understanding of how cloud computing is being leveraged in the real world.
- **Emerging Trends**: Cloud computing isn't static—it's constantly evolving. We'll cover exciting innovations like **5G**, **edge computing**, and **AI in the cloud**, and explain how these technologies are shaping the future of cloud services.

What You Can Expect

As you read through this book, expect a blend of clear explanations, practical guides, and case studies. My goal is to provide a hands-on, tutorial-driven approach that keeps things practical and actionable. You won't just read about concepts—you'll actively work with them.

Each chapter includes:

- **Hands-on examples**: Tutorials where you'll work directly with cloud platforms to implement what you're learning.
- **Clear visual aids**: Diagrams and flowcharts that will help simplify complex topics and illustrate how cloud services interact in a real-world scenario.
- **Case studies**: Real-world examples from various industries that show how cloud computing is being applied today and where it's heading in the future.

Additionally, this book will give you a solid understanding of **cloud certifications** and the types of cloud jobs available in the market. If you're aiming for a career in cloud computing, we've got you covered with advice on how to get started, earn certifications, and position yourself for success in this exciting field.

A Personal Journey

Cloud computing has changed the way I think about technology, scalability, and infrastructure. Over the years, I've seen how organizations have leveraged the cloud to achieve incredible business outcomes. From automating routine tasks to developing cutting-edge AI applications, the cloud enables incredible innovations. My personal journey with cloud computing has been full of discovery, experimentation, and continuous learning, and I want to share that experience with you.

As I wrote this book, my goal was to make the content as practical and accessible as possible. I've seen firsthand how overwhelming cloud technologies can feel at first, but trust me—once you start connecting the dots and applying these concepts, everything clicks into place. So, whether you're an absolute beginner or someone with intermediate experience, you'll find the tools, knowledge, and resources you need to succeed in the cloud.

This book is just the beginning. The cloud is an ever-evolving landscape, and your journey in cloud computing will be ongoing. As you work through the chapters, I encourage you to experiment, practice, and keep learning. The cloud is vast and filled with possibilities. The more you dive in, the more you'll discover. The skills you develop here will not only open up new career opportunities but also give you the confidence to innovate, build, and contribute to the growing world of cloud computing.

In closing, thank you for choosing this book. I'm excited to join you on this journey into the cloud, and I can't wait to see what you'll build and accomplish as you master cloud technologies. Let's get started!

Table of Contents

Part 1: Introduction to Cloud Computing (For Beginners)

Chapter 1: Understanding Cloud Computing

Cloud computing is one of the most transformative technologies of our time. From small startups to multinational corporations, nearly every business today relies on the cloud in some form. Whether you're storing your data in a cloud service like Google Drive, running complex machine learning models on Amazon Web Services (AWS), or deploying a website via Microsoft Azure, cloud computing has become the backbone of modern IT infrastructure.

In this chapter, we'll break down the basics of cloud computing, its key benefits, the different service and deployment models, and provide a quick introduction to the major cloud providers like AWS, Azure, and Google Cloud.

1.1 What is Cloud Computing?

Cloud computing refers to the delivery of computing services—such as storage, processing, networking, and software—over the internet ("the cloud"). Instead of owning and maintaining physical servers or data centers, businesses and individuals can now rent these services from cloud providers. This "pay-as-you-go" model means you're only paying for the services you use, without the need for upfront investments in hardware or worrying about server maintenance.

Imagine you have a computer at home that you use for various tasks: watching movies, working, or browsing the web. Now, imagine not having to worry about running out of storage space on your device or needing an upgraded graphics card to run new software. This is where cloud computing shines. Instead of relying on your own computer or network, you can store and process data remotely using the vast resources provided by cloud service providers.

Key Concepts:

- **On-Demand Self-Service:** Users can provision resources (such as computing power, storage, etc.) as needed without requiring human intervention from the service provider.
- **Resource Pooling:** Cloud providers use multi-tenant models to pool resources (e.g., servers, storage) to serve multiple customers, maximizing resource utilization.
- **Rapid Elasticity:** Cloud systems can scale resources up or down quickly according to demand. For example, during high traffic periods, a website hosted on the cloud can automatically scale up to handle the load.
- **Measured Service:** Cloud computing is based on a usage-based model, meaning customers pay only for what they use (e.g., computing power, storage).

1.2 Key Benefits of Cloud Computing

Cloud computing offers several advantages that make it an attractive option for businesses and individuals alike. Let's break down some of the key benefits:

1.2.1 Cost Savings

In the past, businesses had to invest in physical hardware, like servers, networking equipment, and data centers. With cloud computing, these upfront costs are significantly reduced, as companies no longer need to purchase and maintain expensive infrastructure. Instead, they can leverage the pay-as-you-go pricing model, paying only for the resources they actually use.

Think of it like paying for a subscription to a gym. You don't have to invest in expensive equipment or worry about maintenance. You simply pay for access to what you need, when you need it.

1.2.2 Scalability

One of the most compelling aspects of cloud computing is scalability. Businesses can quickly scale their computing resources up or down based on demand. For example, if your website sees a sudden spike in visitors during a holiday sale, you can automatically increase your server capacity to handle the traffic. Once the traffic subsides, you can scale back, ensuring you're only paying for the resources you're actively using.

1.2.3 Flexibility

Cloud computing provides incredible flexibility by offering a wide range of services tailored to different needs. Whether you need computing power for running complex algorithms, storage for your files, or advanced machine learning tools, cloud providers offer a variety of services that can be mixed and matched based on your unique requirements.

It's a little like going to a restaurant with a buffet—you choose exactly what you want from a range of options without being restricted to a set menu.

1.2.4 Accessibility

Since cloud services are hosted online, they can be accessed from anywhere, at any time, as long as you have an internet connection. Whether you're at the office, working from home, or traveling abroad, you can access your data and applications from virtually any device, such as a laptop, tablet, or smartphone. This level of accessibility is a huge advantage for businesses with remote teams or those that require employees to be on-the-go.

1.3 Cloud Computing Models

There are three primary models of cloud computing, each providing different levels of control, flexibility, and management. These models are known as **IaaS**, **PaaS**, and **SaaS**.

1.3.1 Infrastructure as a Service (IaaS)

In the IaaS model, the cloud provider delivers **basic infrastructure** services like virtual machines, storage, and networking. It's up to the user to install and manage the operating systems, applications, and development tools they need.

Example: Amazon Web Services (AWS) EC2 is a popular IaaS service that allows you to run virtual servers. You're responsible for setting up the server and managing the software that runs on it.

1.3.2 Platform as a Service (PaaS)

PaaS offers a more **complete platform** for developing and deploying applications. It includes the underlying infrastructure but also provides tools and frameworks for building, testing, and deploying apps. This takes some of the burden off the developer since the platform takes care of the operating system, middleware, and other software layers.

Example: Microsoft Azure's App Service is a PaaS offering that allows developers to deploy applications without managing the infrastructure.

1.3.3 Software as a Service (SaaS)

In the SaaS model, cloud providers deliver **fully managed software applications** over the internet. As a user, you simply log into the application and use it. All infrastructure, maintenance, and software updates are handled by the provider.

Example: Google Workspace (formerly G Suite), which includes Gmail, Docs, Drive, and Calendar, is a popular SaaS platform for personal and business productivity.

1.4 Cloud Deployment Models

Cloud deployment models refer to the **types of cloud environments** that an organization can use to host their applications and data. These models offer varying levels of control, security, and scalability.

1.4.1 Public Cloud

A **public cloud** is owned and operated by a third-party cloud service provider, who makes resources like virtual machines, storage, and networks available to the public. These clouds are shared by multiple organizations, making them cost-effective. However, they may have slightly lower levels of control and security compared to other models.

Example: AWS, Microsoft Azure, and Google Cloud are all examples of public clouds.

1.4.2 Private Cloud

A **private cloud** is a dedicated infrastructure for a single organization, either hosted on-premises or at a third-party provider's data center. This model provides more control over security, but it can be more expensive than the public cloud.

Example: A company may choose a private cloud if they handle sensitive data, like healthcare or financial information, and need a higher level of security and compliance.

1.4.3 Hybrid Cloud

A **hybrid cloud** combines both public and private clouds, allowing data and applications to move between them as needed. This model offers the best of both worlds: the cost-efficiency of public cloud resources with the control and security of private cloud.

Example: A company might use a private cloud for sensitive data and a public cloud for less critical applications.

1.4.4 Community Cloud

A **community cloud** is shared by several organizations with common concerns (e.g., similar compliance requirements or business models). This model offers the benefits of a private cloud while sharing costs among multiple organizations.

Example: A group of healthcare providers may choose a community cloud to store and manage patient data securely, ensuring compliance with healthcare regulations.

1.5 Cloud Service Providers Overview

Let's take a quick look at the three biggest players in the cloud computing space: **AWS**, **Microsoft Azure**, and **Google Cloud**.

1.5.1 AWS (Amazon Web Services)

AWS is the largest and most widely adopted cloud platform, offering a wide range of services such as compute, storage, databases, machine learning, analytics, and much more. AWS is known for its flexibility and vast service offerings, making it a go-to solution for businesses of all sizes.

1.5.2 Microsoft Azure

Azure is a cloud platform developed by Microsoft and is known for its seamless integration with Windows Server, Active Directory, and other Microsoft products. Azure is popular among enterprises that rely heavily on Microsoft products and need a hybrid cloud solution.

1.5.3 Google Cloud

Google Cloud offers a suite of services aimed at artificial intelligence (AI), machine learning (ML), data analytics, and computing. It is known for its **big data and machine learning capabilities**, making it a favorite for companies looking to harness the power of AI in their operations.

In the next chapters, we'll dive deeper into each of these cloud providers and walk you through how to get started with hands-on tutorials. But for now, you have the foundation of cloud computing—its definition, models, benefits, and key players—under your belt.

Remember, whether you're just starting out or looking to scale your business, cloud computing opens up endless possibilities. And with the cloud, all you need is an internet connection to access the world's most powerful computing resources!

Chapter 2: Core Cloud Technologies

In this chapter, we'll explore the core technologies that power cloud computing. These are the building blocks that allow the cloud to deliver on its promises of flexibility, scalability, and cost-efficiency. If you've ever wondered how cloud providers like AWS, Azure, and Google Cloud manage to serve millions of users around the world simultaneously, the answer lies in technologies like **virtualization**, **cloud storage**, **networking**, and **security**.

Let's break these concepts down, step by step, in a way that makes it easy to understand how each technology contributes to the cloud ecosystem. By the end of this chapter, you'll have a clear understanding of these core technologies and how they work together to power the cloud.

2.1 Virtualization Basics

Virtualization is a foundational technology in cloud computing, allowing cloud providers to create efficient, flexible, and scalable infrastructure by using software to divide physical hardware into multiple virtual environments. This technology underpins much of the cloud's power and resource efficiency, and understanding how it works is key to leveraging cloud services effectively.

At its core, **virtualization** allows a single physical machine (a server) to be transformed into multiple **virtual machines (VMs)**, each running its own **operating system (OS)** and applications. The hypervisor manages the distribution of resources to these VMs, ensuring that each operates independently, as though it were on its own physical server.

What is Virtualization?

Imagine a physical server as a hotel building. Traditionally, this building would have a set number of rooms, each reserved for a different guest (application). Virtualization allows you to divide each room into multiple "virtual rooms" (VMs), which can host separate guests, running independently, but all using the same physical space (server resources). The physical building (server) becomes much more efficient by hosting many virtual rooms (VMs), without needing additional space.

This ability to **create virtual instances** from a single physical machine maximizes hardware utilization, offering flexibility, scalability, and resource isolation—all key benefits in cloud computing environments.

How Virtualization Works in Cloud Computing

To grasp the working of virtualization, let's explore the core components and their relationships:

1. **Physical Hardware (Host Machine):**
   This is the actual, physical server, providing essential resources like CPU, RAM, and storage. It's the "foundation" of the virtualization process.
2. **Hypervisor (Virtual Machine Monitor):**
   The **hypervisor** is the software that enables virtualization. It sits between the physical hardware and the virtual machines. The hypervisor allocates the resources of the physical machine (CPU, RAM, storage) to each VM and ensures they operate independently.
   - **Type 1 Hypervisor (Bare-Metal):** Directly installed on the physical hardware, such as VMware ESXi, Microsoft Hyper-V, and Xen.
   - **Type 2 Hypervisor (Hosted):** Runs on top of a traditional operating system, like VMware Workstation and Oracle VirtualBox.
3. **Virtual Machines (VMs):**
   Each VM is an independent, virtualized environment that acts like a separate physical computer. Each VM can run its own guest OS, such as Windows, Linux, or Ubuntu, and host its own set of applications.
4. **Operating Systems and Applications:**
   Inside each virtual machine, an operating system is installed (guest OS), and applications can be run. VMs are isolated from one another, meaning an issue in one VM doesn't affect the others.

The Role of Virtualization in Cloud Computing

Cloud providers like AWS, Microsoft Azure, and Google Cloud use virtualization to deliver scalable computing resources on demand. Virtualization allows them to create virtual instances of servers (VMs) that can be quickly deployed, resized, or terminated based on demand.

Here are the major advantages of virtualization:

- **Resource Efficiency:** Cloud providers use virtualization to run many virtual machines on a single physical server, ensuring that resources are used effectively and eliminating waste.
- **Scalability:** Virtualization enables cloud services to scale rapidly by provisioning additional VMs based on demand. If more compute power is needed, cloud platforms can deploy additional VMs.
- **Isolation and Security:** Each VM is isolated from others, which means they don't interfere with each other, improving both security and stability. For example, if one VM crashes or is compromised, it won't affect others.
- **Cost Efficiency:** By consolidating multiple virtual machines onto a single physical server, cloud providers can maximize their infrastructure and offer cost-effective solutions to customers.

Practical Implementation Example: Virtualization with VMware

Let's walk through a practical example using **VMware ESXi**, a Type 1 hypervisor, which is widely used for virtualization in data centers and cloud environments.

Step-by-Step Guide to Creating a Virtual Machine on VMware ESXi:

1. **Install VMware ESXi:**
   - Install VMware ESXi on the physical server, which will act as the host machine. ESXi provides the platform for virtualization.
2. **Access VMware vSphere Client:**

- o Use the VMware vSphere client to connect to the ESXi server. This allows you to manage and monitor the virtual machines on the host.

3. **Create a New Virtual Machine:**
   - o In the vSphere client, select "Create New Virtual Machine" and follow the wizard. You will need to specify the following:
     - **Select the OS type**: Choose the type of OS you want to install (Windows, Linux, etc.).
     - **Allocate resources**: Assign CPU, RAM, and storage to the VM based on the resources available on the host machine.

4. **Install the Operating System:**
   - o After creating the VM, mount the installation ISO file of the desired operating system (e.g., Windows Server or Ubuntu), then start the VM and proceed with the OS installation.

5. **Run Applications:**
   - o Once the OS is installed, you can begin installing and running applications on the VM, such as a web server or database, just as you would on a physical machine.

Case Study: Virtualization in Action (AWS EC2)

AWS EC2 (Elastic Compute Cloud) is a perfect example of virtualization in the cloud. Let's consider how EC2 instances are launched and managed in AWS:

Scenario: Hosting a Web Application on EC2

1. **Launch an EC2 Instance:**
   - o In AWS, you can launch a virtual server called an EC2 instance. Select the desired instance type, which defines the amount of CPU, memory, and storage for the instance.

2. **Install Web Server Software:**
   - o Once the instance is running, you can SSH into the EC2 instance and install web server software like Apache or Nginx to serve your website.

3. **Scalability:**

- o If the website experiences more traffic, you can scale your EC2 instance by increasing its resources or creating additional instances using auto-scaling.
4. **Cost Efficiency:**
   - o AWS charges based on the resources used, so if you scale up or down, you only pay for what you consume. Virtualization makes this resource allocation efficient and cost-effective.

Text-Based Flowchart: Virtualization Process

Here's a **text-based sketch** of how virtualization works:

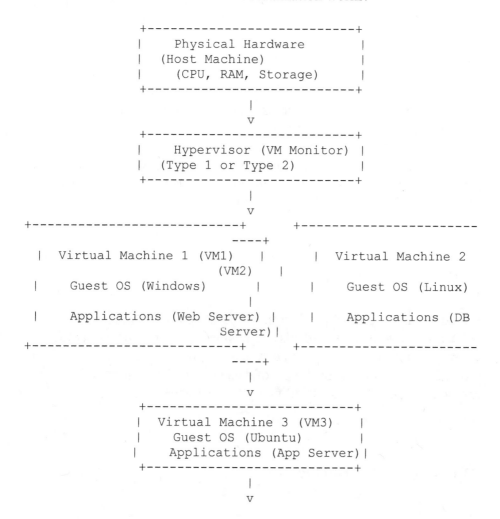

```
         +----------------------------+
         |     Physical Hardware      |
         |    (Host Machine)          |
         |     (CPU, RAM, Storage)    |
         +----------------------------+
                       |
                       v
         +----------------------------+
         |   Hypervisor (VM Monitor)  |
         |   (Type 1 or Type 2)       |
         +----------------------------+
                       |
                       v
+-------------------------------+     +----------------------
                          ----+
|  Virtual Machine 1 (VM1)    |     |  Virtual Machine 2
                     (VM2)    |
|    Guest OS (Windows)       |     |    Guest OS (Linux)
                             |
|   Applications (Web Server) |     |   Applications (DB
                     Server) |
+-------------------------------+     +----------------------
                          ----+
                       |
                       v
         +----------------------------+
         |   Virtual Machine 3 (VM3)  |
         |     Guest OS (Ubuntu)      |
         |    Applications (App Server)|
         +----------------------------+
                       |
                       v
```

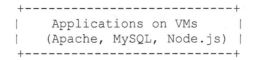

```
+---------------------------+
|     Applications on VMs   |
|   (Apache, MySQL, Node.js)|
+---------------------------+
```

Key Points from the Flowchart:

- **Physical Hardware** is the resource base, providing CPU, memory, and storage.
- The **Hypervisor** manages the virtual machines, allocating hardware resources and ensuring isolation between them.
- **Virtual Machines (VMs)** run on the hypervisor, each with its own guest OS and applications, like web servers, database servers, or application servers.
- **VMs are isolated** from each other, meaning they don't interfere with one another, offering flexibility and security.

Virtualization is the backbone of modern cloud computing. It allows for the efficient allocation of resources, enabling cloud providers to deliver scalable, flexible, and cost-effective solutions. By understanding the basic concepts of virtualization, such as the role of the hypervisor, virtual machines, and how they relate to physical hardware, you can appreciate how cloud services like AWS, Azure, and Google Cloud manage vast amounts of data and workloads efficiently.

2.2 Cloud Storage

Cloud storage is one of the most transformative aspects of cloud computing. It allows individuals and businesses to store data over the internet instead of on local hard drives or physical storage devices. Cloud storage has become the backbone of data storage for a variety of reasons, including scalability, accessibility, cost-effectiveness, and security.

What is Cloud Storage?

Cloud storage is a service that allows users to store data remotely on the internet, provided by third-party cloud service providers like Amazon Web Services (AWS), Microsoft Azure, and Google Cloud. Instead of relying on physical storage devices (like hard drives or on-premise data centers), cloud storage enables data to be stored and accessed over the internet, providing many benefits such as easy accessibility, flexibility, and scalability.

Imagine you have a hard drive with a certain amount of space. The more data you add, the less space you have available. Now, think of cloud storage as a hard drive on the internet that you can expand and shrink according to your needs, without worrying about running out of space or maintaining hardware.

Cloud storage offers three primary types, each suited for different use cases:

- **Object Storage**
- **Block Storage**
- **File Storage**

Let's dive into each of these.

2.2.1 Types of Cloud Storage

Object Storage

Object storage is the most commonly used cloud storage type for storing large amounts of unstructured data. Data is stored as individual objects, each containing the data itself, metadata (information about the data), and a unique identifier. This type of storage is highly scalable, flexible, and cost-effective, making it perfect for storing things like media files, backups, and data archives.

Example: Amazon S3 (Simple Storage Service) is a widely used object storage service, allowing businesses and individuals to store vast amounts of data, such as images, videos, and backups.

How it works:

- **Data is stored as objects**: Each file is treated as an object, with metadata and a unique identifier. This differs from traditional file systems, where files are stored as blocks in directories.
- **Scalability**: You can scale storage capacity effortlessly. Need more storage? Just increase your usage without worrying about running out of space.
- **Redundancy**: Cloud providers store data redundantly across multiple servers and locations, ensuring durability and availability.

Use cases:

- **Backup and Disaster Recovery**: Storing backups in cloud object storage helps ensure that data is safely kept off-site and is easy to retrieve if needed.
- **Media Content**: Streaming platforms store videos, audio files, and images in object storage due to its high scalability and performance.

Block Storage

Block storage is a type of storage that divides data into fixed-size blocks, which are stored across different physical or virtual disks. Each block can be independently managed, which makes it ideal for applications requiring high-performance storage like databases or virtual machines.

Example: Amazon EBS (Elastic Block Store) provides block-level storage for EC2 instances in AWS. It allows users to attach storage volumes to their virtual machines (VMs), ensuring low-latency and high-performance data access.

How it works:

- **Data is stored in blocks**: Block storage splits data into fixed-sized blocks. Each block is independently addressed and can be read or written to separately.
- **Performance**: Since blocks can be read or written to independently, it offers high-performance, low-latency storage ideal for database systems and transactional applications.
- **Persistence**: Unlike object storage, block storage can be attached to a VM, allowing the VM to access the data as though it were on a physical disk.

Use cases:

- **Databases**: Block storage is the go-to option for databases that require fast, low-latency access to data, such as SQL databases.
- **Virtual Machines**: When using cloud-based VMs, block storage is used to provide persistent storage for the VMs, allowing them to retain data even after they are stopped or restarted.

File Storage

File storage is a traditional form of cloud storage where data is stored in a hierarchical structure, similar to how it is stored on your local computer (directories and files). This storage type is often used for applications that need to access files over the network, like content management systems and file-sharing applications.

Example: Azure Files is a managed file share in the cloud, allowing users to store and access files using the SMB (Server Message Block) protocol.

How it works:

- **Data is stored as files in directories**: Just like a local file system, file storage organizes data in directories and files.
- **Network accessibility**: File storage is accessed via network protocols like NFS (Network File System) or SMB, making it ideal for applications that require file sharing and network file access.
- **Collaboration**: It enables file sharing between multiple machines, making it easy to work with teams or share data across an organization.

Use cases:

- **Enterprise File Shares**: Businesses use file storage to store documents, spreadsheets, and other files that need to be accessed by multiple employees.
- **Application Data**: Applications that rely on file systems (like content management systems) use file storage for storing data.

2.2.2 Choosing the Right Type of Cloud Storage

The type of cloud storage you choose depends on the needs of your application or business. Here's a quick breakdown of when to use each type:

Cloud Storage Type	Best For
Object Storage	Large-scale, unstructured data like media files, backups, and archives.
Block Storage	High-performance storage for databases, virtual machines, and transactional applications.
File Storage	File-based applications, collaborative work, or situations requiring shared access to files.

2.2.3 Practical Implementation of Cloud Storage

Let's explore a practical implementation example using **Amazon S3** for object storage. We'll go through the steps to upload a file to S3 and access it.

Step-by-Step Guide to Uploading Files to Amazon S3

1. **Set up an AWS Account and Create an S3 Bucket**:
   - Go to the AWS S3 console and create a new **S3 bucket**. Buckets are containers for storing objects in S3.
   - Choose a unique name for the bucket (e.g., `my-cloud-storage-bucket`) and select a region.
2. **Upload a File to the S3 Bucket**:
   - Once the bucket is created, click on it to open the bucket view.
   - Click on the "Upload" button, and select a file from your computer to upload.
   - After the file is uploaded, it will be stored as an object in the bucket, where you can access it using the S3 URL.
3. **Set Permissions**:
   - To make the file publicly accessible (optional), you can set the permissions for the object. By default, files are private,

but you can adjust the settings to allow public read access if needed.

4. **Access the File**:
   o Once the file is uploaded and permissions are set, you can access it using the generated S3 URL. For example:

```
https://my-cloud-storage-
bucket.s3.amazonaws.com/filename.jpg
```

   o You can download the file using this URL or programmatically access it via the AWS SDK.

Here's an example of uploading a file programmatically using the AWS SDK for Python (Boto3):

```python
import boto3

# Initialize the S3 client
s3 = boto3.client('s3')

# Upload a file
s3.upload_file('localfile.jpg', 'my-cloud-storage-bucket',
'remote-file.jpg')

print("File uploaded successfully!")
```

2.2.4 Case Study: Cloud Storage for Media Streaming

Let's take a look at how cloud storage is used in the **media streaming industry**.

Scenario: Streaming Service Using Object Storage

A media streaming platform needs to store and serve millions of videos to users around the world. The platform chooses Amazon S3 for its object storage due to its scalability, durability, and low cost.

Steps Involved:

1. **Uploading Videos**: The platform stores each video file as an object in S3, ensuring that each video is unique and easily accessible.

2. **Global Delivery**: To ensure fast delivery of content globally, the platform integrates S3 with **Amazon CloudFront** (a CDN service). This caches video content at edge locations worldwide, reducing latency and speeding up delivery.
3. **Scalability**: As the platform grows and more videos are added, the object storage grows seamlessly without the need to worry about capacity planning.

Cloud storage has revolutionized how we manage and store data. Whether you're working with massive datasets, hosting media content, or running high-performance applications, cloud storage provides scalable, cost-effective, and secure solutions. By understanding the differences between object storage, block storage, and file storage, and knowing when to use each type, you can make more informed decisions about how to store and access your data in the cloud.

From **backup and disaster recovery** to **media streaming** and **enterprise file sharing**, cloud storage offers an unparalleled level of flexibility and convenience. Whether you're just getting started with cloud computing or managing a large-scale business, cloud storage is essential for modern data management.

2.3 Networking and Cloud Connectivity

Networking is one of the most fundamental aspects of cloud computing. It ensures that different cloud resources, such as virtual machines, databases, storage, and applications, can communicate with each other and with the outside world. Cloud connectivity is crucial to ensure seamless performance, security, and scalability in cloud-based environments.

What is Cloud Networking?

Cloud networking refers to the design, management, and optimization of networks within a cloud environment. The network forms the foundation that allows resources to communicate, share data, and access services.

Without proper networking, cloud applications, storage systems, and even simple web pages would not be able to function effectively.

Why Cloud Networking Matters

In traditional IT infrastructure, networking happens within the confines of a local area network (LAN). However, in the cloud, resources might be spread across different data centers globally. Cloud networking ensures that resources communicate efficiently, securely, and in a cost-effective manner.

Cloud networking includes:

- **Private and Public Networks**: Segregating data and systems for security.
- **Load Balancing**: Distributing traffic efficiently across multiple servers.
- **Domain Name System (DNS)**: Resolving domain names to IP addresses for accessibility.
- **Content Delivery Networks (CDN)**: Caching content closer to the user for faster delivery.

Let's break down each of these networking concepts in detail.

2.3.1 Virtual Private Cloud (VPC)

A **Virtual Private Cloud (VPC)** is a private, isolated network within a cloud environment, where cloud resources can be launched. It allows you to define your own IP address range, subnets, route tables, and network gateways. It essentially provides a "cloud-based data center" where you control the network infrastructure.

A VPC ensures that your cloud resources are isolated from other users in the same public cloud, ensuring privacy and security.

1. **Subnets**: A VPC can be divided into multiple subnets, which are essentially smaller network segments. Subnets can be **public** (exposed to the internet) or **private** (isolated from the internet).
2. **Routing**: You can control the traffic flow between subnets using **route tables**. This helps in defining how data moves between subnets and to/from the internet.
3. **Internet Gateway (IGW)**: The IGW enables instances within your VPC to communicate with the internet, such as web servers.
4. **NAT Gateway**: The **Network Address Translation (NAT)** gateway allows instances in private subnets to access the internet for tasks like software updates, while still keeping them hidden from public access.
5. **Security Groups and Network ACLs**: Security groups act like firewalls for controlling inbound and outbound traffic at the instance level, while Network ACLs provide an additional layer of security at the subnet level.

Case Study: Setting up a VPC in AWS

Let's walk through the steps of creating a VPC in AWS.

1. **Create a VPC**:
   o Go to the **VPC dashboard** in the AWS Management Console.
   o Click on **Create VPC**, then choose the **CIDR block** (e.g., `10.0.0.0/16`), which defines the IP range for the VPC.
2. **Create Subnets**:
   o Create two subnets: a **public subnet** (for web servers) and a **private subnet** (for databases).
   o Assign a **subnet CIDR** to each, such as `10.0.1.0/24` for the public subnet.
3. **Create an Internet Gateway (IGW)**:
   o In the VPC dashboard, go to **Internet Gateways** and click **Create Internet Gateway**.
   o Attach it to the VPC to enable communication with the internet.
4. **Set up Route Tables**:
   o Create a route table for each subnet. For the public subnet, add a route to the IGW.

o For the private subnet, create a route to a **NAT Gateway** for internet access.
5. **Create EC2 Instances**:
    o Launch EC2 instances in the public subnet (e.g., web servers) and private subnet (e.g., database servers).

By following these steps, you will have a secure, scalable, and isolated network within AWS for hosting your cloud applications.

2.3.2 Load Balancing

In cloud computing, **load balancing** is the process of distributing incoming traffic across multiple servers to ensure that no single server is overwhelmed. This enhances availability and fault tolerance while ensuring optimal resource utilization.

How it Works

- **Traffic Distribution**: Load balancers monitor the health of servers in a server pool and route traffic only to healthy servers. This prevents downtime and ensures that users are always connected to responsive servers.
- **Types of Load Balancers**:
    o **Layer 4 Load Balancer (TCP/UDP)**: Operates at the transport layer, directing traffic based on IP address and port.
    o **Layer 7 Load Balancer (HTTP/HTTPS)**: Operates at the application layer, directing traffic based on HTTP headers, URLs, cookies, and other application data.

Example: AWS Elastic Load Balancer (ELB)

AWS ELB automatically distributes incoming application traffic across multiple targets, such as EC2 instances. Here's how you can configure it:

1. **Create an ELB**:
    o Navigate to **EC2 Dashboard** → **Load Balancers** → **Create Load Balancer**.

o Choose between **Classic Load Balancer, Application Load Balancer**, or **Network Load Balancer** based on your needs.
2. **Configure Listeners**:
   o Specify protocols (HTTP/HTTPS) and ports (80/443) for your load balancer to listen for incoming traffic.
3. **Add Targets**:
   o Choose the instances (e.g., web servers) that will receive traffic. These will be automatically registered as targets for the load balancer.
4. **Health Checks**:
   o Configure health checks to ensure that only healthy instances receive traffic.

2.3.3 Domain Name System (DNS)

The **Domain Name System (DNS)** is the system that translates domain names (like `www.example.com`) into IP addresses (like `192.168.1.1`). DNS is essential for making websites and services accessible using human-readable names instead of numerical IP addresses.

How it Works

- When a user enters a domain name in a web browser, the DNS resolver looks up the corresponding IP address from a DNS server. The browser then uses this IP address to connect to the server hosting the website.
- **DNS Record Types**:
  o **A Record**: Maps a domain to an IP address.
  o **CNAME Record**: Aliases one domain to another (e.g., `www.example.com` to `example.com`).
  o **MX Record**: Specifies mail servers for a domain.

Example: Setting up DNS in AWS Route 53

1. **Create a Hosted Zone**:
   o Navigate to **Route 53** in the AWS Console and create a hosted zone for your domain (e.g., `example.com`).

2. **Add DNS Records**:
   - o Add **A records** to map your domain to the IP address of your EC2 instance.
   - o Add **CNAME records** for subdomains like www to point to the root domain.
3. **Use Route 53 for Health Checks**:
   - o Route 53 can perform health checks on your endpoints (e.g., EC2 instances) and automatically route traffic away from unhealthy instances.

2.3.4 Content Delivery Networks (CDN)

A **Content Delivery Network (CDN)** is a network of distributed servers that deliver web content (such as videos, images, and scripts) to users based on their geographic location. CDNs reduce latency and speed up content delivery by caching content closer to end-users.

How it Works

- **Edge Locations**: A CDN caches content in edge locations, which are data centers located around the world.
- **Caching**: When a user requests content, the CDN checks the nearest edge location to serve it. If the content is not cached, the CDN fetches it from the origin server and stores it in the edge location for future requests.

Example: Using AWS CloudFront

1. **Create a CloudFront Distribution**:
   - o Go to the **CloudFront Console** in AWS and click **Create Distribution**.
   - o Choose the **Origin** (e.g., an S3 bucket or web server) where your content is stored.
2. **Configure Distribution Settings**:
   - o Set cache behaviors to determine how CloudFront caches your content.
   - o You can also configure security settings (SSL/TLS) for secure connections.
3. **Distribute Content**:

- o Once set up, CloudFront will automatically cache and serve content to users from the nearest edge location.

Cloud networking is essential for ensuring that cloud resources communicate efficiently, securely, and reliably. By understanding how **Virtual Private Clouds (VPCs)**, **load balancing**, **DNS**, and **CDNs** work, you can design a cloud network that is both robust and scalable.

From isolating your cloud resources within a VPC to using load balancers for traffic distribution, cloud networking enables high performance, high availability, and security. Whether you're building an enterprise application or hosting a website, mastering cloud networking is key to optimizing your cloud infrastructure and delivering a seamless experience to your users.

2.4 Introduction to Cloud Security

Cloud security is one of the most critical aspects of cloud computing, as it ensures the protection of data, applications, and services within a cloud environment. As organizations increasingly migrate their workloads to the cloud, safeguarding sensitive information and ensuring the availability of services becomes paramount. Cloud security is not just about protecting data from cyberattacks; it is about creating a robust framework that prevents unauthorized access, ensures data integrity, maintains confidentiality, and guarantees the availability of services. Whether you are a developer, system administrator, or business leader, understanding cloud security is essential for building resilient and secure cloud-based applications.

What is Cloud Security?

Cloud security refers to the policies, technologies, and controls used to protect data, applications, and services hosted in the cloud. Unlike traditional on-premises IT security, cloud security involves multiple stakeholders: the **cloud service provider (CSP)**, the **cloud customer**, and often, third-party security tools or services.

Cloud security encompasses a wide range of techniques and principles, including encryption, identity and access management (IAM), multi-factor authentication (MFA), network security, and compliance.

Think of cloud security as a multi-layered defense system: the provider secures the infrastructure (physical security, data centers), while the customer is responsible for securing their own applications, data, and user access.

Why is Cloud Security Important?

1. **Data Breaches**: As more data moves to the cloud, the risk of breaches and unauthorized access increases. A breach could expose sensitive information, leading to financial losses and reputational damage.
2. **Regulatory Compliance**: Many industries are subject to regulations (such as GDPR, HIPAA, PCI-DSS) that require strict data protection standards. Cloud security ensures compliance with these standards.
3. **Data Availability**: With cloud services being accessible from anywhere, security measures must ensure that the data remains available and intact, even in the face of potential cyber threats.
4. **Shared Responsibility Model**: In cloud environments, security is a shared responsibility between the customer and the cloud provider. Understanding this model is crucial for ensuring proper security measures.

2.4.1 Core Principles of Cloud Security

Let's break down the key principles that form the foundation of cloud security:

1. Confidentiality

Confidentiality ensures that sensitive data is only accessible to those authorized to view it. Encryption plays a crucial role in confidentiality by encoding data so that only users with the decryption key can access it.

Example: In AWS, **Amazon S3** provides server-side encryption to ensure that data stored in buckets is encrypted before being written to disk. Only users with the correct permissions can decrypt and access this data.

2. Integrity

Integrity ensures that data remains accurate, consistent, and unaltered during storage or transmission. Hashing and digital signatures are commonly used techniques to verify data integrity.

Example: When sending data over the internet, cloud providers use **TLS/SSL encryption** to ensure that data isn't tampered with during transmission. Digital signatures can be used to verify the integrity of the data when it reaches its destination.

3. Availability

Availability ensures that cloud services and data are accessible to authorized users whenever needed. This principle is vital for cloud applications that must be up and running 24/7.

Example: **AWS Elastic Load Balancer (ELB)** can distribute incoming application traffic across multiple servers, ensuring that if one server fails, others can handle the traffic, thereby maintaining availability.

2.4.2 Key Components of Cloud Security

To implement cloud security effectively, there are several critical components that need to be addressed. Let's look at each of these in more detail.

1. Identity and Access Management (IAM)

IAM is a framework for managing digital identities and controlling user access to cloud resources. IAM ensures that only authorized individuals or services can access resources and data within a cloud environment.

- **Roles and Permissions**: Assigning specific roles to users or groups to ensure they have the correct level of access.
- **Policy Management**: Cloud providers like AWS, Azure, and Google Cloud allow the creation of access policies that determine who can access what resources and what actions they can perform.

Example: In **AWS IAM**, administrators can create IAM roles with specific permissions (e.g., `AdministratorAccess` or `ReadOnlyAccess`) and assign those roles to users or services.

Code Example: In AWS, to create an IAM role with `S3ReadOnlyAccess`, you can use the following code snippet (via AWS CLI):

```
aws iam create-role --role-name ReadOnlyRole \
--assume-role-policy-document file://trust-policy.json

aws iam attach-role-policy --role-name ReadOnlyRole \
--policy-arn arn:aws:iam::aws:policy/AmazonS3ReadOnlyAccess
```

This sets up a role that gives users only read access to S3 buckets.

2. Encryption

Encryption is one of the cornerstones of cloud security. It ensures that data is unreadable to unauthorized users, even if they gain access to it. Both **data-at-rest** and **data-in-transit** should be encrypted.

- **Data-at-rest**: Data stored on disk or in databases.
- **Data-in-transit**: Data being transferred across networks.

Cloud providers like AWS, Google Cloud, and Azure offer built-in encryption mechanisms for both types of data.

Example: AWS offers **AWS Key Management Service (KMS)**, which allows customers to create and manage encryption keys for their data, enabling both data-at-rest and data-in-transit encryption.

3. Multi-Factor Authentication (MFA)

MFA is a security measure that requires users to provide two or more verification factors to gain access to a system, making it harder for unauthorized users to breach accounts.

- **Something you know**: A password or PIN.
- **Something you have**: A smartphone app or hardware token for generating verification codes.
- **Something you are**: Biometric data like fingerprints or facial recognition.

Example: In AWS, users can enable MFA to protect their accounts. When logging in, users are required to provide their password and a one-time code generated by their MFA device.

4. Network Security

Network security in the cloud includes measures to prevent unauthorized access to cloud services over the network. This is typically achieved through **firewalls, VPNs,** and **Virtual Private Networks (VPCs).**

- **Security Groups**: Firewalls that control traffic at the instance level.
- **Network Access Control Lists (ACLs)**: Control traffic at the subnet level.
- **Virtual Private Networks (VPNs)**: Secure communication channels between the on-premise environment and the cloud.

Example: In **AWS, Security Groups** act as virtual firewalls to control inbound and outbound traffic for EC2 instances.

5. Monitoring and Logging

Effective monitoring and logging are essential to detect security incidents and maintain compliance. Cloud providers offer services to monitor activities and generate logs that can be analyzed to identify unusual behaviors.

- **CloudTrail (AWS)**: Provides logs of all API calls made within the AWS environment.

- **Azure Monitor**: Collects and analyzes data from Azure resources.

Example: Using **AWS CloudTrail**, you can track API calls made to your AWS resources, such as creating or deleting EC2 instances, and investigate suspicious activity.

```
aws cloudtrail lookup-events --lookup-attributes
AttributeKey=EventName,AttributeValue=CreateBucket
```

This command will retrieve logs of all events related to creating an S3 bucket.

2.4.3 Cloud Security Best Practices

To help organizations implement effective cloud security, here are some best practices:

1. **Apply the Principle of Least Privilege**: Ensure that users and services have only the minimum level of access necessary to perform their jobs.
2. **Regularly Rotate Keys and Passwords**: Rotate access keys and passwords regularly to minimize the risk of credential theft.
3. **Use Encryption Everywhere**: Always encrypt sensitive data both in transit and at rest, using strong encryption algorithms.
4. **Monitor and Audit Activities**: Implement continuous monitoring and audit logging to detect and respond to suspicious activity quickly.
5. **Implement MFA**: Require multi-factor authentication for all users, especially those with administrative privileges.

2.4.4 Case Study: Cloud Security in E-Commerce

Let's consider an e-commerce platform that migrates its infrastructure to AWS. The platform sells high-value items, such as electronics, and needs to comply with PCI-DSS (Payment Card Industry Data Security Standard) regulations.

Steps Taken:

1. **VPC Setup**: The e-commerce platform sets up a VPC with private subnets for databases and public subnets for web servers.
2. **Encryption**: The platform uses **AWS KMS** to encrypt sensitive customer data at rest and **SSL/TLS** for encrypting data in transit.
3. **IAM Roles**: Specific IAM roles are created with strict permissions for employees accessing the system. Only authorized employees can access payment information.
4. **MFA**: MFA is enabled for all administrative accounts to add an extra layer of protection.
5. **Continuous Monitoring**: **AWS CloudTrail** and **AWS GuardDuty** are used to monitor API calls and detect any unauthorized access attempts.

Result:

By implementing these security measures, the e-commerce platform ensures that sensitive customer data is secure, complies with PCI-DSS, and can handle large traffic spikes while minimizing the risk of data breaches.

Cloud security is an ongoing process that requires a mix of technical measures, policies, and best practices. By understanding the core principles of **confidentiality**, **integrity**, and **availability**, and by implementing strong security controls such as IAM, encryption, MFA, and network security, you can build a robust security posture in the cloud. The key is to stay vigilant and continuously monitor your cloud environment to identify and address potential threats.

As cloud computing evolves, so too must our approach to security. Adopting a layered security model that includes both preventive and detective controls will ensure that your cloud infrastructure remains secure and resilient in the face of an ever-changing threat landscape.

Part 2: Hands-on Tutorials with AWS, Azure, and Google Cloud (Intermediate Level)

Chapter 3: Getting Started with Amazon Web Services (AWS)

Welcome to the world of Amazon Web Services (AWS), the most widely adopted cloud platform globally. Whether you're building a website, hosting applications, or managing databases, AWS offers a comprehensive set of tools to get you started. In this chapter, we'll dive into the practical aspects of using AWS, walking you through setting up your account, launching your first EC2 instance, and working with some of AWS's most essential services like S3 and VPC.

This chapter is designed for beginners and intermediate users, so if you're new to AWS or cloud computing in general, you're in the right place. Let's get started!

3.1 Creating an AWS Account

Before you can begin using Amazon Web Services (AWS), you need to create an AWS account. This is the first step in harnessing the full power of cloud computing, whether you're a small business, a developer, or part of a large enterprise. Setting up an account is straightforward, but understanding the process and the services you'll use as part of your AWS journey is key to making the most out of your cloud experience.

Step 1: Visit the AWS Website

Start by going to the official AWS website:
https://aws.amazon.com

Once you're there, click on the **"Create a Free Account"** button. AWS provides a Free Tier for new users, which allows you to use many AWS services for free up to a certain limit. This is an excellent way to get started and experiment with various services without worrying about charges (at least, until you exceed the Free Tier limits).

Step 2: Enter Your Email Address and Set Up a Password

After clicking **Create a Free Account**, AWS will prompt you for the following details:

1. **Email Address**: Enter your email address that will be associated with your AWS account. This is the main communication channel for AWS notifications, such as billing updates, service changes, and promotions.
2. **Password**: Choose a secure password. Make sure your password is strong—ideally, use a combination of uppercase and lowercase letters, numbers, and special characters to create a unique, secure password.
3. **AWS Account Name**: This is the name that will represent your AWS account. You can choose any name, but it should be something meaningful to you or your organization, such as the name of your business or project.

Step 3: Enter Billing Information

AWS requires you to provide billing information, including a **credit card** or **debit card** number, even for new users on the Free Tier. Don't worry, AWS won't charge you unless you exceed the Free Tier limits. However, you still need to enter your payment details to verify your identity and for possible future usage.

1. **Credit or Debit Card Information**: Enter your card details (such as the card number, expiration date, and CVV). AWS accepts major credit and debit cards, including Visa, MasterCard, and American Express.
2. **Billing Address**: Provide your billing address to help AWS verify your identity. This is standard for any online service that requires payment details.

3. **Phone Number**: AWS requires you to verify your identity via phone. This verification step is part of AWS's security measures to ensure that the person creating the account is legitimate.

Step 4: Identity Verification

AWS performs a **phone verification** as part of the account creation process. You'll be asked to provide your phone number, and AWS will send you a verification code via **text message (SMS)** or **voice call**.

1. **Choose Verification Method**: AWS gives you the option to verify via SMS or voice call. Select the option that works best for you and enter the code when prompted.
2. **Complete Verification**: Once you receive the verification code, enter it in the appropriate field and click **Verify**. This step ensures that you're a legitimate user and not a bot.

Step 5: Select a Support Plan

AWS offers several **support plans** that provide varying levels of support. For new users, you can start with the **Basic Support Plan**, which is **free** and provides access to AWS documentation, FAQs, and community forums.

- **Basic Support**: This is free and includes access to 24/7 customer service, access to documentation, and limited support for AWS services.
- **Developer Support**: This plan provides 12-hour response times for non-critical issues and costs around **$29/month**.
- **Business Support**: Includes 24/7 support and more personalized help, costing approximately **$100/month**.
- **Enterprise Support**: Tailored to large enterprises, with dedicated technical account managers and 24/7 support, starting at **$15,000/month**.

If you're just starting out, stick with the **Basic Support Plan**. You can always upgrade later as your needs grow.

Step 6: Complete the Sign-Up Process

After completing all the steps above, click **Complete Sign-Up**. AWS will review the information you've entered, and your account will be set up within a few minutes. You'll receive an email confirming that your account is ready.

At this stage, you can log into your **AWS Management Console**, which is the interface you'll use to create and manage all your AWS resources.

Step 7: Log in to the AWS Management Console

Once your account is set up, return to the AWS homepage and click on **Sign in to the Console**. You'll use the email and password you set during the sign-up process to log in.

When you log in, you'll be taken to the **AWS Management Console**, a web interface where you can manage all your AWS services.

Understanding the AWS Management Console

When you first enter the **AWS Management Console**, it may seem overwhelming due to the vast array of services and tools available. However, once you understand the layout, it's easy to navigate and begin utilizing AWS.

Here's a breakdown of the key elements you'll interact with:

1. **Search Bar**: At the top of the screen, you'll find a search bar. This allows you to quickly find services or documentation. For example, typing **EC2** will direct you to the **EC2 Dashboard** for launching and managing virtual machines.
2. **Services Menu**: On the left side, you'll see a list of AWS services categorized into different sections like **Compute**, **Storage**,

Networking, **Databases**, and **Security**. This is your gateway to all AWS resources.

3. **Dashboard**: The main screen will provide an overview of your AWS account. You can check things like your **usage** (under the Free Tier), **billing**, and **recent activity**.

4. **Resource Management**: When you select a specific service, such as EC2 or S3, you'll be taken to the **dashboard** for that service, where you can create, configure, and manage resources.

Managing Your AWS Account and Free Tier

AWS offers a **Free Tier** that allows new users to explore and use many services for free up to specific limits. The Free Tier is perfect for getting hands-on experience without incurring charges. Here's a quick breakdown of what's included in the AWS Free Tier:

- **Amazon EC2**: 750 hours of **t2.micro** instance usage per month for 12 months.
- **Amazon S3**: 5 GB of standard storage and 20,000 GET requests and 2,000 PUT requests per month.
- **AWS Lambda**: 1 million free requests and 400,000 GB-seconds of compute time each month.

You can monitor your Free Tier usage by visiting the **Billing Dashboard** in the AWS Management Console. This will give you an overview of your usage across all services and help ensure you don't go over the Free Tier limits.

Security and Account Settings

Now that you've created your AWS account, it's essential to secure it. Here are some tips to help you do that:

1. **Enable Multi-Factor Authentication (MFA)**: This is an additional layer of security. It ensures that even if someone has your password, they won't be able to access your account without a second authentication factor (e.g., a code sent to your phone).

2. **Create IAM Users**: Instead of using your root account for everyday activities, create **IAM users** with appropriate permissions. This minimizes the risk of accidentally changing critical settings or compromising your account.
3. **Set Up Billing Alerts**: To avoid unexpected costs, set up billing alerts to notify you if you're approaching the Free Tier limits or if your usage exceeds a certain threshold.

Case Study: Setting Up an AWS Account for a New Startup

Let's consider a startup, **TechSolutions**, that's just getting started with cloud computing. They decide to set up an AWS account to host their website and store files for internal use.

Steps Taken:

1. **Account Creation**: The founder, Sarah, creates an AWS account using her business email and credit card details. She selects the **Basic Support Plan** and enables **multi-factor authentication** to ensure account security.
2. **Free Tier Exploration**: Sarah starts by exploring the **Free Tier**, launching an EC2 instance to test hosting their website. She also uploads some files to **Amazon S3** for internal document storage.
3. **Security Setup**: Sarah configures **IAM roles** to limit access to sensitive resources. She assigns her development team to use the **DeveloperAccess** role, restricting them from accessing billing or administrative resources.
4. **Monitoring Costs**: She sets up billing alerts to monitor the usage of EC2 and S3, ensuring the startup stays within the Free Tier's limits.

By following these steps, TechSolutions successfully launched its website and secured its cloud environment while keeping costs low.

Creating an AWS account is the first step toward building and managing your cloud resources. By following the steps outlined in this guide, you can quickly get your AWS account set up, start using the Free Tier, and explore the powerful services AWS has to offer.

3.2 Introduction to AWS Console and Dashboard

The **AWS Management Console** is the web-based interface through which you manage your AWS services. It's where you'll spend most of your time when creating, configuring, and monitoring AWS resources. Understanding how to navigate the AWS Console and make the most of its features is key to efficiently using AWS and managing your cloud infrastructure.

What is the AWS Management Console?

The **AWS Management Console** is a user-friendly web interface that enables you to interact with AWS services. It provides you with a visual overview of your cloud resources, enabling you to deploy, manage, and monitor them from a central location.

- **Web-based**: It runs in any modern web browser and doesn't require any special installation.
- **Comprehensive**: It supports a wide range of AWS services, including compute, storage, networking, security, and more.
- **Interactive**: You can view dashboards, launch new resources, set up services, and monitor the health of your applications with just a few clicks.

How to Access the AWS Management Console

1. **Sign In**:
   Go to *AWS Management Console* and click **Sign In**. Enter your

email address and password to access your account. Once signed in, you'll land on the Console's homepage.

2. **Console Home**:
   The homepage displays an overview of your AWS environment, including any recent activity, key metrics, and a list of recently used services. If you're new to AWS, this is where you'll find shortcuts to get started with popular services.

Main Components of the AWS Console

Let's break down the key sections you'll encounter in the AWS Console and explore how they can be used to manage your cloud infrastructure.

---

1. Navigation Bar and Search

At the top of the screen, you'll find the **Navigation Bar**, which includes:

- **Search Bar**:
  This is your shortcut to finding AWS services. You can type the name of any service, and the Console will show you relevant results. For example, if you type "EC2," it will direct you to the **EC2 Dashboard**.
- **Region Selector**:
  AWS operates in multiple regions globally, and the region selector allows you to choose the geographic region where you want to deploy your resources. This is important because AWS services are region-specific, and choosing the right region minimizes latency and improves performance for your users.
- **Notifications**:
  You'll receive notifications about your AWS account activity, billing updates, or security alerts. Clicking on the notification icon provides a summary of recent events and any actions you may need to take.

---

2. Services Menu and Categories

On the left-hand side of the Console, you'll see the **Services Menu**. This is where all AWS services are listed, categorized into specific groups based on their functionality.

- **Categories**:
  Services are organized into broad categories, such as:
    - **Compute**: EC2, Lambda, Elastic Beanstalk, etc.
    - **Storage**: S3, EBS, Glacier, etc.
    - **Databases**: RDS, DynamoDB, Redshift, etc.
    - **Networking**: VPC, Route 53, CloudFront, etc.
    - **Security & Identity**: IAM, AWS Shield, WAF, etc.
    - **Machine Learning**: SageMaker, Lex, Rekognition, etc.
- **Pinned Services**:
  As you use services more frequently, you can **pin** them to your dashboard for easy access. For example, if you're using EC2 often, you can pin it to the top for quick navigation.

Personal Insight:
The AWS services menu is incredibly vast, and as a beginner, it may feel overwhelming. My suggestion is to focus on the core services you'll use the most, such as **EC2** (for compute), **S3** (for storage), and **IAM** (for identity management). Once you're comfortable with these, you can start exploring other services as needed.

---

3. AWS Dashboard

The **Dashboard** is your overview page. When you first log into the Console, this page shows you an interactive summary of your resources and their current status. It includes:

- **Resource Overview**:
  The dashboard gives you a high-level view of the resources you have running, such as EC2 instances, S3 buckets, and RDS databases. You'll also see any alerts or notifications related to your AWS usage.
- **Quick Actions**:
  You'll find shortcuts to key services here. For example, you can

launch a new EC2 instance, create an S3 bucket, or configure an IAM role, all from the Dashboard.

- **Billing and Cost Management**:
  On the dashboard, you can easily access your **AWS Billing Dashboard**. This allows you to keep track of your AWS usage and cost to ensure that you are within your budget, especially if you are using services beyond the Free Tier.

---

4. Using AWS Services: Step-by-Step Example

Let's walk through a practical implementation by using the **EC2** service (virtual machines) and **S3** (cloud storage). These two services are among the most commonly used in AWS, and understanding them will give you a solid foundation for working with AWS.

Launching an EC2 Instance:

1. **Go to EC2**:
   In the Services Menu, click on **EC2** under **Compute**. This takes you to the EC2 Dashboard.
2. **Launch Instance**:
   On the EC2 Dashboard, click on **Launch Instance**. This will guide you through the process of creating a new virtual machine (EC2 instance).
3. **Select an AMI (Amazon Machine Image)**:
   Choose an AMI based on your operating system (for example, **Amazon Linux 2** or **Ubuntu**).
4. **Choose an Instance Type**:
   Select an instance type based on your needs. For beginners, the **t2.micro** instance is perfect and falls under the Free Tier.
5. **Configure Instance**:
   Choose your desired configurations, such as VPC settings and network options. For now, you can stick with the default VPC.
6. **Add Storage**:
   The default storage size is typically enough for simple applications. You can adjust this based on your needs.
7. **Configure Security Group**:
   A **Security Group** is like a firewall. For the default configuration, allow SSH access (port 22) so you can connect to your instance.

8. **Launch**:
   After reviewing your selections, click **Launch**. Don't forget to create or select an existing **Key Pair** for SSH access.

Once your instance is up, you'll be able to connect to it via SSH using the key pair you created.

Creating an S3 Bucket:

1. **Go to S3**:
   In the Services Menu, click on **S3** under **Storage**.
2. **Create a Bucket**:
   Click on the **Create Bucket** button to create a new storage container. You'll need to provide a globally unique name for the bucket.
3. **Set Region**:
   Select a region where your bucket will be stored. This should ideally be close to your user base to minimize latency.
4. **Configure Options**:
   For now, you can leave the default options. S3 will handle your storage requirements automatically.
5. **Set Permissions**:
   You can set your bucket's permissions to control who has access to it. By default, it's private, meaning only you can access it.
6. **Upload Files**:
   After your bucket is created, you can upload files to it. Simply click on **Upload**, drag files, and click **Next**.

5. Monitoring and Managing Resources

The **AWS CloudWatch** service allows you to monitor your AWS resources, such as EC2 instances, RDS databases, and more. You can set up **alarms** to notify you when certain thresholds (e.g., CPU usage or disk space) are exceeded, helping you maintain a healthy cloud environment.

- **CloudWatch Dashboard**:
  Provides real-time metrics about your AWS resources.

- **CloudWatch Alarms**:
  Allows you to set custom alerts for resource usage, ensuring you can act before issues arise.

6. Billing and Cost Management

The **Billing Dashboard** is a crucial part of the AWS Console for tracking your spending. With AWS's **Free Tier**, you get limited usage of certain services for free, but if you exceed the limits, you'll be charged.

- **Cost Explorer**:
  Use this tool to track your AWS spending and usage trends. You can see how much you've used and what services are generating costs.
- **Budgets**:
  AWS allows you to set a budget for your usage and receive alerts when you approach or exceed that budget.

Visual Aid: AWS Console Layout

Below is a simple **text-based sketch** illustrating the key components of the AWS Management Console:

```
+-----------------------------------------------------------
                    -----+
    | AWS Management Console (Top Navigation Bar)
                    |
    | - Search Bar | Region Selector | Notifications
                    |
+------------------- ---------------------------------------
                    -----+
             | Services Menu:
                    |
        | - Compute (EC2, Lambda, etc.)
                    |
        | - Storage (S3, EBS, Glacier)
                    |
        | - Databases (RDS, DynamoDB)
                    |
```

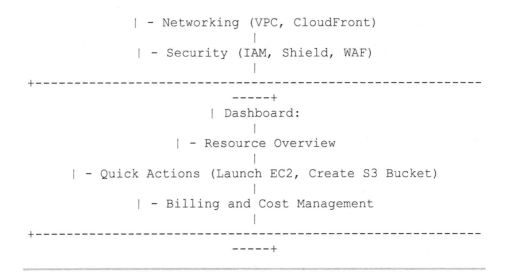

```
                |  - Networking (VPC, CloudFront)
                              |
                |  - Security (IAM, Shield, WAF)
                              |
+-----------------------------------------------------------
                          -----+
                    | Dashboard:
                              |
                    |  - Resource Overview
                              |
        |  - Quick Actions (Launch EC2, Create S3 Bucket)
                              |
                |  - Billing and Cost Management
                              |
+-----------------------------------------------------------
                          -----+
```

Case Study: A Startup's First AWS Project

Company: **TechStart**
Goal: Host a simple website and store user-uploaded images.

Steps Taken:

1. **AWS Account Creation**:
   Sarah, the founder, creates an AWS account using her business email and credit card details.
2. **Launching EC2 for the Website**:
   Sarah launches a **t2.micro EC2 instance** using the **Amazon Linux 2 AMI**. She installs a web server and sets up a basic HTML website.
3. **Using S3 for File Storage**:
   Sarah uses **Amazon S3** to store user-uploaded images. She configures the permissions to keep the bucket private but allows access through the web application.
4. **Monitoring with CloudWatch**:
   Sarah sets up CloudWatch to monitor the EC2 instance's CPU usage. She creates an alarm to notify her if the usage exceeds 70%.

The AWS Management Console is your gateway to managing and configuring AWS resources. By learning how to navigate the Console, search for services, create and manage resources like EC2 and S3, and monitor your usage, you'll be well-equipped to leverage AWS for your cloud-based applications. The Console provides an intuitive interface, but it's important to take the time to explore and understand its capabilities to make the most of AWS's extensive feature set.

3.3 Launching Your First EC2 Instance

Welcome to the world of **Amazon EC2 (Elastic Compute Cloud)**, one of the most powerful and flexible services offered by AWS. With EC2, you can rent virtual machines (VMs) called **instances** to run applications, host websites, and more, all while scaling as needed. In this guide, we'll walk you through the process of launching your first EC2 instance, covering everything from selecting the right instance type to configuring your instance for security and remote access.

What is Amazon EC2?

Amazon EC2 is a core service in AWS that allows you to run **virtual servers** in the cloud. These virtual servers, called **instances**, can run various operating systems, such as Linux, Windows, and custom Amazon Machine Images (AMIs). EC2 instances come with various configurations for CPU, memory, and storage, which can be scaled up or down depending on your needs.

Key features of EC2:

- **On-demand instances**: You can spin up and shut down instances as needed, only paying for what you use.
- **Scalability**: Easily scale up or down based on your requirements.
- **Elasticity**: Automatically adjust the number of instances running based on demand.
- **Secure**: EC2 instances are isolated within your virtual private network (VPC) and can be accessed securely using SSH or RDP.

Step-by-Step Guide to Launching Your First EC2 Instance

Let's walk through the process of launching an EC2 instance from start to finish. For this tutorial, we'll use **Amazon Linux 2** (a free, Amazon-maintained operating system) and the **t2.micro instance type**, which is eligible for the AWS Free Tier.

Step 1: Sign in to the AWS Console

1. Open <u>AWS Management Console</u>.
2. Log in using your AWS account credentials.
3. Once logged in, search for **EC2** in the search bar and select **EC2** under **Compute**.

Step 2: Launch Instance

Once you're in the EC2 Dashboard, follow these steps to launch a new instance:

1. **Click "Launch Instance"**:
   In the EC2 Dashboard, click the **Launch Instance** button to begin creating a new instance.

Step 3: Choose an Amazon Machine Image (AMI)

The next screen will prompt you to choose an AMI. An AMI is a pre-configured image that includes an operating system and any additional software needed to run the instance.

- **Choose Amazon Linux 2**:
  Amazon Linux 2 is a free, lightweight, and secure operating system that is optimized for EC2. It's perfect for running web servers, databases, or applications.

Select **Amazon Linux 2 AMI** and click **Select**.

Step 4: Choose an Instance Type

Next, you'll need to select the type of instance you want to run. This decision is based on your computing needs (CPU, memory, storage).

- **Choose t2.micro**:
  For beginners, **t2.micro** is the best choice because it's eligible for the AWS Free Tier, meaning it won't cost you anything as long as you stay within the Free Tier limits.

  Select **t2.micro** and click **Next: Configure Instance Details**.

Step 5: Configure Instance Details

On this screen, you'll configure the instance's settings, such as network and subnet.

- **Network**: By default, EC2 instances will be placed in a **default VPC** (Virtual Private Cloud) and **default subnet**. This is usually fine for a simple project.
- **Auto-assign Public IP**: For most use cases, you'll want to ensure that the instance gets a public IP address so you can access it from the internet. Make sure this option is set to **Enable**.

Once you're done with the settings, click **Next: Add Storage**.

Step 6: Add Storage

EC2 instances use **EBS (Elastic Block Store)** for persistent storage, meaning your data will remain intact even if you stop and start the instance.

- **Storage Settings**:
  By default, a **8 GB General Purpose SSD (gp2)** volume is created for you, which is typically sufficient for small applications.
- **Modify Volume Size**: If you need more storage, you can increase the volume size here.

Click **Next: Add Tags** when you're ready.

Step 7: Add Tags

Tags help you identify and organize your AWS resources.

- **Add a Name Tag**:
  Click **Add Tag**, enter **Name** as the key, and give it a value like **MyFirstEC2**. This makes it easier to identify the instance later.

Click **Next: Configure Security Group** to continue.

Step 8: Configure Security Group

A **Security Group** acts as a virtual firewall for your EC2 instance. It controls incoming and outgoing traffic to/from the instance. You'll need to set up a **security group** that allows you to connect to your instance.

- **Create a new Security Group**:
  - Name it **MyFirstEC2-SG**.
  - Add a rule to allow **SSH (port 22)** from your **IP address**. This will enable you to connect to your EC2 instance via SSH.
  - Optional: You can add more rules for HTTP (port 80) if you plan to host a web server, but for now, SSH is sufficient.

Click **Review and Launch** to proceed.

Step 9: Review and Launch

Here's a summary of all your instance configurations. Review everything to ensure that everything is set up correctly.

- **Key Pair**:
  AWS will ask you to select or create a new **key pair**. This key pair is used to securely access your EC2 instance via SSH.
  - If you don't have a key pair yet, click on **Create a new key pair**, give it a name (e.g., **MyKeyPair**), and download the **.pem file**. This is your private key file, and you'll use it to connect to your instance securely.

Once you've reviewed everything, click **Launch**.

Step 10: Accessing Your EC2 Instance

After launching your instance, it will take a few minutes for it to be provisioned and started. Once it's running, you can access it using **SSH**.

1. **Find the Public IP Address**:
   Go to the EC2 Dashboard, select your instance, and find the **Public IP** listed in the details.
2. **Connect via SSH**:
   Open your terminal (or use **PuTTY** if you're on Windows), and run the following SSH command:

```
ssh -i "path/to/MyKeyPair.pem" ec2-user@<Your-Instance-Public-IP>
```

Replace with the actual IP address of your instance.

3. **Access the Instance**:
   You should now be logged into your EC2 instance. From here, you can install software, run applications, and configure the system as needed.

Additional Insights:

1. **Stop vs Terminate**:
   - **Stopping** an EC2 instance allows you to pause it and later resume it. The instance's data will remain intact, but you're still charged for storage.
   - **Terminating** an instance will delete it permanently, including all data on the instance unless you've configured persistent storage (like EBS) separately.
2. **Elastic IP**:
   If you need a static IP for your instance that remains the same even if the instance is stopped and restarted, you can allocate an **Elastic IP** to it.

Case Study: Hosting a Simple Website with EC2

Company: TechSolutions
Goal: Host a static website on EC2.

Steps Taken:

1. **Launch EC2 Instance**:
   Sarah from TechSolutions followed the steps above to launch an EC2 instance using Amazon Linux 2. She chose a **t2.micro** instance and configured it for SSH access.
2. **Install Web Server**:
   After SSH'ing into the instance, Sarah installed **Apache Web Server**:

```
sudo yum update -y
sudo yum install httpd -y
sudo service httpd start
```

3. **Upload Website Files**:
   Sarah uploaded her HTML files to the **/var/www/html** directory, which is the default directory for Apache on Amazon Linux 2.
4. **Access the Website**:
   Using the EC2 instance's public IP address, Sarah was able to

access the website by entering the IP in her browser (e.g., `http://<Your-Instance-Public-IP>`).

Congratulations, you've successfully launched your first EC2 instance! By following these steps, you've created a virtual machine on AWS, configured it for SSH access, and even hosted a simple website. EC2 provides the flexibility and scalability to handle virtually any workload, from small websites to large, complex applications.

3.4 Working with S3 Storage

Amazon S3 (Simple Storage Service) is one of the most widely used AWS services, offering scalable, high-durability object storage for a variety of use cases, from simple file storage to complex data lake architectures. Whether you're storing static website files, backups, or big data, S3 is the go-to solution for secure, scalable cloud storage.

What is Amazon S3?

Amazon S3 is an object storage service that allows you to store and retrieve any amount of data at any time from anywhere on the web. Unlike file systems or block storage, S3 organizes data into **objects**, which are composed of the following:

- **Data**: The actual content or file you upload (e.g., a PDF, image, video, etc.).
- **Metadata**: Additional information about the object, such as its size, type, or creation date.
- **Unique Identifier**: Each object is assigned a unique ID within a **bucket**.

S3 offers virtually unlimited storage and provides 99.999999999% durability, ensuring that your data is safe and reliably accessible. You only pay for the storage you use, making it an incredibly cost-effective solution for businesses of all sizes.

Key Features of Amazon S3

- **Scalability**: S3 is designed to scale automatically to accommodate data growth. There's no need to worry about running out of space.
- **Data Durability**: S3 automatically stores your data across multiple devices within a region to ensure redundancy and fault tolerance.
- **Security**: S3 provides robust security controls, such as encryption (both in transit and at rest) and access management through IAM policies and bucket policies.
- **Accessibility**: You can access your data anywhere via the internet using URLs, SDKs, or APIs.

Step-by-Step Guide to Working with S3

Let's go through the steps to create a bucket, upload files, manage permissions, and retrieve data from S3.

Step 1: Creating an S3 Bucket

An S3 bucket is a container for storing objects. You need to create a bucket before you can start uploading files.

1. **Log into AWS Console**:
   From the AWS Management Console, search for **S3** in the search bar and select **S3** to navigate to the S3 dashboard.
2. **Create a New Bucket**:
   o Click on the **Create Bucket** button.
   o **Bucket Name**: Choose a globally unique name for your bucket (e.g., `mycompany-backups`).
   o **Region**: Select the AWS region where you want the bucket to reside. For example, if you're based in North America, you might choose **US East (N. Virginia)**.

- Configure Options: Leave most of the settings at their defaults unless you have specific requirements. For simplicity, you can leave the **Versioning**, **Logging**, and **Tags** options turned off for now.
- Set Permissions: AWS will automatically configure the bucket to be private, meaning only you can access it by default. You can modify permissions later if you need public access to the bucket (e.g., for serving website content).

3. **Click "Create"**:
   After reviewing the settings, click **Create** to finalize your bucket creation.

Step 2: Uploading Files to S3

Once your bucket is created, it's time to start uploading data. Amazon S3 supports various methods for uploading files, including the web console, AWS CLI, and SDKs. We'll begin with a simple web-based upload.

1. **Select Your Bucket**:
   In the S3 dashboard, click on the name of the bucket you just created.
2. **Upload Files**:
   - Click on the **Upload** button to start uploading files.
   - Drag and drop the files you want to upload, or click **Add Files** to browse and select them from your local machine.
   - Click **Next** to proceed.
3. **Configure Permissions (Optional)**:
   - If you want to make the uploaded files publicly accessible, you can configure permissions here.
   - For now, we'll leave the default private setting.
4. **Review and Upload**:
   After reviewing your settings, click **Upload** to begin uploading the files. Once uploaded, the files will appear in the bucket.

Step 3: Managing S3 Objects

After uploading data to S3, you'll want to manage the files (i.e., organize, update, delete, and control access to them). Here's how you can do that.

Organizing with Folders:

While S3 is technically a flat storage system, you can simulate folders by naming your objects with slashes (e.g., `images/pic1.jpg`). This helps organize your data, especially if you have many files.

- To create a "folder," simply click on **Create folder** within the S3 bucket and give it a name (e.g., `documents/`).
- Upload files directly into these "folders."

Setting Permissions:

S3 permissions are controlled via **bucket policies** and **IAM** roles. By default, all objects are private. You can grant access by:

- **Bucket Policy**: Define who can access the objects within the bucket.
- **IAM**: Control permissions at a more granular level by assigning roles and policies to specific users.

Example: To allow public read access to a specific file, you can modify the object's permissions to allow **Everyone** to have **Read** access. To do this:

- Select the object, go to the **Permissions** tab, and add the **Everyone** group with **Read** permissions.

Versioning:

To keep multiple versions of an object in the same bucket, you can enable **Versioning** on the bucket. This allows you to preserve, retrieve, and restore every version of every object in the bucket. It's useful when you need to keep track of file changes or ensure data durability.

To enable versioning:

1. Go to the **Bucket Settings**.
2. In the **Properties** section, enable **Versioning**.
3. After this, S3 will keep multiple versions of objects when they're overwritten.

Lifecycle Policies:

S3 allows you to automate the management of your data by setting up **Lifecycle Policies**. You can configure S3 to automatically transition objects between storage classes (e.g., from **Standard** to **Glacier** for archiving) or delete files after a certain period.

For example, if you want to archive files that haven't been accessed in 30 days:

1. Go to the **Management** tab in your bucket.
2. Click **Create lifecycle rule**.
3. Define the rule (e.g., transition to Glacier after 30 days).
4. Click **Save**.

Step 4: Retrieving Data from S3

Once your data is stored in S3, retrieving it is just as easy as uploading it.

1. **Accessing the Object URL**:
   After uploading an object to S3, you can access it via a URL. To get the URL:
   - Select the object in your bucket.
   - Go to the **Object URL** section in the **Overview** tab. It will look like this:
   - `https://my-bucket-name.s3.amazonaws.com/path/to/object`
2. **Downloading an Object**:
   To download the object, simply click on the file name in the S3 console, and you will see an option to **Download** the file.
3. **Using the AWS CLI**:
   You can also retrieve objects programmatically using the **AWS CLI**. To download a file from S3, use the following command:

```
aws s3 cp s3://my-bucket-name/path/to/object
/local/path/to/download
```

Best Practices for Using S3

1. **Use the Right Storage Class**:
   S3 offers multiple storage classes tailored to different use cases,
   such as **Standard, Infrequent Access**, and **Glacier** for archiving.
   Use the appropriate class for your data to optimize costs.
2. **Enable Encryption**:
   To secure your data, enable encryption for both data at rest (using
   SSE-S3 or **SSE-KMS**) and data in transit (using **SSL/TLS**). AWS
   makes this easy to enable when uploading or configuring your
   bucket.
3. **Use Bucket Policies**:
   Apply bucket policies to control access at the bucket level,
   ensuring that only authorized users or services can access sensitive
   data. Make sure to follow the principle of least privilege.
4. **Monitor with CloudWatch**:
   Use **Amazon CloudWatch** to monitor S3 activity, including
   upload/download actions, error logs, and other metrics. This is
   useful for auditing and managing performance.
5. **Leverage Versioning for Critical Data**:
   Enable versioning on buckets that store critical data. This allows
   you to recover from accidental deletions or overwrites.

Case Study: Hosting a Static Website on S3

Scenario: A small business, **WebDesignCo**, wants to host a static website
on AWS without the overhead of managing servers.

Steps Taken:

1. **Create an S3 Bucket**:
   WebDesignCo creates an S3 bucket named `webdesignco-website`
   with public read access enabled for the bucket.

2. **Upload Website Files**:
   The company uploads HTML, CSS, and image files into the S3 bucket.
3. **Enable Static Website Hosting**:
   They enable static website hosting on the bucket and configure the **index.html** file as the entry point.
4. **Access the Website**:
   The website is now accessible using the **S3 bucket endpoint URL**: `http://webdesignco-website.s3-website-us-east-1.amazonaws.com`.

Amazon S3 is a powerful, flexible, and cost-effective cloud storage solution. By understanding how to create buckets, upload files, set permissions, and manage data with S3's advanced features like versioning and lifecycle policies, you can make the most of this essential AWS service.

3.5 Basic Networking with AWS VPC

When you launch an application in the cloud, one of the first things you need to consider is networking. In AWS, **VPC (Virtual Private Cloud)** is the service that enables you to create a logically isolated section of the AWS Cloud where you can launch and manage AWS resources in a secure environment. VPC allows you to define and control your network configuration, including IP address ranges, subnets, route tables, and network gateways.

By the end of this tutorial, you'll be familiar with key VPC concepts and will have created your own VPC network in AWS, ready for deployment of your applications and services.

What is an AWS VPC?

An **AWS Virtual Private Cloud (VPC)** is a virtual network that you define within AWS, isolated from other networks in the AWS Cloud. It gives you complete control over your network settings, including:

- **Subnets**: Divide your VPC into sub-networks to segment resources.
- **IP Address Range**: You can specify your own IP address range (using CIDR blocks).
- **Route Tables**: Control how traffic moves between subnets and outside the VPC.
- **Internet Gateway (IGW)**: Allow resources in your VPC to access the internet.
- **NAT Gateway**: Provide internet access to instances in private subnets.
- **Security Groups** and **Network ACLs**: Provide security control to control inbound and outbound traffic.

VPC gives you the ability to launch instances in a secure, isolated environment, configure firewall rules, and manage traffic routing, all within your own customized virtual network.

Step-by-Step Guide to Setting Up a Basic VPC

In this section, we'll walk through the process of creating a VPC, adding subnets, configuring a route table, and ensuring internet access to your resources. We'll also explore the importance of **public** and **private subnets** in VPC.

Step 1: Creating a VPC

1. **Log in to the AWS Management Console**:
   - Search for **VPC** in the search bar, then select **VPC** from the list of services.
2. **Create VPC**:
   - In the **VPC Dashboard**, click **Create VPC**.
   - Provide the following details:

- **Name**: Give your VPC a name, such as
  `MyFirstVPC`.
- **IPv4 CIDR block**: Choose an IP range for your
  VPC (e.g., `10.0.0.0/16`). This range will
  determine how many IP addresses your VPC can
  use (a `/16` block gives you 65,536 possible IP
  addresses).
- **IPv6 CIDR block**: For simplicity, you can leave
  this **No IPv6 CIDR Block**.
- **Tenancy**: Select **Default** unless you have specific
  requirements for dedicated instances.

3. **Review and Create**:
   - Review your VPC settings, and click **Create VPC**.

Step 2: Creating Subnets

After creating a VPC, the next step is to create **subnets** within that VPC.
Subnets allow you to segment your network based on use case (e.g.,
public-facing web servers vs. private databases).

1. **Navigate to Subnets**:
   - In the VPC Dashboard, click on **Subnets** and then **Create
     Subnet**.
2. **Configure Subnet Details**:
   - Choose the **VPC** you just created.
   - **Subnet Name**: Name your subnet (e.g., `PublicSubnet`).
   - **Availability Zone**: Select an availability zone (e.g., `us-
     east-1a`).
   - **IPv4 CIDR block**: Select a range of IP addresses for the
     subnet (e.g., `10.0.1.0/24` for the public subnet). This
     provides up to 256 IP addresses for your subnet.
   - **Subnet Type**: Choose whether the subnet will be **Public** or
     Private. For now, we'll create a public subnet, which can
     route traffic to/from the internet.
3. **Create Another Subnet (Private Subnet)**:
   - Repeat the process for creating a private subnet with a
     CIDR block such as `10.0.2.0/24`. This subnet will not be
     directly accessible from the internet.

4. **Create Subnets**:
   Click **Create** after reviewing your subnet settings.

Step 3: Creating a Route Table and Internet Gateway

To allow instances in the public subnet to access the internet, we need to configure a **route table** and associate it with the public subnet.

1. **Navigate to Route Tables**:
   - o In the VPC Dashboard, click on **Route Tables**, then click **Create Route Table**.
2. **Configure Route Table**:
   - o Choose the **VPC** you just created.
   - o Name the route table (e.g., `PublicRouteTable`).
   - o Click **Create**.
3. **Add a Route for Internet Access**:
   - o Select your route table, then click **Edit Routes** and **Add Route**.
   - o In the **Destination** field, type `0.0.0.0/0` (this route covers all traffic to and from the internet).
   - o In the **Target** field, select **Internet Gateway** (if you haven't already created one, create one from the **Internet Gateways** section).
   - o Click **Save Routes**.
4. **Associate the Route Table with the Public Subnet**:
   - o In the **Subnet Associations** tab, click **Edit subnet associations**.
   - o Select the **public subnet** you created earlier and click **Save**.

Step 4: Creating an Internet Gateway (IGW)

The **Internet Gateway** allows instances in your public subnet to communicate with the internet. This is essential for enabling access to web servers, for example.

1. **Navigate to Internet Gateways**:
   - o In the VPC Dashboard, click **Internet Gateways**, then **Create Internet Gateway**.

2. **Create and Attach the Internet Gateway**:
   - Give the gateway a name (e.g., `MyInternetGateway`).
   - Click **Create** and then select the newly created Internet Gateway.
   - Click **Actions** > **Attach to VPC**, and choose the VPC you created earlier.

Step 5: Launching an EC2 Instance in the Public Subnet

Now that your network is set up, you can launch an EC2 instance in the **public subnet**.

1. **Launch EC2 Instance**:
   - Go to the **EC2 Dashboard**, and click **Launch Instance**.
   - Choose an AMI (e.g., **Amazon Linux 2 AMI**).
   - Select **t2.micro** (eligible for the Free Tier).
   - Under **Network**, select the VPC and the public subnet you created earlier.
   - Choose **Auto-assign Public IP** as **Enable** to ensure the instance is assigned a public IP address.
   - Configure security groups to allow **SSH** access (port 22).
   - Review and launch the instance.
2. **Connect to EC2 Instance**:
   - After the instance is running, go to the EC2 Dashboard and select the instance.
   - Copy the **Public IP** address.
   - Use **SSH** to connect to your EC2 instance using the command:
   - `ssh -i "path/to/your-key.pem" ec2-user@<Public-IP>`

Step 6: Verifying the Setup

1. **Test Internet Connectivity**:
   Once you've SSHed into your EC2 instance, you can verify internet access by running a simple `ping` command:
2. `ping google.com`

If you receive responses, your EC2 instance is successfully connected to the internet.

3. **Test Access from Private Subnet**:
   You won't be able to directly connect to instances in the **private subnet** via SSH because they don't have direct internet access. However, you can set up a **NAT Gateway** (to be covered later) to allow the private subnet to access the internet.

Visual Aid: Basic VPC Architecture

Below is a simple **text-based flowchart** illustrating the basic architecture of the VPC we just created:

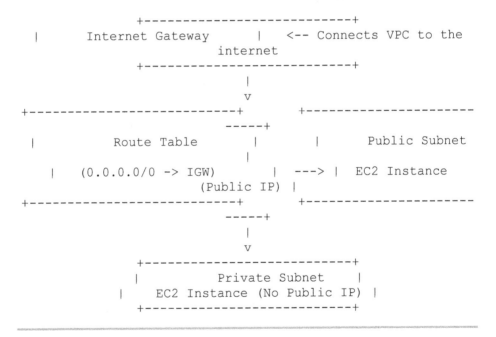

Best Practices for AWS VPC

1. **Use Multiple Availability Zones**:
   To increase fault tolerance, deploy instances in multiple Availability Zones (AZs) within a region. This helps ensure that even if one AZ goes down, your application remains available.

2. **Isolate Critical Resources**:
   Use private subnets for sensitive resources like databases or application servers that don't need internet access. This adds a layer of security by isolating them from direct exposure to the internet.
3. **Use Security Groups and NACLs**:
   Use **Security Groups** to control inbound and outbound traffic to EC2 instances. For more granular control, **Network ACLs** can be used at the subnet level.
4. **Implement Monitoring with CloudWatch**:
   Enable **CloudWatch Logs** and **CloudWatch Alarms** to monitor the health and performance of your VPC resources, such as EC2 instances and load balancers.

Case Study: Deploying a Secure Web Application

Scenario: A small business, **TechSolutions**, wants to deploy a secure web application in AWS using a VPC.

Steps Taken:

1. **VPC Creation**:
   Sarah, the founder, creates a VPC with a CIDR block of `10.0.0.0/16`, then adds a public subnet and a private subnet.
2. **Web Server in Public Subnet**:
   She launches an EC2 instance in the public subnet and installs **Apache** to host the web application.
3. **Database in Private Subnet**:
   Sarah creates a MySQL database in the private subnet, ensuring it is not directly accessible from the internet.
4. **NAT Gateway for Outbound Traffic**:
   To allow the EC2 instance in the private subnet to access the internet for software updates, Sarah sets up a **NAT Gateway** in the public subnet.
5. **Security Groups and IAM**:
   Sarah configures security groups to restrict SSH access to the web server and IAM roles to grant specific permissions to the EC2 instances.

Creating a basic VPC in AWS is an essential first step in setting up secure and scalable cloud infrastructure. VPCs provide the flexibility to segment your network, control access, and connect your resources securely to the internet. By following this guide, you now understand how to create VPCs, subnets, and route tables, and launch instances in a secure network environment.

3.6 Managing Security and Access with IAM (Identity and Access Management)

AWS Identity and Access Management (IAM) is a critical security feature that helps you control who can access your AWS resources and what actions they can perform. IAM is foundational to cloud security in AWS, and understanding how it works is crucial for managing your AWS infrastructure securely.

What is AWS IAM?

AWS **IAM** is a service that allows you to control who can access your AWS resources, what actions they can take, and under what conditions. IAM provides fine-grained access control, which is essential for maintaining security in a shared environment.

Key IAM concepts:

- **Users**: Individuals or services that need to access your AWS resources.
- **Groups**: Collections of users that share the same permissions.
- **Roles**: Temporary access permissions that can be assumed by AWS services or users.
- **Policies**: JSON documents that define what actions are allowed or denied on AWS resources.

By using IAM, you can ensure that only authorized users can perform actions on your AWS resources, and you can enforce the principle of **least privilege**—granting only the permissions needed to perform a specific task.

IAM Components and How They Work

IAM is built around several key components that allow you to manage access and security in AWS.

1. IAM Users

An **IAM User** is an entity that represents a person or a service. Each user can be assigned specific permissions to access AWS resources.

- **Creating IAM Users**:
  IAM users are created within your AWS account. Once created, you can assign them permissions via policies to control what resources they can access.
- **Credentials**:
  Each user has **credentials** that allow them to authenticate to AWS, such as an **access key ID and secret access key** (for programmatic access) or a **password** (for console access).

Example: To create an IAM user with programmatic access, follow these steps:

1. **Go to the IAM Console**: In the AWS Management Console, go to **IAM** under the **Security, Identity, & Compliance** section.
2. **Create User**: In the IAM dashboard, click **Add user**.
   - Enter a **username**.
   - Select **Programmatic access** (if they need access to the AWS CLI or API).
   - Optionally, enable **AWS Management Console access**.
3. **Set Permissions**: Assign permissions (directly or via groups).
4. **Review and Create**: Review settings and click **Create user**.

2. IAM Groups

IAM Groups are collections of IAM users that share common permissions. Groups allow you to manage permissions at the group level rather than for individual users. For example, you might have a **Developers** group with permissions to access EC2 instances, or an **Admins** group with full access to all AWS resources.

- **Creating IAM Groups**:
  To create a group, follow these steps:
  1. **Navigate to IAM**: Go to **IAM** in the AWS Console.
  2. **Create Group**: In the IAM dashboard, click **Groups** and then **Create New Group**.
  3. **Assign Permissions**: Choose the policies to apply to the group. For instance, the **AmazonEC2FullAccess** policy can be attached to the Developers group.
  4. **Add Users**: You can then add IAM users to the group. Any user in this group will inherit the permissions associated with the group.

3. IAM Roles

An **IAM Role** is similar to a user, but instead of being associated with a specific person, a role is intended to be assumed by anyone or any service that needs temporary access. IAM roles are often used for **AWS services** (like EC2 instances or Lambda functions) to grant them the permissions needed to perform specific actions.

- **Creating an IAM Role for EC2**:
  You might want to assign an IAM role to an EC2 instance so that it can access other AWS resources, such as an S3 bucket.
  1. **Go to IAM Console**: In the **IAM Console**, click **Roles**, then click **Create role**.
  2. **Select Trusted Entity**: Choose **AWS service**, and then select **EC2** as the service that will assume the role.
  3. **Attach Policies**: Choose the policies that define what the EC2 instance can access. For example, select the

AmazonS3ReadOnlyAccess policy to give the EC2 instance read-only access to S3.

4. **Review and Create**: After reviewing, click **Create role**.

Once the role is created, you can assign it to an EC2 instance by selecting the instance, navigating to **Actions > Security > Modify IAM role**.

4. IAM Policies

IAM Policies define what actions are allowed or denied on AWS resources. Policies are attached to IAM users, groups, or roles and are written in **JSON** format. They consist of statements that specify the permissions for specific AWS actions.

- **Policy Structure**: Each policy consists of the following elements:
  - **Version**: The policy version (always set to 2012-10-17 for AWS).
  - **Statement**: A list of permissions, with conditions like **Action**, **Resource**, and **Effect**.

Example Policy: Below is an example policy that grants read-only access to an S3 bucket:

```
{
  "Version": "2012-10-17",
  "Statement": [
    {
      "Effect": "Allow",
      "Action": "s3:GetObject",
      "Resource": "arn:aws:s3:::my-bucket/*"
    }
  ]
}
```

This policy allows users or services to **get objects** from the my-bucket S3 bucket, but it doesn't allow any other actions (like uploading or deleting objects).

- **Creating a Policy**: To create an IAM policy, follow these steps:
  1. **Navigate to IAM Console**.
  2. Click on **Policies > Create Policy**.

3. Choose **JSON** or **Visual editor** to write the policy.
4. Review and click **Create policy**.

Step-by-Step Example: Granting Permissions with IAM

Let's walk through a practical example where we create an IAM user, assign it to a group, and apply a policy.

Step 1: Create an IAM User

1. In the **IAM Console**, click **Add User**.
2. Enter a user name (e.g., `john.doe`).
3. Select **Programmatic access** (for AWS CLI or SDK) and **AWS Management Console access** (for console login).
4. Set a password for console access and choose **Require password reset** for better security.

Step 2: Create an IAM Group

1. Go to **Groups** > **Create New Group**.
2. Name the group (e.g., `Developers`).
3. Attach the **AmazonEC2FullAccess** policy to the group to allow users in the group full access to EC2 instances.
4. Click **Create Group**.

Step 3: Add User to Group

1. After creating the user, add the user to the **Developers** group.
2. Review the user and group settings and click **Create User**.

IAM Best Practices

1. **Follow the Principle of Least Privilege**:
   Always grant users only the permissions they need to perform their job. Avoid giving users unnecessary permissions, especially full access to resources.

2. **Enable Multi-Factor Authentication (MFA)**:
   Enable MFA for all users with console access, especially users with administrative privileges. This provides an additional layer of security.
3. **Use Roles for AWS Services**:
   Instead of embedding AWS credentials in your applications, use IAM roles to grant AWS services the permissions they need to interact with other resources.
4. **Use Group-Based Access**:
   Create IAM groups based on roles (e.g., **Developers**, **Admins**, etc.) and assign policies to those groups. Assign users to groups rather than directly assigning permissions to individual users.
5. **Audit and Review Permissions Regularly**:
   Periodically review IAM user permissions and remove access for users who no longer need it. Use **IAM Access Analyzer** to check for unused permissions.

Case Study: Managing Access for a Development Team

Scenario: **TechStart** is a software development company that needs to manage access for its team members. The team is split into two roles: Developers and Admins.

Steps Taken:

1. **Create Groups**:
   TechStart creates two groups: **Developers** and **Admins**. Developers get **read-write** access to EC2 and S3, while Admins get **full access** to all AWS resources.
2. **Create IAM Users**:
   Individual users are created for each team member. Developers are assigned to the **Developers** group, and Admins to the **Admins** group.
3. **Enable MFA**:
   Multi-factor authentication is enabled for all users, especially those in the Admins group.
4. **Use Roles for EC2 Instances**:
   The DevOps team creates an IAM role for EC2 instances, granting

them the necessary permissions to access S3 buckets and CloudWatch logs. This is done via the **EC2 instance role**.

By implementing IAM in this way, TechStart ensures that only the right people have access to the right resources, minimizing security risks and adhering to best practices for cloud access management.

IAM is the backbone of security in AWS. By using IAM, you can control who can access your resources, what actions they can perform, and ensure that your AWS infrastructure remains secure. As you continue working with AWS, it's important to understand IAM's components—users, groups, roles, and policies—and how to configure them effectively to manage access.

Chapter 4: Exploring Microsoft Azure

Microsoft Azure is a powerful cloud platform that offers a wide range of services for building, deploying, and managing applications through Microsoft's global network of data centers. In this chapter, we'll guide you through the essential aspects of Azure, from setting up an account to deploying and managing virtual machines, using storage solutions, configuring virtual networks, and leveraging Azure Active Directory for identity management.

Whether you're new to Azure or looking to expand your cloud knowledge, this chapter will provide practical, step-by-step tutorials to help you navigate the Azure ecosystem.

4.1 Setting Up an Azure Account

Before you can dive into creating and managing resources in Azure, you first need to set up an **Azure account**. Setting up your account is the first step in unlocking the vast range of cloud computing resources that Azure offers, from virtual machines and storage to advanced AI and machine learning tools. The process is straightforward, and Azure provides many helpful features, including a **free tier** to get you started without immediate costs.

What is an Azure Account?

An **Azure account** is your gateway to the Microsoft Azure cloud platform. It allows you to access all Azure resources, such as virtual machines, databases, networking, and storage, as well as manage permissions and security.

When you set up an Azure account, you're provided with access to Azure's web-based management interface known as the **Azure Portal**, where you can create, manage, and monitor resources. You also get access to other services such as Azure CLI, PowerShell, and SDKs for programmatic access to resources.

Key Benefits of an Azure Account:

1. **Comprehensive cloud services**: Access compute, storage, networking, and AI tools for building, deploying, and managing applications.
2. **Scalability**: Azure services are designed to scale up or down based on demand, making it ideal for both small projects and enterprise-level workloads.
3. **Security**: Azure provides built-in security tools, including encryption, multi-factor authentication, and identity management through **Azure Active Directory**.
4. **Free tier access**: With an Azure free account, you can explore and experiment with many services free of charge, making it a perfect option for developers, small businesses, and learners.

Steps to Set Up Your Azure Account

Setting up an Azure account is simple and quick. Here's a step-by-step guide to help you through the process.

Step 1: Sign Up for an Azure Free Account

1. **Go to the Azure Website**:
   Visit the official Azure website: https://azure.microsoft.com.
   o On the homepage, click on the **Start free** button to begin the process.
2. **Sign in with a Microsoft Account**:
   o You need a **Microsoft account** (e.g., **Outlook, Hotmail, Live**, or any Microsoft-associated email account) to sign up for Azure.
   o If you don't have one, you can easily create a new Microsoft account by clicking on **Create one**.
3. **Fill in Your Information**:

- Enter your **name**, **email address**, and **phone number**. Azure will use these details to verify your identity and communicate with you regarding your account.
- Microsoft will send you a **verification code** to your phone number via **SMS** or **voice call**. Enter this code to proceed.

4. **Provide Billing Information**:
   - **Credit Card Information**: While the **Azure Free Account** gives you $200 of credits for the first 30 days, you'll need to provide a valid credit card to verify your identity.
   - **No Charges Unless Exceeding Free Tier**: Microsoft will not charge your credit card unless you exceed the free usage limits. You can also set up **spending caps** to avoid unexpected charges.

5. **Agree to the Terms**:
   - Review the **Microsoft Azure Agreement** and **Privacy Statement**.
   - Accept the terms and click **Sign Up** to create your account.

Step 2: Verify Your Identity

After filling in your information and agreeing to the terms, Microsoft will verify your identity using the **phone number** and **credit card** you provided. This verification process is a standard security measure to ensure that the account is valid.

1. **Receive Verification Code**:
   You'll receive an **SMS or voice call** from Microsoft with a verification code.
2. **Enter the Code**:
   Enter the verification code to confirm your identity. This will help secure your account and prevent fraudulent activities.

Step 3: Access the Azure Portal

Once you've completed the sign-up and verification process, you can access the **Azure Portal**.

1. **Login to the Portal**:
   Go to https://portal.azure.com and sign in with your **Microsoft account** credentials.
2. **Explore the Azure Dashboard**:
   After logging in, you'll be directed to the **Azure Dashboard**, which is the home interface of the Azure Portal. Here, you can access your resources, monitor usage, and navigate to different Azure services.

Azure Free Account

When you sign up for an Azure account, Microsoft provides a **Free Tier** with various benefits:

- **$200 in credits** for the first 30 days.
- **12-month free services**: Includes popular services like **Azure Virtual Machines**, **Azure Blob Storage**, and **Azure SQL Database**, with some limitations.
- **Always free services**: Services such as **Azure Functions, Azure App Services**, and **Azure Active Directory** (for basic usage) are always free within certain limits.

The **free credits** and **free services** allow you to experiment and get hands-on experience with Azure without incurring any costs.

Step 4: Configuring Your Azure Account Settings

Now that you've set up your Azure account, it's time to configure a few essential settings to ensure smooth management and optimal use of Azure services.

1. **Set Up Billing Alerts**:
   - It's a good idea to set up billing alerts to keep track of your free credits and usage. In the Azure Portal, go to the **Cost Management + Billing** section.
   - Set up alerts to notify you if your free credits are nearing their limit.

2. **Enable Multi-Factor Authentication (MFA)**:
   - For added security, enable **MFA** on your Azure account to require two forms of authentication before accessing sensitive resources. This step is especially critical for any production environments.
   - To enable MFA, go to **Azure Active Directory** > **Security** > **MFA** settings.
3. **Configure Subscriptions**:
   - In the **Cost Management + Billing** section, you can organize and manage your subscriptions, ensuring you stay within your budget. If you're using different services or resources, you can set up multiple subscriptions to separate environments (e.g., production, development).
4. **Set Up Azure Active Directory**:
   - Azure Active Directory (Azure AD) allows you to manage users, groups, and their access to Azure resources. Configure your Azure AD to securely manage identity and access for all team members or services.
   - To create users and assign roles, go to **Azure Active Directory** > **Users** and **Groups**.

Additional Insights and Tips

1. **Free Services to Get Started**:
   - Microsoft provides a **Free Tier** for a wide range of Azure services. To get started, try services like **Azure App Service** (for web apps), **Azure Blob Storage**, and **Azure Functions**.
   - Use the free services to experiment with building applications and managing cloud resources without incurring any costs.
2. **Explore the Azure Marketplace**:
   - The **Azure Marketplace** offers third-party services and applications that you can easily deploy on Azure. From security tools to machine learning models, the marketplace is a treasure trove of additional resources.
3. **Azure Mobile App**:
   - The **Azure mobile app** allows you to monitor your resources, receive alerts, and manage your services from

anywhere. It's especially useful when you need to keep track of important notifications on the go.

4. **Documentation and Support**:
   o If you're ever unsure about something, Azure has a comprehensive documentation library available at https://docs.microsoft.com/en-us/azure/.
   o Azure also provides various **support plans** if you require more technical assistance. The **Basic Support Plan** is free and provides 24/7 customer support, though it's limited in scope compared to higher-tier plans.

Case Study: Setting Up an Azure Account for a Startup

Let's look at how a small company, **TechSolutions**, sets up an Azure account to host their web application and manage their development and production environments.

Steps Taken:

1. **Create a Free Account**:
   The founder, Sarah, signs up for an Azure account using her **Microsoft account** and enters her payment details for identity verification.
2. **Configure the Portal**:
   After logging into the Azure Portal, Sarah configures billing alerts to track usage and sets up **multi-factor authentication (MFA)** for security.
3. **Explore Free Services**:
   Sarah uses the **$200 credits** to experiment with **Azure App Services** and **Azure Storage**. She deploys a **web app** and starts using **Azure Blob Storage** to manage static assets.
4. **Set Up Azure Active Directory**:
   Sarah creates **users and groups** in **Azure Active Directory** to manage access for her development team. She assigns them different roles, ensuring that developers have limited access and admins can manage everything.

Conclusion

Creating an Azure account is the first step to unlocking the power of Microsoft's cloud platform. With an Azure account, you can easily access the vast array of services offered by Azure and begin building, deploying, and managing your applications securely. By taking advantage of the free services, setting up MFA, and organizing your resources effectively, you can get the most out of your Azure experience.

Now that your account is set up, you're ready to dive into more advanced Azure services, such as **virtual machines**, **storage solutions**, and **virtual networks**. Azure offers a flexible and secure cloud platform for a wide range of use cases, and with this foundational setup, you're well on your way to mastering it. Happy cloud computing!

4.2 Navigating the Azure Portal

The **Azure Portal** is your primary interface for managing and monitoring all your resources in Microsoft Azure. As an essential tool for cloud management, it provides a user-friendly, web-based interface that allows you to access, deploy, configure, and monitor all Azure services. Whether you're deploying virtual machines, setting up databases, or managing storage accounts, the Azure Portal is where it all happens.

In this guide, we will walk you through how to effectively navigate the Azure Portal, understand its features, and make the most of it to manage your cloud infrastructure. We'll also provide practical, real-world examples to demonstrate how to use the portal efficiently.

What is the Azure Portal?

The **Azure Portal** is a web-based console that provides a graphical interface for interacting with your Azure account. It allows you to:

- **Create and manage resources**: Easily create and configure resources like virtual machines, databases, networks, and more.

- **Monitor usage and performance**: View metrics and diagnostics for resources, ensuring that your applications are running smoothly.
- **Configure and manage security**: Set up identity management, access controls, and security policies.
- **Automate tasks**: Use tools like Azure Resource Manager (ARM) templates to automate the deployment of resources.

The portal is designed to be intuitive and flexible, allowing you to work with a range of services—from basic compute resources to advanced AI tools—all from one place.

Key Features of the Azure Portal

When you first log into the **Azure Portal**, you'll be greeted with a powerful, customizable dashboard that provides access to your resources and services. Let's break down the major components of the portal and how they help you manage your Azure environment.

1. Azure Dashboard

The **Azure Dashboard** is the first thing you see when logging into the portal. It's a customizable page that gives you a quick overview of your Azure resources and services.

- **Overview of Resources**: The dashboard displays tiles for your most used services and resources. You can customize this layout to match your workflow.
- **Resource Groups**: Here, you can manage collections of related resources, which can simplify management and security configurations.

Customization Tip: You can drag and drop tiles on the dashboard to organize them. This makes it easy to create a personalized workspace, especially if you're managing a wide range of resources.

2. Navigation Panel

On the left side of the portal, you'll find the **Navigation Panel**. This panel provides quick links to all major Azure services and resources. It's where you'll spend most of your time as you manage your resources.

Key sections in the navigation panel:

- **Home**: Brings you back to your dashboard.
- **Create a resource**: Quickly start new resources such as virtual machines, databases, or storage accounts.
- **All services**: A list of all available Azure services (compute, storage, networking, AI, etc.).
- **Resource groups**: Allows you to manage resources that are grouped together for easier administration.
- **Subscriptions**: Manage billing and view the status of your Azure subscriptions.
- **Azure Active Directory**: Manage users, groups, roles, and access policies in your Azure directory.
- **Security Center**: Offers a centralized view of the security health of your Azure resources.

The **All services** section can be searched or filtered by category. You can also pin services that you use frequently for quick access.

---

3. Search Bar

The **Search Bar** at the top of the portal allows you to quickly find resources, services, and documentation. If you're looking for something specific, just start typing, and Azure will show relevant results. It's much faster than manually browsing through the navigation panel.

For example, typing "Virtual Machines" in the search bar will take you directly to the **Virtual Machines** section, where you can manage or create new VMs.

---

4. Resource and Service Management

Once you've selected a specific resource or service, such as a **Virtual Machine** or **SQL Database**, the portal provides you with detailed management options. You can:

- **View resource details**: Get an overview of the resource's health, usage, and configurations.
- **Configure settings**: Change the properties, networking options, and other settings of the resource.
- **Monitor performance**: View metrics like CPU usage, memory usage, and disk I/O to ensure your resources are running smoothly.
- **Set alerts**: Configure automated alerts for resource performance or specific events (e.g., resource usage exceeding certain thresholds).

5. Notifications and Alerts

The **bell icon** in the upper right corner of the portal notifies you about important account updates, service health issues, or resource status changes. For example, if there's an issue with a deployed VM or a subscription nearing its resource limits, Azure will alert you here.

You can also configure **alerts** for specific events in your resources. For instance, if your virtual machine's disk usage exceeds a certain limit, you can set an alert to notify you automatically.

6. Azure CLI and Cloud Shell

The **Cloud Shell** is an integrated, browser-based shell that allows you to run **Azure CLI** commands without needing to set up anything on your local machine.

- **Cloud Shell Access**: You can open Cloud Shell by clicking the **Cloud Shell icon** (the terminal icon) at the top of the portal.
- **Preconfigured Environment**: Cloud Shell comes preconfigured with the Azure CLI, Azure PowerShell, and a variety of other tools, such as **Git** and **Terraform**. It also gives you access to a

temporary **home directory** to store files, scripts, and other resources.

This is particularly useful if you prefer working with command-line tools or need to automate Azure tasks.

Step-by-Step Example: Creating a Virtual Machine Using the Azure Portal

Let's walk through a simple example of how to create a **Virtual Machine (VM)** in the Azure Portal.

Step 1: Open the Virtual Machines Service

1. In the **Navigation Panel**, search for **Virtual Machines** and select it.
2. Click on **+ Add** to start creating a new VM.

Step 2: Configure Basic Settings

1. **Subscription**: Select your Azure subscription (for a new user, there's usually one subscription by default).
2. **Resource Group**: Either select an existing resource group or create a new one (e.g., `myResourceGroup`).
3. **Virtual Machine Name**: Give your VM a name, such as `MyFirstVM`.
4. **Region**: Select the region where you want your VM to be deployed (e.g., **East US**).
5. **Image**: Choose the OS for the VM, such as **Ubuntu 20.04 LTS**.
6. **Size**: Select the size of the VM. For this example, choose the **Standard B1s** size, which is eligible for the **Free Tier**.
7. **Authentication Type**: Choose **SSH public key** for Linux VMs. You'll need to provide an SSH key, which you can generate using:
8. `ssh-keygen -t rsa -b 2048`

1. **Virtual Network**: You can create a new **Virtual Network (VNet)** or use an existing one. A VNet allows your VM to communicate securely with other resources.
2. **Subnet**: Select a subnet for your VM. For simplicity, you can use the default subnet in the newly created VNet.
3. **Public IP**: Ensure the **Public IP** option is set to **Dynamic** (this will allow the VM to be accessed via a public IP address).
4. **Network Security Group**: Choose to create a new **Network Security Group (NSG)**, which acts like a firewall, or use an existing one. Make sure to allow **SSH** access on port 22 to connect to the Linux VM.

Step 4: Review and Create

- **Review** all the settings you've chosen.
- Click **Create**. Azure will validate the settings, and once everything is correct, it will begin deploying the virtual machine.

Azure Resources and Monitoring

The Azure Portal offers robust tools to monitor the health and performance of your resources, helping ensure that everything runs smoothly. For example, with **Virtual Machines**, you can:

- **Monitor metrics** such as CPU usage, disk I/O, and memory usage.
- **Set up alerts** for specific conditions (e.g., if the CPU usage exceeds 80% for more than 5 minutes).
- **View diagnostics logs** to troubleshoot issues and optimize performance.

To access these tools, go to your resource (e.g., your Virtual Machine) in the portal, and under the **Monitoring** section, you will find **Metrics**, **Logs**, and **Alerts**.

Visual Aid: Azure Portal Overview

Below is a text-based diagram illustrating the layout of the Azure Portal:

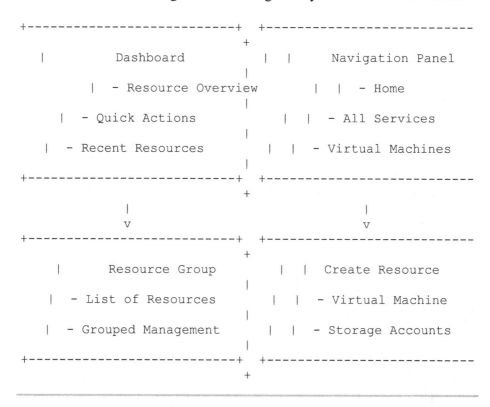

Case Study: Launching a Web Application

Scenario: **WebDesignCo**, a small startup, wants to launch a web application on Azure.

Steps Taken:

1. **Azure Subscription**:
   The founder, Sarah, creates a free Azure account and logs into the portal.
2. **Create a Virtual Machine**:
   Sarah uses the Azure Portal to deploy an **Ubuntu 20.04** virtual machine. She configures it with an **SSH key** for secure access.

3. **Install Web Server**:
   After logging into the VM via SSH, Sarah installs **Apache** to serve the web application.
4. **Monitor and Scale**:
   Sarah uses the **Azure Monitor** and **Alerts** to keep track of the VM's CPU usage and set an alert to notify her if it exceeds 80%.

The Azure Portal is a powerful tool for managing your cloud infrastructure. With its easy-to-use interface, customizable dashboard, and comprehensive management features, it allows you to deploy, monitor, and manage resources with ease. By understanding its key components— such as the navigation panel, dashboard, and resource management tools—you'll be well-equipped to navigate the Azure cloud efficiently.

4.3 Creating and Managing Virtual Machines in Azure

Virtual Machines (VMs) in Azure are one of the core components of **Azure Compute** services. A **Virtual Machine** is a software-based emulation of a physical computer, with its own operating system (OS) and application software. In Azure, VMs allow you to run your applications, websites, and services in a highly scalable and secure environment. The beauty of Azure's VM offering lies in its flexibility, scalability, and ability to integrate with a wide range of other Azure services.

What is a Virtual Machine (VM) in Azure?

An **Azure Virtual Machine** is an on-demand, scalable computing resource that can run both Windows and Linux operating systems. VMs are ideal for scenarios where you need full control over the OS, applications, and configurations, similar to running your own server in a data center.

Key Features of Azure VMs:

- **Choice of OS**: Azure supports both **Windows** and **Linux** operating systems. You can choose from various OS versions such as **Windows Server**, **Ubuntu**, **Red Hat**, **CentOS**, and more.
- **Scalability**: VMs can be resized easily based on performance needs. You can scale up (increase CPU, RAM, etc.) or scale out (add more VMs).
- **Customization**: You can install any software or configure the VM to suit your specific needs.
- **Networking**: Azure VMs can be connected to other Azure services like **Azure Virtual Network**, **Azure Load Balancer**, and **VPN**.
- **Pricing**: You pay for the VM based on the size, region, and usage, with hourly or monthly billing options.

Step-by-Step Guide to Creating a Virtual Machine in Azure

Now, let's walk through the process of creating a Virtual Machine (VM) using the **Azure Portal**. This is the most common and user-friendly method for deploying VMs in Azure.

Step 1: Access the Azure Portal

1. Log in to the **Azure Portal** at https://portal.azure.com.
2. If you don't have an account yet, you can create one (you may also use the free tier to start experimenting with VMs).

Step 2: Start the VM Creation Process

1. In the Azure Portal, search for **Virtual Machines** in the search bar.
2. Click on **Virtual Machines** in the search results to open the Virtual Machines dashboard.
3. Click on the **+ Add** button to start the process of creating a new virtual machine.

Step 3: Configure Basic Settings

1. **Subscription**: Select the subscription under which this VM will be created (for example, if you're using a free account, it will default to your free subscription).
2. **Resource Group**: Choose an existing resource group or create a new one. Resource groups allow you to manage related resources together. For example, you might create a new resource group called `MyVMResourceGroup`.
3. **VM Name**: Provide a unique name for your virtual machine (e.g., `MyVM`).
4. **Region**: Choose the Azure region where you want to deploy your VM. Make sure to select a region close to your users for lower latency.
5. **Availability Options**:
   o For basic workloads, you can select **No infrastructure redundancy required**.
   o For production workloads, consider selecting **Availability Zone** or **Availability Set** to increase fault tolerance.

Step 4: Select the Operating System

1. **Image**: Select the image of the operating system you want to run on your VM. For this example, let's choose **Ubuntu 20.04 LTS**.
2. **Version**: You can select the specific version or use the default latest version.
3. **Size**: Choose a size based on your workload. For testing purposes, select the **Standard B1s** size (1 vCPU, 1 GB RAM). This is a small, cost-effective instance that is eligible for the free tier.

Step 5: Configure Authentication

1. **Authentication Type**:
   o For Linux VMs, select **SSH public key** as the authentication method. This is more secure than using a password and allows you to SSH into your VM using your private key.
   o If you're using a Windows VM, you'll use **Password** authentication by setting a username and password.
2. **SSH Key Pair**:

- If you selected SSH, you'll need to either upload an existing **SSH public key** or generate a new one. You can generate an SSH key using the following command on Linux/Mac:
- `ssh-keygen -t rsa -b 2048`

  For Windows, you can use tools like **PuTTYgen** to generate SSH keys.

Step 6: Configure Networking

1. **Virtual Network (VNet)**: Choose an existing **Virtual Network** or create a new one. A VNet enables communication between your resources in a secure, isolated network.
2. **Subnet**: Select a subnet within the VNet. If you don't have any subnets, Azure will create one for you by default.
3. **Public IP**: If you need to connect to your VM from the internet (e.g., to SSH into a Linux server), select **Dynamic** for the public IP. This will allocate an IP that can be accessed externally.
4. **Network Security Group (NSG)**: You'll need to create or select an existing **Network Security Group**. This acts as a virtual firewall for your VM to control inbound and outbound traffic. You can add rules such as **Allow SSH (Port 22)** for Linux or **Allow RDP (Port 3389)** for Windows.

Step 7: Configure Additional Settings (Optional)

1. **Disks**:
   - By default, Azure creates an **OS disk** (for the operating system) and **temporary disk** (for caching purposes).
   - You can also attach **additional data disks** if needed for storage.
2. **Monitoring**: Enable monitoring features like **Boot diagnostics**, **Guest OS diagnostics**, and **Azure Monitor** to help keep track of the VM's performance and health.
3. **Management**: Configure automatic **backup**, **auto-shutdown** to save costs when the VM is not in use, and other features to optimize the VM's management.

- Review all your settings and configurations. Azure will validate your configuration to ensure everything is set up properly.
- Once validation is successful, click on **Create**. Azure will begin provisioning your VM.

Step-by-Step Example: SSH Into a Linux VM

After the VM is deployed, you can **SSH** into it to start managing it.

1. **Find the Public IP Address**:
   After the VM is created, go to the **Virtual Machines** dashboard and click on your VM. Copy the **Public IP address** listed in the overview section.
2. **Connect to the VM via SSH**: Open a terminal on your local machine and use the following command:

```
ssh -i /path/to/your/private/key.pem azureuser@<Public-IP>
```

   Replace /path/to/your/private/key.pem with the actual path to your private key, and <Public-IP> with the public IP address of your VM.

3. **Start Using the VM**:
   Once connected, you can start using your VM just like you would with any Linux server. You can install software, configure the system, and deploy your application.

Managing Virtual Machines in Azure

Once your VM is up and running, managing it becomes a vital task. Here's how you can monitor and scale your VM.

1. Monitoring the VM

Azure provides several tools to monitor your VM's health and performance:

- **Metrics**: View CPU usage, disk performance, network performance, etc.
- **Logs**: Check the logs for system activities or any errors.
- **Azure Monitor**: Set up automated alerts and monitor the VM continuously.

2. Scaling the VM

If you need more power for your VM:

1. Go to the **VM dashboard** and click **Size** under **Settings**.
2. Select a new size based on your requirements (e.g., more CPUs or memory).

For **VM Scale Sets**, Azure can automatically scale your VM instances based on demand. This is ideal for applications with fluctuating traffic.

3. Stopping and Restarting VMs

You can stop or restart a VM directly from the Azure Portal:

- To **stop** a VM, click **Stop** in the VM's management interface.
- To **restart**, click **Restart**.

Stopping a VM shuts it down but retains its configuration. If you want to **terminate** the VM, you can delete it.

Best Practices for Managing VMs in Azure

1. **Use Availability Sets for High Availability**:
   When deploying production workloads, use **Availability Sets** to distribute your VMs across different fault and update domains.

This ensures that your VMs remain available in case of hardware failure or planned maintenance.

2. **Implement Backup and Recovery**:
   Use **Azure Backup** to automatically back up your VMs to ensure data safety. Implement **site recovery** to facilitate disaster recovery in case of failure.

3. **Use Managed Disks**:
   Always use **Managed Disks** to simplify disk management and ensure better performance and scalability.

4. **Automate VM Deployment**:
   For large-scale VM deployments, use **Azure Resource Manager (ARM) templates** or **Azure Automation** to automate the provisioning process.

5. **Use Tags for Resource Management**:
   Tagging your resources helps you organize and manage VMs more effectively, especially when working with multiple projects or teams.

Case Study: Deploying a Web Application on Azure

Scenario: **TechSolutions**, a web development company, needs to deploy a production-ready web application on Azure. Here's how they use **Azure VMs**:

Steps Taken:

1. **Create a Virtual Machine**:
   Sarah, the lead developer, creates a **Windows Server 2019** VM with 2 vCPUs and 4 GB of RAM. She selects a **Standard B2ms** size for the VM to meet the performance requirements.

2. **Install Web Server**:
   Sarah SSHs into the VM and installs **IIS** (Internet Information Services) to serve the web application. She also installs necessary application dependencies like **SQL Server** for database management.

3. **Set Up Load Balancing**:
   As traffic increases, Sarah uses **Azure Load Balancer** to distribute requests between multiple VMs running the web application, ensuring high availability and performance.

4. **Scale and Monitor**:
   The team uses **Azure Monitor** to keep track of the VM's performance and set alerts for any resource overuse. Based on demand, they scale the VMs vertically (adding more memory) and horizontally (adding more VMs).

Creating and managing virtual machines in Azure is a powerful way to leverage cloud computing for a wide range of applications. From setting up your VM to configuring networking, security, and scaling, Azure provides a flexible and robust platform for hosting your workloads.

4.4 Azure Storage Solutions

Azure Storage is a comprehensive and highly scalable cloud storage solution designed to meet a wide range of storage needs, including storing structured data, unstructured data, backups, and much more. Azure offers various storage types, each tailored to specific use cases. Understanding the available options and knowing when to use them is crucial for efficient and cost-effective cloud storage.

What is Azure Storage?

Azure Storage provides cloud storage services to store and manage data in a variety of formats. It offers a secure, durable, and highly available platform for storing data, with integrated features like encryption, access control, and redundancy.

Azure Storage includes multiple services:

1. **Blob Storage**: For storing unstructured data, such as text and binary data (images, videos, backups).
2. **Disk Storage**: For persistent storage of virtual machine (VM) data (OS disks and data disks).
3. **File Storage**: A managed file share service that provides access to files using SMB protocol.

4. **Queue Storage**: For storing and managing queues of messages used in cloud applications.
5. **Table Storage**: A NoSQL key-value store for structured data.

In this guide, we will focus on **Blob Storage** and **Disk Storage**, two of the most commonly used services for data storage in Azure.

---

1. Azure Blob Storage: Object Storage for Unstructured Data

Azure Blob Storage is designed for storing unstructured data such as documents, images, videos, backups, and logs. It is highly scalable and can handle petabytes of data. The service is optimized for storing large amounts of data, and it's used in a variety of applications, from websites to big data analytics.

Key Features of Azure Blob Storage:

- **Scalability**: Handles massive amounts of data, making it ideal for big data, data lakes, and backups.
- **Redundancy**: Offers multiple redundancy options to ensure data durability, such as **LRS (Locally Redundant Storage)** and **GRS (Geo-Redundant Storage)**.
- **Access Control**: Supports access control through **Azure Active Directory (Azure AD)**, **shared access signatures (SAS)**, and **role-based access control (RBAC)**.
- **Lifecycle Management**: Supports automated management of data lifecycle, including transitioning data between storage tiers (hot, cool, and archive).

Blob Storage Components:

1. **Containers**: Containers are like folders in a traditional file system. They group blobs (objects) together within a storage account.
2. **Blobs**: Blobs are the actual data objects. Azure Blob Storage supports three types of blobs:
    - **Block blobs**: Optimized for storing large amounts of data, such as media files, images, and backups.

- **Append blobs**: Ideal for logging data that needs to be appended continuously.
- **Page blobs**: Used for storing virtual hard disks (VHDs) for Azure VMs.

Steps to Create and Work with Blob Storage

Let's go through the steps to create a **Blob Storage account** and interact with it via the Azure Portal.

1. **Create a Storage Account**:
   - Navigate to the **Azure Portal** and search for **Storage Accounts**.
   - Click **+ Add** to create a new storage account.
   - Choose your **Subscription** and **Resource Group**. Name your storage account (e.g., `myblobstorage`) and choose a region.
   - Select the **Performance** and **Replication** options (e.g., **Standard performance** with **LRS replication**).
2. **Create a Blob Container**:
   - Once your storage account is created, go to the **Containers** section within the storage account.
   - Click **+ Container** and name your container (e.g., `mycontainer`).
   - Set the **Access level** to either **Private** (default), **Blob** (public read access to blobs), or **Container** (public read access to container and blobs).
3. **Upload Data to Blob Storage**:
   - Inside the container, click on **Upload** to upload files from your local machine.
   - Select the files you want to upload and click **Upload** to add them to the container.
4. **Access Data from Blob Storage**:
   - You can access the blob data using the **Azure Portal** or through **Azure Storage SDKs** (e.g., Python, .NET, Java).
   - To download the file, click on the file name and then click **Download**.
5. **Set Up Blob Lifecycle Management**:

- To manage the lifecycle of your blobs, go to the **Lifecycle management** section within the storage account and configure rules for transitioning blobs to different tiers (hot, cool, archive) based on the data's age or usage.

---

2. Azure Disk Storage: Persistent Storage for Virtual Machines

Azure Disk Storage is used for persistent storage for your virtual machines (VMs). It provides high-performance, durable storage for VM operating systems, data disks, and temporary storage. Disk storage is primarily used for workloads that require high throughput, low latency, and fast access to data.

Key Features of Azure Disk Storage:

- **High Performance**: Offers multiple disk types, including **Standard HDD**, **Standard SSD**, and **Premium SSD**, to match your performance requirements.
- **Durability**: Data on Azure disks is automatically replicated to ensure durability. Premium SSDs provide low-latency, high-performance storage, while Standard SSDs and HDDs are cost-effective for less performance-demanding workloads.
- **Snapshot and Backup**: You can create **snapshots** of your disks for backup and disaster recovery purposes.
- **Encryption**: Azure provides built-in encryption for both data at rest (using **Azure Storage Service Encryption**) and in transit (using **TLS/SSL**).

Steps to Create and Work with Azure Disk Storage

1. **Create a Managed Disk**:
   - In the Azure Portal, search for **Disks** and click **+ Add**.
   - Choose the **Subscription**, **Resource Group**, and **Disk Name**.
   - Select the **Disk Type** (Standard HDD, Standard SSD, Premium SSD).
   - Specify the **Size** of the disk (in GB).

2. **Attach a Disk to a Virtual Machine**:
   o After creating the disk, navigate to **Virtual Machines** and select the VM to which you want to attach the disk.
   o In the **Disks** section of the VM, click + **Add data disk** and select the disk you created earlier.
3. **Create a Snapshot of a Disk**:
   o To create a snapshot of a disk for backup purposes, go to the **Disks** section, select the disk, and click **Create snapshot**.
   o Choose the **Snapshot Name** and specify the **Storage Type**.
4. **Access Disk Data**:
   o The data on disks can be accessed through the operating system running on the attached VM. For instance, if you attach a data disk to a Linux VM, you can mount it like any other Linux disk.

Choosing Between Blob Storage and Disk Storage

While both **Blob Storage** and **Disk Storage** are used for storing data in Azure, they serve different purposes:

- **Blob Storage** is ideal for:
  o Storing unstructured data like documents, media files, and backups.
  o Serving large amounts of data to applications or users (e.g., static website hosting, data lakes).
  o Archiving data and managing its lifecycle (transitioning between hot, cool, and archive tiers).
- **Disk Storage** is best for:
  o Storing the operating system disk and data disks for Azure virtual machines.
  o Performance-critical applications that require high throughput and low latency (e.g., databases, enterprise applications).
  o Data that needs to be attached to running VMs for processing.

Case Study: Using Azure Storage for a Web Application

Scenario: **WebDesignCo**, a web development company, needs to host a web application on Azure. They choose to use **Blob Storage** for static content (images, CSS, JS files) and **Disk Storage** for their VM's data and backups.

Steps Taken:

1. **Blob Storage for Static Files**:
   - WebDesignCo creates an **Azure Blob Storage account** and sets up a container for storing static assets.
   - They upload images, JavaScript, and CSS files to the container and configure public access for these files to be served to users visiting the website.
2. **Azure VM for Hosting the Web App**:
   - They deploy a **Linux-based VM** on Azure to host the web application.
   - They attach an **Azure Disk** to the VM to store dynamic content and user data (e.g., database backups, application logs).
3. **Snapshots for Backup**:
   - Regular snapshots of the disk are created to back up the web app's data, ensuring they can quickly restore in case of failure.
4. **Scaling and Redundancy**:
   - To ensure high availability and performance, WebDesignCo uses **Premium SSD disks** for their VM's data and **Geo-Redundant Storage (GRS)** for their Blob Storage to ensure that the data is replicated across multiple regions.

Azure provides a robust and flexible storage solution with a variety of services tailored to different use cases. Whether you need to store unstructured data with **Blob Storage**, persist VM data with **Disk Storage**, or manage backups and logs, Azure's storage options allow you to scale and manage your data efficiently.

4.5 Managing Virtual Networks in Azure

In cloud computing, **networking** is a critical element for ensuring that resources can securely and efficiently communicate with one another. Azure provides a variety of networking tools to help you securely connect your resources, both within Azure and externally. One of the key networking tools in Azure is **Virtual Networks (VNets)**, which allow you to define and manage your private network in the Azure cloud.

What is an Azure Virtual Network (VNet)?

An **Azure Virtual Network (VNet)** is a logically isolated network within the Azure cloud where you can deploy and manage your resources. It's similar to a traditional on-premises network but with the scalability, security, and flexibility of the cloud.

A **VNet** allows you to:

- **Segment resources**: Organize resources into different subnets for better security and management.
- **Isolate traffic**: Control traffic between your resources using network security groups and route tables.
- **Connect on-premises networks**: Use **VPN Gateway** or **ExpressRoute** to connect your Azure VNet to your on-premises infrastructure securely.
- **Communicate between Azure resources**: Enable secure communication between VMs, databases, and other Azure resources that reside within the VNet.

Key Components of an Azure Virtual Network

Before diving into creating and managing VNets, let's take a look at the key components that make up an Azure Virtual Network:

1. **Subnets**:
   A **VNet** can be divided into smaller segments called **subnets**. Each

subnet can host different types of resources, such as VMs, web applications, or databases. Subnets allow you to group related resources together for easier management and better network performance.

2. **IP Addressing**:
When you create a VNet, you assign it a **CIDR block** (e.g., 10.0.0.0/16). This defines the range of IP addresses that will be used within the VNet. Each subnet will have its own portion of the IP range, ensuring resources can communicate without conflicting IP addresses.

3. **Network Security Groups (NSGs)**:
NSGs are used to control inbound and outbound traffic to resources within a subnet or VNet. You define **rules** (allow or deny) based on IP address, port, and protocol. For example, you can use an NSG to restrict access to a subnet that contains sensitive data.

4. **Route Tables**:
Route tables define how traffic flows within the VNet and between subnets. You can customize routing rules to allow or block traffic to specific destinations, improving security and traffic management.

5. **Public and Private IP Addresses**:
Resources within a VNet can either use **private IP addresses** (for internal communication) or **public IP addresses** (for internet-facing services).

6. **VPN Gateway**:
Azure allows you to create a **VPN Gateway** to securely connect your on-premises network to your Azure VNet over a public internet connection.

Step-by-Step Guide to Creating a Virtual Network in Azure

Now, let's go through the process of creating an Azure VNet, adding subnets, and configuring security.

Step 1: Create a Virtual Network (VNet)

1. **Go to the Azure Portal**:
   Log into the **Azure Portal** at https://portal.azure.com.
2. **Create a New Virtual Network**:
   - In the search bar, type **Virtual Networks** and click on **Virtual Networks** under **Networking**.
   - Click + **Add** to create a new VNet.
3. **Configure the VNet Settings**:
   - **Subscription**: Select your Azure subscription.
   - **Resource Group**: Either select an existing resource group or create a new one (e.g., `MyNetworkResourceGroup`).
   - **Region**: Choose the region where your VNet will reside (e.g., **East US**).
   - **Name**: Enter a name for your VNet (e.g., `MyFirstVNet`).
   - **Address Space**: Define the CIDR block for your VNet (e.g., `10.0.0.0/16`). This range will determine the available IP addresses within your VNet.
4. **Create the VNet**:
   After configuring the settings, click **Review + Create**, review the information, and then click **Create**. Azure will now deploy your VNet.

Step 2: Add Subnets to Your VNet

Subnets are used to logically separate resources within your VNet. For example, you might create a **Public Subnet** for web servers and a **Private Subnet** for databases.

1. **Go to Subnets**:
   After the VNet is created, go to the **Subnets** section in the VNet overview page.
2. **Add Subnets**:
   - Click on + **Subnet** to add a new subnet.
   - **Name**: Enter a name for the subnet (e.g., `PublicSubnet`).
   - **Subnet Address Range**: Choose an address range within the VNet's CIDR block (e.g., `10.0.1.0/24`).
   - **Security Settings**: You can choose to associate the subnet with a **Network Security Group (NSG)** to control access.

3. **Create Additional Subnets**:
    You can add multiple subnets as needed, such as **PrivateSubnet** for internal applications, with different IP ranges.

Step 3: Configure Network Security Groups (NSG)

NSGs control inbound and outbound traffic for Azure resources. By default, a VNet's resources are open to all traffic, but you can restrict access using NSGs.

1. **Create a Network Security Group**:
    o In the Azure Portal, search for **Network Security Groups** and click on + **Add**.
    o Choose your **Subscription** and **Resource Group**.
    o **Name**: Name the NSG (e.g., MyNSG).
    o **Region**: Select the same region as your VNet.
    o Click **Create** to deploy the NSG.
2. **Configure NSG Rules**:
    o Once the NSG is created, go to the **Inbound security rules** and **Outbound security rules** sections to create new rules.
    o For example, to allow HTTP traffic to a **public subnet**:
        ▪ Add an inbound rule with:
            ▪ **Source**: Any
            ▪ **Source port ranges**: *
            ▪ **Destination**: Any
            ▪ **Destination port ranges**: 80 (HTTP)
            ▪ **Protocol**: TCP
            ▪ **Action**: Allow
3. **Associate NSG with Subnet**:
    o Go to the **Subnets** section of your VNet and click on the **Subnet** you want to associate the NSG with.
    o Under **Network Security Group**, select the NSG you created earlier.

Step 4: Configure a VPN Gateway (Optional)

A **VPN Gateway** allows you to securely connect your on-premises network to Azure. This can be useful for hybrid cloud setups.

1. **Create a Virtual Network Gateway**:
   o In the Azure Portal, search for **Virtual Network Gateway** and click **+ Add**.
   o Choose your **Subscription**, **Resource Group**, and **Region**.
   o **Name**: Provide a name for the gateway (e.g., `MyVPNGateway`).
   o **VPN Type**: Choose **Route-based** (recommended).
   o **SKU**: Select the SKU that fits your performance and cost requirements.
2. **Configure the VPN Connection**:
   o After the gateway is deployed, you can configure the **VPN Connection** to your on-premises network using either **IPsec/IKE** or **ExpressRoute**.

Step 5: Set Up Peering (Optional)

VNet Peering allows two VNets to communicate with each other securely and privately. This is useful when you want resources in different VNets to communicate.

1. **Create VNet Peering**:
   o In the Azure Portal, go to your first VNet.
   o Under **Settings**, select **Peerings** and click **+ Add**.
   o Choose the second VNet you want to peer with and configure the peering settings.
   o This enables communication between the VNets through private IPs.

Best Practices for Managing Azure Virtual Networks

1. **Use Subnets to Segregate Resources**:
   Create separate subnets for different types of resources (e.g., web servers, databases, and application servers) to improve security and manageability.
2. **Use Network Security Groups (NSGs) Wisely**:
   Apply **least privilege** to NSG rules by allowing only the necessary

traffic to your resources. For example, restrict access to databases by only allowing internal traffic.

3. **Leverage Private IP Addresses**:
   Use **private IPs** for internal communication within the VNet. Only expose resources that require external communication (like web servers) via **public IPs**.

4. **Consider Azure Bastion**:
   For enhanced security, use **Azure Bastion** to securely connect to your VMs over **RDP** or **SSH** without exposing them to the public internet.

5. **Use VNet Peering for Multi-VNet Communication**:
   Use **VNet Peering** to allow secure communication between VNets in different regions or subscriptions, enabling hybrid architectures.

Case Study: Deploying a Multi-Tier Application with Azure VNets

Scenario: A company, **TechSolutions**, is deploying a web application in Azure that consists of three layers: a **web layer**, an **application layer**, and a **database layer**.

Steps Taken:

1. **Create a VNet**:
   TechSolutions creates a VNet with the address range `10.0.0.0/16`. They then divide the network into three subnets:
   - **WebSubnet** (for web servers)
   - **AppSubnet** (for application servers)
   - **DBSubnet** (for database servers)

2. **Apply NSGs**:
   TechSolutions applies a restrictive NSG to the **DBSubnet**, allowing only traffic from the **AppSubnet**. The **WebSubnet** has an open NSG to allow incoming HTTP traffic.

3. **Set Up Peering**:
   TechSolutions sets up **VNet Peering** between their production VNet and a separate **test VNet** to facilitate testing in a separate environment while keeping them connected securely.

4. **Configure VPN Gateway**:
   TechSolutions connects their on-premises network to Azure using a **VPN Gateway** for secure communication with internal systems.

Managing Virtual Networks in Azure is fundamental for building secure, scalable cloud applications. By understanding the core components like VNets, subnets, NSGs, and VPN Gateways, you can effectively design and manage your Azure networking environment.

As you grow your cloud infrastructure, consider using advanced features like **VNet Peering**, **ExpressRoute**, and **Network Virtual Appliances** to extend your network and optimize communication between Azure resources and on-premises systems.

4.6 Introduction to Azure Active Directory (AAD)

Azure Active Directory (AAD) is a cloud-based identity and access management service from Microsoft. It is designed to provide secure access to applications and resources for users and devices within an organization. With Azure AD, you can manage identities, control access, and ensure security across your cloud and on-premises environments.

What is Azure Active Directory (AAD)?

Azure Active Directory (AAD) is Microsoft's cloud-based identity and access management (IAM) service. It provides a unified platform for managing identities, authentication, and permissions across Microsoft services, third-party apps, and on-premises systems. Unlike traditional Active Directory (AD), which operates in an on-premises environment, Azure AD is designed for cloud-first architectures.

Core Benefits of Azure AD:

1. **Identity Management**: AAD stores user identities and provides authentication and authorization for cloud resources.
2. **Single Sign-On (SSO)**: AAD enables SSO for applications, allowing users to authenticate once and access a wide range of applications without re-entering credentials.
3. **Multi-Factor Authentication (MFA)**: Enhances security by requiring multiple forms of verification before granting access to sensitive resources.
4. **Role-Based Access Control (RBAC)**: AAD allows organizations to assign permissions based on roles, ensuring that users have the appropriate access levels for their tasks.
5. **Integration with Azure Resources**: AAD integrates seamlessly with other Azure services, making it the backbone of security and user management for any organization using Azure.

Key Features of Azure Active Directory

Azure Active Directory offers a variety of powerful features that support security, compliance, and efficient identity management. Let's take a closer look at some of the most important features.

1. Identity Management

Azure AD provides centralized identity management, allowing you to create, update, and delete users and groups across your organization.

- **Users**: You can create individual user accounts for employees, contractors, and partners. These accounts are used for accessing resources both on-premises and in the cloud.
- **Groups**: Grouping users into **security groups** or **Microsoft 365 groups** simplifies management and access control by enabling you to assign permissions to entire sets of users at once.

Creating a User in Azure AD: To create a user in Azure AD, follow these steps:

1. In the Azure Portal, go to **Azure Active Directory**.
2. Under **Manage**, click on **Users** and then click **+ New user**.

3. Enter the user's **username**, **name**, and **password**. You can also set up **multi-factor authentication** and **roles** for the user here.

Example: Creating a new user with the username `jane.doe@company.com` and assigning her to the **Sales Group**.

2. Authentication

Azure AD supports multiple forms of authentication, including traditional password-based login, **multi-factor authentication (MFA)**, and **passwordless authentication**.

- **Single Sign-On (SSO)**: With Azure AD SSO, users can sign in once and gain access to all integrated applications, both cloud-based (like Office 365, SharePoint) and on-premises applications.
- **Passwordless Authentication**: Azure AD allows for **passwordless authentication** using methods like **Windows Hello**, **FIDO2 security keys**, or **Microsoft Authenticator**.

MFA Setup Example:

1. In the Azure portal, go to **Azure Active Directory > Security > Multi-Factor Authentication**.
2. Set up the **MFA settings**, including preferred verification methods like text messages, mobile apps, or email.

3. Conditional Access

Azure AD provides **Conditional Access** policies that help enforce security by applying specific rules for accessing applications or resources based on conditions like:

- **User location** (e.g., only allowing access from trusted countries).
- **Device compliance** (e.g., requiring a device to be compliant with security policies).
- **Risk level** (e.g., requiring additional verification if Azure detects unusual sign-in activity).

For example, you can create a rule that requires **MFA** if a user is accessing an application from an unfamiliar location or device.

Example of Creating a Conditional Access Policy:

1. Go to **Azure Active Directory** > **Security** > **Conditional Access**.
2. Click **+ New policy** and define the conditions (e.g., apply to **All Users** or specific groups).
3. Set the **conditions** (e.g., location or device compliance).
4. Choose **Grant** to enforce MFA for access.

4. Azure AD Roles and Permissions

Azure AD uses **Role-Based Access Control (RBAC)** to manage who can access resources and what actions they can perform. Roles in Azure AD define a user's permissions.

- **Built-in Roles**: Azure AD includes predefined roles like **Global Administrator**, **User Administrator**, **Application Administrator**, etc.
- **Custom Roles**: You can create custom roles if the built-in roles don't meet your requirements.

Assigning a Role:

1. In the **Azure Portal**, navigate to **Azure Active Directory** > **Roles and administrators**.
2. Select a role (e.g., **Global Administrator**).
3. Click **+ Add assignment** and select the user to assign the role.

Step-by-Step Example: Managing Users and Groups in Azure AD

Let's walk through the process of managing users and groups in Azure AD.

Step 1: Create a New User

1. In the **Azure Portal**, go to **Azure Active Directory**.
2. Click **Users** under **Manage** and select **+ New user**.

3. Enter the user's **name, user principal name** (e.g., `jane.doe@company.com`), and set a password.
4. Click **Create** to add the new user.

1. In **Azure Active Directory**, click on **Groups** under **Manage**.
2. Click **+ New Group** and choose **Security** or **Microsoft 365** for the group type.
3. Provide a **Group Name** and click **Create**.
4. To add users to the group, go to the group's settings and click **Members** > **+ Add members**, then select the users to add.

Step 3: Assign a Role to a User

1. Go to **Azure Active Directory** > **Roles and administrators**.
2. Select a built-in role (e.g., **Global Administrator**).
3. Click **+ Add assignment**, select the user (e.g., `jane.doe@company.com`), and assign the role.

Integration of Azure AD with External Applications

Azure AD provides seamless integration with a wide range of applications and services, including both Microsoft and third-party applications.

- **Office 365**: Azure AD is tightly integrated with Microsoft services like **Office 365**, enabling you to manage users, licenses, and security settings across all Office applications.
- **Third-Party Applications**: You can integrate external applications with Azure AD for single sign-on (SSO) and access management using **SAML, OAuth**, or **OpenID Connect**.

Example of Integrating a Third-Party Application (e.g., Salesforce):

1. In the **Azure Portal**, navigate to **Azure Active Directory** > **Enterprise applications** > **+ New application**.
2. Select **Salesforce** from the list of applications, or use **Custom app** for a non-listed app.

3. Configure the necessary settings (e.g., enable SSO using **SAML**), and assign users or groups who should have access to the app.

Case Study: Implementing Azure AD for a Web Application

Scenario: A company, **WebDevCo**, wants to implement Azure AD to manage user access to their internal web application.

Steps Taken:

1. **Create a Tenant**:
   WebDevCo creates an **Azure AD Tenant** for managing identities.
2. **Add Users**:
   They create individual user accounts for each employee using the **New User** feature in Azure AD.
3. **Create a Security Group**:
   They create a **Developers** group in Azure AD, which will allow their development team to access specific applications.
4. **Assign Roles**:
   Developers are assigned the **Application Administrator** role to configure and manage the internal web application's settings.
5. **Enable SSO**:
   WebDevCo integrates the **web application** with Azure AD using **SSO** for seamless login. Users can now log in once to access not only the internal app but also other Office 365 services.
6. **MFA and Conditional Access**:
   For enhanced security, they enable **MFA** for all users and configure **Conditional Access** to require MFA for access from unfamiliar locations.

Best Practices for Managing Azure Active Directory

1. **Use Multi-Factor Authentication (MFA)**:
   Always enable MFA for added security, especially for users with administrative privileges or those accessing sensitive resources.

2. **Leverage Conditional Access Policies**:
   Apply conditional access policies based on user location, device compliance, and risk level to ensure secure access to your resources.
3. **Organize Users and Groups Efficiently**:
   Use **groups** for role-based access control and manage permissions effectively. This reduces administrative overhead and ensures users have appropriate access levels.
4. **Implement Role-Based Access Control (RBAC)**:
   Use **built-in roles** for access management, and create **custom roles** for more granular control over permissions.
5. **Regularly Review and Audit Access**:
   Regularly review user access and roles to ensure that users have the correct permissions. Utilize **Azure AD reporting** to track sign-ins, changes, and potential security risks.

Azure Active Directory (AAD) is a critical component for managing identity and access in the Azure cloud. It provides a unified platform for managing user identities, authenticating users, and controlling access to resources across both Azure and external applications. By leveraging features like **single sign-on (SSO), multi-factor authentication (MFA),** and **conditional access**, you can ensure that your resources are secure and that users have the appropriate level of access.

Chapter 5: Getting Hands-On with Google Cloud

Google Cloud Platform (GCP) is one of the leading cloud computing platforms, offering a range of powerful services that help developers and businesses deploy, manage, and scale applications on the cloud. With Google's focus on high-performance infrastructure, innovative machine learning tools, and a rich suite of cloud services, GCP is an ideal platform for those looking to harness the power of the cloud.

In this chapter, we will walk through the key components of Google Cloud, starting with setting up your Google Cloud account and moving through practical exercises on deploying virtual machines, managing storage, and understanding networking in GCP.

5.1 Creating a Google Cloud Account

Creating a **Google Cloud account** is the first step in unlocking the full potential of Google Cloud Platform (GCP). Google Cloud provides an extensive suite of tools for computing, storage, networking, machine learning, and more. Whether you're a developer, data scientist, or business leader, GCP allows you to harness powerful cloud computing services to build scalable applications and manage resources efficiently.

Why Choose Google Cloud?

Before diving into the account creation process, it's helpful to understand why you might choose **Google Cloud** for your projects. GCP offers:

- **Scalable Infrastructure**: Google Cloud runs on the same infrastructure that powers Google's services (like **YouTube**, **Search**, and **Gmail**), ensuring high performance, reliability, and security.

- **Powerful Services**: GCP provides a wide range of services such as **Compute Engine** for VMs, **Kubernetes Engine** for container orchestration, **BigQuery** for data analytics, and **Cloud Storage** for scalable file storage.
- **Machine Learning and AI**: Google's leadership in AI and machine learning is reflected in its **AI Platform**, which provides pre-built models and a platform for training custom models.
- **Global Reach**: GCP's global network ensures low-latency access to your resources, no matter where you are in the world.

Step-by-Step Guide to Creating Your Google Cloud Account

Let's get started with the process of creating a Google Cloud account, which can be done in just a few minutes. This guide will walk you through each step with screenshots, practical insights, and key tips.

Step 1: Visit Google Cloud's Website

1. Open your browser and navigate to Google Cloud's website.
2. On the homepage, you'll see a **"Get started for free"** button. This will allow you to sign up for a **free tier** with $300 in credits for 90 days, so you can experiment with Google Cloud without incurring charges.

Step 2: Sign In with Your Google Account

1. **Google Account**: If you already have a **Google account** (e.g., Gmail), you can sign in using your existing credentials. If not, you'll need to create a new Google account by clicking on **Create account**.
2. **Create Account**: Follow the prompts to create a Google account, including providing your email address, password, and phone number for account verification.

Google Cloud requires billing information to verify your identity. However, you won't be charged unless you exceed the free tier's limits.

1. **Billing Account**: After signing in, you'll be asked to enter your **billing information** (credit or debit card details). Don't worry— Google offers a **$300 free credit** for new users, so you'll only incur charges once the credit is exhausted or the 90-day period ends.
2. **Verification**: Google uses your billing information to verify your account, ensuring that only valid users can access the cloud resources.

Personal Insight: Even though the billing information is required for verification, your account is **not automatically charged** during the free trial period. Google Cloud's billing dashboard allows you to easily track your usage and credits, so you can avoid surprise charges.

Step 4: Create a New Project

A **Google Cloud project** is a logical container that holds your resources. Every action or resource you create in GCP is associated with a project. When you first sign up, you'll be prompted to create a new project.

1. **Project Name**: Choose a meaningful name for your project. For example, `MyFirstGCPProject` or `CloudAppDev`.
2. **Billing Account**: Select the billing account you entered earlier (it should be pre-selected by default).
3. **Location**: Select the location (region) of your project resources. Google Cloud offers data centers in multiple regions across the globe. Choose a region that is closest to your primary user base to minimize latency.

Once your project is created, you'll be directed to the **Google Cloud Console**, which is the web interface for managing all your cloud resources.

Step 5: Google Cloud Console Overview

The **Google Cloud Console** is where you'll manage and monitor all your resources. When you first log in, you'll be greeted with the following:

1. **Dashboard**: This is the default view, where you can quickly see your active projects, services, and billing information.
2. **Navigation Menu**: Located on the left side of the console, this menu allows you to access different services such as **Compute Engine**, **Cloud Storage**, **BigQuery**, and more.
3. **Cloud Shell**: Google Cloud Console provides an integrated **Cloud Shell** (a terminal window in your browser) that you can use to interact with your Google Cloud resources using the **gcloud CLI**.

Personal Insight: As a beginner, I highly recommend exploring the **Cloud Shell**. It's pre-configured with the **Google Cloud SDK** and provides access to a **command-line interface** right from the console, making it easy to interact with GCP resources without setting up anything on your local machine.

Understanding Google Cloud's Pricing Model

Google Cloud operates on a **pay-as-you-go** pricing model, which means you only pay for the resources you use. However, it's crucial to understand the components of Google Cloud's pricing to manage costs effectively.

1. Free Tier and Free Trial Credit

- **$300 Free Credit**: New users get **$300** in free credit for 90 days. This credit can be used for any Google Cloud services, and it allows you to experiment with a wide range of tools, from virtual machines to storage and machine learning services.
- **Always Free**: Google Cloud offers a range of services that are always free within certain usage limits, including **Cloud Functions**, **App Engine**, **BigQuery**, and **Cloud Storage** (with limited storage and usage).

- Google Cloud's pricing is typically divided into **compute resources** (e.g., **virtual machines**), **storage** (e.g., **Cloud Storage**), and **networking**. Each service has its own pricing, which is based on factors such as:
    - **Compute**: For services like Compute Engine, pricing depends on the size of the instance (e.g., **CPUs, RAM**) and usage duration (e.g., per hour).
    - **Storage**: Services like **Cloud Storage** and **Persistent Disks** charge based on the amount of data stored and data retrieval requests.
    - **Network**: Networking charges are based on the data transfer between regions, egress data (data leaving Google Cloud), and load balancing.

3. Pricing Calculator

Google provides a **pricing calculator** that helps you estimate the cost of your services based on your expected usage. It's a great tool for estimating costs before you commit to resources.

- You can access it at: Google Cloud Pricing Calculator.

Personal Insight: Use the **Google Cloud Pricing Calculator** before deploying resources. This will help you understand how different configurations, such as selecting different machine types or regions, can affect your cost.

Step 6: Exploring the Google Cloud Free Tier

The **Google Cloud Free Tier** is a great way to explore the platform without incurring costs. Here's a breakdown of the free offerings available:

- **Compute Engine**:
    - One **f1-micro instance** per month in the **U.S. regions** (free tier eligible) with **30 GB of HDD** storage.
    - 1 GB of **network egress** to the internet.

- **Cloud Storage**:
  - **5 GB** of **Regional Storage** for free, with **standard class** and up to **1 GB of outbound data** per month.
- **BigQuery**:
  - 1 TB of queries per month for free, which is perfect for small analytics workloads.
- **Cloud Functions**:
  - 2 million invocations per month.

Case Study: Setting Up a Google Cloud Project for Web Hosting

Let's walk through a simple case study of how to set up a Google Cloud project to host a basic web application. The goal is to use **Google Compute Engine** for hosting and **Cloud Storage** for static assets.

1. **Create a Project**:
   Start by creating a new Google Cloud project called `MyWebHostingProject`.
2. **Set Up Compute Engine**:
   Create a new **f1-micro instance** using **Ubuntu** as the operating system. This instance will host your web application (e.g., **Nginx** or **Apache**).
   - Use the **free-tier eligible instance** to keep costs low.
   - Set up the web server and configure the firewall to allow HTTP traffic.
3. **Add Storage**:
   Create a **Cloud Storage bucket** to store your static assets (e.g., images, CSS, JavaScript files).
   - Upload your assets to the bucket and make them publicly accessible.
   - Link the storage bucket to your web application for serving static files.
4. **Deploy the App**:
   With the server and storage set up, deploy your application and test it. Use the instance's public IP to access the web application.

Creating a Google Cloud account is the first step toward exploring the vast array of cloud services that Google offers. With the **$300 free credit** and **free-tier services**, you have a great opportunity to experiment without incurring significant costs. Once your account is set up, dive into the **Google Cloud Console**, create projects, and start experimenting with services like **Compute Engine**, **Cloud Storage**, and **BigQuery**.

Remember, Google Cloud offers a flexible **pay-as-you-go** pricing model, but using the **pricing

---

5.2 Google Cloud Console Overview

The **Google Cloud Console** is the primary interface for managing all of your Google Cloud resources. It provides a web-based dashboard where you can create, configure, and monitor services such as **Compute Engine**, **Cloud Storage**, **BigQuery**, **AI tools**, and more. The console allows you to interact with Google Cloud using a **graphical interface**, as well as a **command-line interface** (via Cloud Shell).

Why Use Google Cloud Console?

The Google Cloud Console is an essential tool for anyone working with Google Cloud Platform (GCP). It provides a user-friendly interface that helps developers, administrators, and other cloud professionals:

- **Create and manage resources**: Easily provision and configure cloud services, including virtual machines, storage, databases, and networking.
- **Monitor usage and performance**: View key metrics and logs, set up alerts, and monitor the health of your cloud infrastructure.
- **Collaborate and manage access**: Implement security policies and permissions to ensure the correct access controls are in place for your team members.
- **Integrate with Google Cloud services**: Directly interact with **AI**, **machine learning**, and **analytics** tools through the console.

By the end of this guide, you'll understand how to navigate the Google Cloud Console and leverage its features to manage your cloud resources efficiently.

Key Components of the Google Cloud Console

1. Dashboard

When you first log in to the Google Cloud Console, you'll be presented with the **Dashboard**. The dashboard gives you an overview of your projects and resources, allowing you to quickly access services and monitor your usage. It's your starting point when managing Google Cloud.

- **Resource Overview**: View the total number of active resources, like virtual machines, storage buckets, and databases, across all your projects.
- **Recent Activity**: Check recent actions, including resource creation, updates, and deletions, to stay on top of changes to your cloud environment.
- **Notifications**: The **bell icon** at the top of the console displays alerts about your resources, billing, or security issues.

Personal Insight: The Dashboard is an essential part of the Cloud Console. If you have multiple projects, you can customize this view to focus on specific resources or services.

---

2. Navigation Menu

The **Navigation Menu** is located on the left side of the Google Cloud Console and allows you to quickly access all of Google Cloud's services.

- **Home**: The starting point for your Google Cloud environment, where you can see your projects and dashboard.
- **IAM & Admin**: Manage identities, access, and roles for users in your organization.
- **Compute Engine**: Provision virtual machines and manage compute instances.
- **Storage**: Access and manage services like **Cloud Storage**, **Cloud SQL**, **BigQuery**, and **Persistent Disks**.
- **Networking**: Configure networking services like **Virtual Private Cloud (VPC)**, **Load Balancing**, and **Cloud DNS**.

- **BigQuery**: Manage and query large datasets stored in Google Cloud's data warehouse solution.
- **AI & Machine Learning**: Access services like **AI Platform**, **AutoML**, and **TensorFlow** for building machine learning models.

Example: When you click on **Compute Engine**, you'll be able to create and manage virtual machines directly from the console, making it easy to launch cloud infrastructure on the fly.

---

3. Project Selector

Google Cloud projects act as containers for your cloud resources. Each project is isolated, which means you can have different billing, access policies, and settings for each project. The **Project Selector** in the console allows you to switch between different projects.

- **Active Project**: The top of the console always shows the name of the currently active project. This is where all your resources will be created and managed.
- **Create or Select a Project**: You can click on the **project name** in the console header to create a new project or switch to an existing project.

Personal Insight: When working on multiple environments (e.g., development, staging, and production), it's a good idea to organize resources by project to keep things clean and secure.

---

4. Cloud Shell

Cloud Shell is a browser-based **command-line interface (CLI)** that allows you to interact with your Google Cloud resources directly from the console. It comes pre-configured with the **Google Cloud SDK** and other essential tools, so you can manage your resources without needing to install anything locally.

- **Interactive CLI**: Cloud Shell is fully interactive, enabling you to execute commands, manage resources, and automate tasks directly from your browser.

- **Pre-configured Environment**: Cloud Shell comes with pre-installed tools like **kubectl**, **gcloud**, and **Terraform**, making it easy to work with Google Cloud's infrastructure.

Example: You can use Cloud Shell to manage Google Kubernetes Engine (GKE) clusters or to automate VM provisioning using the `gcloud` CLI.

---

5. Billing and Account Management

Google Cloud has a robust billing system that allows you to track your usage, set up budgets, and view invoices. The **Billing** section of the console gives you full visibility into your costs and usage across your Google Cloud projects.

- **Billing Dashboard**: Track your active usage, view estimated costs, and analyze billing reports.
- **Budgets and Alerts**: Set up **budgets** to track costs over time and create **alerts** to notify you when you're close to exceeding a defined budget.
- **Invoices and Payments**: Access your billing history and download invoices for reporting purposes.

Example: You can set up a budget for your project to ensure that you don't accidentally exceed your expected cloud costs. The alert system will notify you via email if you're approaching the budget limit.

---

6. IAM & Admin

Identity and Access Management (IAM) is critical for securing your Google Cloud resources. The **IAM & Admin** section allows you to define who has access to your resources and what level of access they have.

- **Users and Permissions**: Add users, assign roles, and set permissions for each project or resource.
- **Roles**: Google Cloud uses **roles** to manage permissions. You can assign predefined roles, like **Viewer**, **Editor**, or **Owner**, or create custom roles to suit your organization's needs.

- **Audit Logs**: Review activity logs to monitor who is accessing what resources and what changes have been made.

Example: You can assign the **Viewer** role to team members who need read-only access to your cloud infrastructure, while giving admins the **Owner** role to manage resources and settings.

Navigating Google Cloud Services

Now that you understand the basic components of the Google Cloud Console, let's walk through the process of navigating and using some of the most common services.

1. Deploying a Virtual Machine (VM) on Compute Engine

Google Compute Engine allows you to create and manage virtual machines (VMs) on Google's infrastructure.

1. **Access Compute Engine**:
   - In the **Navigation Menu**, click on **Compute Engine** and select **VM instances**.
2. **Create a New VM**:
   - Click the **Create Instance** button.
   - Configure your instance by selecting an image (e.g., **Ubuntu 20.04 LTS**), machine type (e.g., **e2-medium**), and zone (e.g., **us-central1-a**).
   - Set up the firewall rules to allow HTTP/HTTPS traffic if you're hosting a web app.
3. **Access the VM**:
   - After the VM is created, you can SSH into it directly from the console by clicking the **SSH** button next to your instance.

2. Setting Up Cloud Storage

Google Cloud Storage provides scalable object storage for your data.

1. **Navigate to Cloud Storage**:

- In the **Navigation Menu**, click on **Storage** and select **Browser** to manage your buckets.
2. **Create a New Bucket**:
   - Click the **Create Bucket** button, provide a unique name, select a region, and choose the storage class (e.g., **Standard**).
3. **Upload Files**:
   - After creating your bucket, click on it and use the **Upload Files** button to upload data, such as images, logs, or backups.

Personal Insights and Tips for Navigating the Google Cloud Console

- **Organize Projects Effectively**: As your organization grows, you might need to manage multiple projects. Create separate projects for different environments (e.g., development, staging, and production) to ensure clean segregation of resources and proper security management.
- **Use the Cloud Shell for CLI Access**: Cloud Shell is incredibly useful when you want to quickly interact with your resources via the command line without installing the Google Cloud SDK on your machine. It's a great way to work on the go.
- **Track Costs with Budgets and Alerts**: Google Cloud's pricing model is based on usage, so it's important to monitor costs. Set up budgets and alerts to avoid unexpected expenses, especially when experimenting with new services.
- **Leverage Documentation and Help Resources**: If you're unsure about something, Google Cloud provides extensive documentation and tutorials to guide you. Use the **Help** section of the console to search for solutions.

Case Study: Managing Resources for a Web App in Google Cloud

Scenario: A startup, **TechTastic**, is hosting a web app in Google Cloud. Here's how they use the Google Cloud Console to manage their resources:

1. **Create Projects**:
   TechTastic creates three projects—**dev**, **staging**, and **prod**—to isolate their environments.
2. **Deploy VMs for Web Servers**:
   They use **Compute Engine** to create VMs in the **prod** environment for hosting their web application. They configure firewalls to allow HTTP/HTTPS traffic.
3. **Manage Storage**:
   For storing media files, TechTastic uses **Cloud Storage**.

5.3 Deploying Google Compute Engine Instances

Google **Compute Engine** is one of the core services of **Google Cloud Platform (GCP)**. It allows you to provision and manage virtual machines (VMs) that run on Google's infrastructure. Whether you need to host a website, run a business application, or process large datasets, Google Compute Engine provides scalable, flexible, and secure environments to meet your needs.

What is Google Compute Engine?

Google Compute Engine (GCE) provides scalable virtual machines (VMs) that run on Google's highly reliable infrastructure. With GCE, you can launch virtual machines, manage resources, and scale workloads quickly.

Key features of Google Compute Engine:

- **Scalable Compute Resources**: Choose machine types based on CPU, RAM, and disk needs.

- **Customizable VMs**: Select from predefined machine types or create custom configurations.
- **Global Network**: Leverage Google's global network to run your VMs in any region and zone.
- **Persistent Storage**: Attach persistent disks to VMs for reliable storage that remains intact even if the VM is shut down.
- **Integrated with Google Cloud Services**: Easily integrate VMs with other GCP services, including storage, databases, and machine learning tools.

Step-by-Step Guide to Deploy a Google Compute Engine Instance

Step 1: Set Up Your Google Cloud Environment

Before you deploy your first VM, ensure that you've created a **Google Cloud Project** and set up billing information. If you haven't done so yet, refer to the earlier section in this book on **creating a Google Cloud account**.

1. **Navigate to the Google Cloud Console**:
   o Go to Google Cloud Console.
   o Sign in with your Google account.
   o Select or create a **Google Cloud project**.
2. **Set up billing**: Google offers **$300 in free credits** for new users to try out the cloud services.
3. **Activate the Compute Engine API**: The **Compute Engine API** is enabled by default in most cases, but if it isn't, you can manually enable it by going to the **API & Services** section in the Google Cloud Console.

Step 2: Create a Virtual Machine (VM) Instance

Now that you have everything set up, let's deploy a VM using **Google Compute Engine**.

1. **Navigate to Compute Engine**:

- o In the **Google Cloud Console**, click the **hamburger menu** in the top left corner, go to **Compute Engine**, and then select **VM instances**.
2. **Create a New VM Instance**:
   - o Click **Create Instance**.
   - o This will open the **Create an Instance** page where you can configure your virtual machine.
3. **Configure Your VM Instance**:
   - o **Name**: Give your VM a name (e.g., `my-first-vm`).
   - o **Region and Zone**: Choose a **region** and **zone** for your VM. Google Cloud has data centers worldwide, and you can choose the one closest to your users for better performance. For example, choose **us-central1-a** for a US-based server.
   - o **Machine Type**: Select a machine type based on your performance needs. For small workloads, you can choose the **e2-micro** machine, which is eligible for the **Google Cloud free tier**.
   - o **Boot Disk**: Select an operating system for your VM. Google Cloud offers a variety of Linux distributions (such as **Ubuntu**, **CentOS**, **Debian**) and Windows Server versions. For this guide, we'll choose **Ubuntu 20.04 LTS**.
   - o **Firewall**: Check the boxes for **Allow HTTP traffic** and **Allow HTTPS traffic** to allow your VM to serve web traffic.
4. **Additional Configuration Options**:
   - o You can customize settings such as **Disk Size**, **Network Settings**, and **Startup Scripts** based on your use case.
   - o Under **Management, Security, Disks, Networking, Sole-tenant nodes**, you can configure advanced features like auto-start, SSH keys, and others, but for now, the default settings should work.
5. **Create the VM**: After you've configured your VM, click the **Create** button. Google Cloud will provision the virtual machine in the selected region and zone.

Step 3: Access Your Virtual Machine

Once the VM is created, you'll see it listed in the **VM instances** dashboard.

1. **SSH Access**:
   o To access your VM, click the **SSH** button next to the instance. This will open a **browser-based terminal** where you can interact with the instance directly.
   o Alternatively, you can use **Google Cloud SDK** on your local machine to SSH into the VM. The command is:
   o `gcloud compute ssh my-first-vm --zone=us-central1-a`

   This will open an SSH session into your VM.

Step 4: Installing Software on the VM

Once you have SSH access to your VM, you can install the software you need. For example, let's install **Nginx**, a popular web server.

1. **Update the Package List**: Run the following command to update the package list:

```
sudo apt-get update
```

2. **Install Nginx**: Run the following command to install Nginx:

```
sudo apt-get install nginx -y
```

3. **Start and Enable Nginx**: After the installation is complete, start the Nginx service:

```
sudo systemctl start nginx
sudo systemctl enable nginx
```

4. **Verify Nginx Installation**: Open your browser and go to your VM's **external IP address**. You should see the default Nginx welcome page.

Step 5: Configuring Networking and Security

Now that you have a VM running, it's essential to configure networking and security for your instance.

1. **Assign a Static IP Address**: By default, Google Cloud assigns your VM a dynamic IP address, which changes if the VM is stopped and restarted. To assign a **static IP**, go to **VM instances > External IP > Reserve a static address**.
2. **Create Firewall Rules**: If you need to restrict access to your VM, you can define custom firewall rules. For instance, you may want to allow **SSH** (port 22) and **HTTP** (port 80) traffic while blocking other ports.

   To create a custom firewall rule:

   o   Go to the **Firewall rules** section in the Google Cloud Console.
   o   Click **Create firewall rule**.
   o   Define the rule by specifying:
       ▪   **Name** (e.g., `allow-ssh-http`).
       ▪   **Source IP** (e.g., **0.0.0.0/0** to allow access from anywhere).
       ▪   **Allowed protocols and ports** (e.g., `tcp:22,80`).
3. **Secure Access with SSH Keys**: For better security, instead of using a password to access your VM, you can configure **SSH keys**. This allows you to authenticate without exposing your credentials. When you create a VM, you can either provide an existing public SSH key or let Google Cloud generate one for you.

Step 6: Managing VM Instances

As you begin to use your Google Compute Engine instances, you may need to manage them. This includes actions like:

1. **Stopping, Starting, or Restarting VMs**:
   o   You can stop, start, or restart your VM by going to the **VM instances** page in the Google Cloud Console and clicking the appropriate buttons next to your instance.

2. **Scaling Your VM**: If your application requires more power, you can resize your VM to a larger machine type. Go to **VM instances**, select the VM, and click **Edit** to change the machine type.
3. **Snapshots and Backups**: To create a backup of your VM, use **snapshots**. A snapshot is a point-in-time copy of your disk that you can use for backup or to create a new VM with the same configuration.
    o Go to **Disks** > select the disk you want to snapshot > click **Create snapshot**.

Personal Insights and Best Practices

- **Start Small**: Begin with small VM instances to keep costs low, especially when experimenting. You can always scale up later if needed.
- **Use Preemptible VMs**: For workloads that are fault-tolerant and don't require high availability, consider using **Preemptible VMs**. These are cost-effective instances that Google can terminate at any time but are much cheaper than regular instances.
- **Monitor Performance**: Use **Stackdriver Monitoring** (now integrated into **Google Cloud Operations Suite**) to track your VM's health and performance, including CPU usage, memory, and disk I/O.
- **Automation**: Automate repetitive tasks by using **Google Cloud's Deployment Manager** or **Terraform** to manage your infrastructure as code.

Case Study: Hosting a Web Application

Scenario: **TechX** is a small company that wants to host a simple **static website** on Google Cloud using **Compute Engine**.

Steps Taken:

1. **Create a VM**: TechX creates a **f1-micro instance** with **Ubuntu 20.04 LTS** as the OS.

2. **Install Web Server**: They install **Nginx** on the VM to serve the website.
3. **Set up Firewall Rules**: TechX configures firewall rules to allow **HTTP** and **SSH** traffic.
4. **Reserve Static IP**: They assign a **static IP** to ensure that the IP address remains the same even if the VM is stopped and restarted.
5. **Upload Website Files**: The team uploads the HTML files to the VM's web directory and verifies that the website is accessible by visiting the static IP address in their browser.

Google Compute Engine is a powerful and flexible service for provisioning virtual machines on Google Cloud. By following this guide, you now understand how to create a VM, configure networking and security, manage resources, and scale your infrastructure as needed. Compute Engine is perfect for a wide range of applications, from simple websites to complex machine learning workflows. As you grow your cloud-based infrastructure, leveraging the best practices outlined here will help you optimize your usage, enhance security, and reduce costs.

5.4 Managing Storage with Google Cloud Storage

Google Cloud Storage is one of the most important and versatile services offered by Google Cloud Platform (GCP). It provides a highly scalable, secure, and durable object storage service for managing data in the cloud. Whether you're storing small files, backup data, or massive datasets, Google Cloud Storage can meet your needs.

What is Google Cloud Storage?

Google Cloud Storage is an **object storage service** that allows you to store and manage large amounts of unstructured data, such as documents, images, videos, backups, and logs. It offers high availability and durability, with multiple redundancy options.

Key benefits of Google Cloud Storage:

- **Scalability**: Store and retrieve unlimited amounts of data.
- **Durability**: Data is redundantly stored across multiple locations to ensure durability and availability.
- **Security**: Data is automatically encrypted at rest and in transit, with options for fine-grained access control.
- **Global Accessibility**: Access your data from anywhere in the world, thanks to Google's global network infrastructure.
- **Storage Classes**: Google Cloud offers multiple storage classes tailored to different use cases (e.g., standard, archival).

Core Components of Google Cloud Storage

Before diving into usage, it's essential to understand the key components of Google Cloud Storage:

1. **Buckets**: A bucket is a container for your data. Buckets store your objects (files) and are the highest-level containers within Google Cloud Storage.
2. **Objects**: Objects are the actual data stored within a bucket. Objects can be any type of file, like images, video files, backup data, etc.
3. **Storage Classes**: Google Cloud Storage offers different storage classes that determine the cost, availability, and durability of your data. These include:
   - **Standard**: Best for frequently accessed data.
   - **Nearline**: For data accessed less than once a month.
   - **Coldline**: For long-term storage of infrequently accessed data.
   - **Archive**: For data that is rarely accessed and needs to be stored for long periods.

Step-by-Step Guide: Managing Storage with Google Cloud Storage

In this section, we will walk through the process of setting up Google Cloud Storage, creating buckets, uploading data, and managing access.

Step 1: Create a Google Cloud Storage Bucket

1. **Navigate to Cloud Storage**:
   o In the **Google Cloud Console**, use the **hamburger menu** (top left) to go to **Storage > Browser**.
2. **Create a New Bucket**:
   o Click on **Create Bucket**.
   o **Bucket Name**: Choose a globally unique name for your bucket (e.g., `my-cloud-storage-bucket`).
   o **Location**: Choose the **Location Type** (e.g., **Multi-region** for global access or **Region** for localized storage).
   o **Storage Class**: Choose the **storage class** (e.g., **Standard** for frequently accessed data).
   o **Access Control**: Choose between **Uniform bucket-level access** (recommended) or **Fine-grained access**.
   o Click **Create** to create your bucket.

Step 2: Upload Files to Your Bucket

Now that we have a bucket, let's upload some files into it.

1. **Upload Files**:
   o Once your bucket is created, click on the bucket name to enter it.
   o Click on **Upload Files** and select the files you want to upload from your local system.
   o You can also drag and drop files directly into the browser window.
2. **Organize Files with Folders**:
   o While Google Cloud Storage doesn't have traditional folder structures, you can simulate folders by including slashes (/) in your object names. For example, if you upload a file named `images/photo.jpg`, it will appear in the **images** folder.
3. **Monitor Upload Progress**:

o   You can monitor the upload process in the console. Once completed, the uploaded files will be listed under the **Objects** section of the bucket.

Step 3: Manage Bucket Permissions

One of the key features of Google Cloud Storage is the ability to set fine-grained access control for your buckets and objects.

1. **IAM Policies**:
    o   Google Cloud uses **IAM (Identity and Access Management)** to define roles and permissions for your resources. In the **Google Cloud Console**, go to **IAM & Admin > IAM** to manage roles for your team members.
    o   Assign roles such as **Storage Object Viewer** or **Storage Admin** to users, groups, or service accounts for managing access to the storage.
2. **Bucket-Level Permissions**:
    o   To set bucket-level permissions, go to your **bucket** in the console and click on **Permissions**.
    o   Here, you can set permissions for individual users, service accounts, or groups, controlling what actions they can take (e.g., **read, write, delete**).
3. **Access Control Lists (ACLs)**:
    o   Google Cloud Storage also provides **ACLs** to control access at the object level. For example, you can make specific objects publicly accessible or restrict access to certain users only.

Step 4: Using Google Cloud Storage with gsutil

While the **Google Cloud Console** is convenient for basic tasks, many users prefer the command-line tool **gsutil** for scripting and automation tasks.

1. **Install gsutil**:
    o   If you haven't already, install **gsutil** by following the instructions on the Google Cloud SDK page. This allows

you to interact with Google Cloud Storage from the command line.

2. **Authenticate gsutil**:
   - o Run the following command to authenticate your session:
   - o `gcloud auth login`

3. **Basic gsutil Commands**:
   - o **Create a Bucket**:
   - o `gsutil mb gs://my-cloud-storage-bucket`
   - o **Upload a File**:
   - o `gsutil cp /path/to/local/file gs://my-cloud-storage-bucket`
   - o **Download a File**:
   - o `gsutil cp gs://my-cloud-storage-bucket/file.txt /path/to/local/directory`
   - o **List Files in a Bucket**:
   - o `gsutil ls gs://my-cloud-storage-bucket`

4. **Using gsutil for Bulk Operations**:
   - o **Copy Multiple Files**: To copy multiple files, you can use wildcard characters:
   - o `gsutil cp gs://my-cloud-storage-bucket/images/*.jpg /path/to/local/directory`
   - o **Synchronize Directories**: Use `gsutil rsync` to sync files between local directories and your Cloud Storage bucket:
   - o `gsutil -m rsync -r /local/directory gs://my-cloud-storage-bucket`

Step 5: Monitor and Manage Data Usage

Google Cloud Storage provides several tools to monitor and manage your usage.

1. **Usage Statistics**:
   - o In the **Google Cloud Console**, go to **Storage** > **Browser**, then select a bucket. Under the **Overview** tab, you can view storage usage statistics, including how much data you've stored and how many operations (uploads, downloads, etc.) have occurred.

2. **Billing**:
   - o Use the **Google Cloud Billing Console** to track costs associated with your Cloud Storage usage. You can set budgets and alerts to prevent unexpected charges.

3. **Object Lifecycle Management**:

- Google Cloud Storage allows you to automate the transition of objects to different storage classes or even delete them after a specified period. For example, you can set rules to move files to **Coldline** storage after 30 days.

To set up lifecycle management, go to the **Lifecycle** section of the bucket and define your rules based on age, access frequency, or other criteria.

Personal Insights and Best Practices

- **Understand Your Storage Needs**: When choosing a storage class, consider how frequently you will access your data. For high-frequency data, use **Standard** storage; for archival data, consider **Coldline** or **Archive** storage to reduce costs.
- **Automation with gsutil**: If you're working with large datasets or managing cloud storage programmatically, **gsutil** is an essential tool. It allows you to automate backup processes, synchronize directories, and move data between your local system and Google Cloud Storage.
- **Monitoring Costs**: While Cloud Storage is a cost-effective solution, keep track of your usage to avoid unnecessary costs. The **Pricing Calculator** can help estimate costs for storage and data transfer.
- **Security First**: Use **IAM roles** and **bucket-level permissions** to control access to your data. Apply **principle of least privilege** to minimize the risk of unauthorized access.

Case Study: Storing User-Uploaded Files in Google Cloud Storage

Scenario: **PhotoShare**, a startup that provides a photo-sharing service, needs a scalable solution for storing user-uploaded images.

Steps Taken:

1. **Create a Storage Bucket**:
   PhotoShare creates a **multi-region** bucket for storing images and sets the storage class to **Standard** for frequent access.
2. **Upload and Organize Files**:
   They organize the images into directories (e.g., `user_photos/user1/`) and use the **gsutil cp** command to upload large batches of images efficiently.
3. **Access Control**:
   PhotoShare configures **ACLs** and **IAM roles** to ensure that only authenticated users can upload and download their photos, while the public can only access shared images.
4. **Optimize Costs**:
   After a month, PhotoShare moves less-frequently accessed images to **Nearline** storage to reduce costs, while keeping the most popular images

5.5 Networking with Google Cloud VPC

In cloud computing, **networking** is a critical part of setting up an infrastructure that ensures secure, high-performance communication between your resources. Google Cloud Platform (GCP) offers **Virtual Private Cloud (VPC)** as the fundamental building block for networking. A VPC enables you to define your own private network within Google Cloud, providing secure communication between resources and control over traffic flow, security policies, and scalability.

What is Google Cloud VPC?

Google Cloud VPC is a flexible, scalable private network that allows you to manage networking for your Google Cloud resources. A VPC is like a traditional network, but it is deployed in the cloud, providing several key advantages:

- **Isolation**: VPCs are isolated from one another, ensuring that your resources are separated securely.
- **Global Reach**: Unlike traditional networks, Google Cloud's VPC is global. Resources across multiple regions can communicate seamlessly within the same VPC.
- **Customizable Network Design**: You have complete control over IP address ranges, subnets, routes, and firewall settings.

A VPC network enables several essential capabilities, including:

- Private IP communication between virtual machines (VMs) and other resources.
- Securely connecting on-premises infrastructure to Google Cloud via **VPN** or **Interconnect**.
- Managing traffic between different components using **firewall rules**, **routes**, and **network policies**.
- Peering multiple VPCs to allow communication between separate environments.

Core Components of Google Cloud VPC

To build a network in Google Cloud, it's important to understand the core components that make up a VPC:

1. **VPC Network**: The main container for your network, providing isolation and routing. It spans across all regions of Google Cloud, meaning it's not confined to a single region.
2. **Subnets**: A VPC is subdivided into **subnets** that span specific **regions**. Each subnet has a range of IP addresses, and the resources within that subnet communicate using private IPs.
3. **Firewall Rules**: **Firewall rules** control the flow of traffic to and from resources within a VPC. Google Cloud offers highly granular control over which resources can communicate with each other.
4. **Routes**: Routes control how traffic is directed within a VPC. You can define custom routes to guide traffic to specific destinations, either within the VPC or externally.
5. **External IP Addresses**: Resources within a VPC can be assigned external IPs to make them accessible from the public internet (for web servers, for example).

6. **Cloud VPN**: **VPN** enables secure connections between your on-premises infrastructure and Google Cloud resources.
7. **VPC Peering**: **VPC Peering** allows private communication between two VPC networks, either within the same project or across different projects.

Step-by-Step Guide: Setting Up Google Cloud VPC

Now that we understand the core components of a VPC, let's walk through the process of creating and configuring a VPC in Google Cloud.

Step 1: Create a VPC Network

1. **Access Google Cloud Console**:
   o Navigate to the **Google Cloud Console** at https://console.cloud.google.com.
   o From the **Navigation menu**, go to **VPC network** under **Networking**.
2. **Create a New VPC**:
   o Click + **Create VPC Network**.
   o Choose **Custom** under **Subnet creation mode** to manually configure subnets (for greater control over your network).
   o Provide a **name** for your VPC (e.g., `my-first-vpc`).
3. **Configure Subnets**:
   o Add your first subnet by selecting a **Region** (e.g., `us-central1`).
   o Define the **IP range** for your subnet (e.g., `10.0.0.0/24`). This range should be within the overall IP range of your VPC.
   o Click **Add subnet** if you want to create more subnets in other regions.
4. **Set Up Firewall Rules**:
   o By default, Google Cloud creates firewall rules that allow **SSH, RDP**, and **ICMP** traffic. You can add custom rules to restrict or allow specific traffic based on your needs.
5. **Create the VPC**:
   o Once you've configured your VPC network, click **Create**. Your VPC network is now ready to use.

Once your VPC is set up, you can create virtual machines (VMs) within the subnets you've configured. Here's how to create a VM instance in your newly created VPC:

1. **Navigate to Compute Engine**:
    o   In the **Google Cloud Console**, go to **Compute Engine > VM instances**.
2. **Create a New VM Instance**:
    o   Click **Create Instance**.
    o   Choose the **Region** and **Zone** for your VM (ensure it matches the region of your subnet).
    o   Under **Networking**, select the **VPC network** you created earlier (e.g., my-first-vpc), and select the subnet for the VM (e.g., us-central1).
3. **Set VM Configuration**:
    o   Choose the **machine type** (e.g., **e2-medium** for a small instance).
    o   Select the **OS** image (e.g., **Ubuntu 20.04 LTS**).
    o   Adjust **firewall settings** (allow **HTTP** and **HTTPS** if needed).
4. **Create the VM**:
    o   After configuring the settings, click **Create**. Your VM will be provisioned and connected to the subnet within your VPC.

Step 3: Setting Up VPC Peering

If you need to connect two VPC networks, you can use **VPC Peering**. This allows resources in separate VPCs to communicate securely.

1. **Navigate to VPC Peering**:
    o   In the **Google Cloud Console**, go to **VPC Network > Peering**.
    o   Click **+ Create Peering Connection**.
2. **Configure Peering**:
    o   Provide a **name** for the peering connection.

- o Select the **VPC network** that you want to peer with.
- o Choose the **project** that contains the VPC to be peered.
- o Select **Private Google Access** for private access between VPCs, if needed.
3. **Create Peering Connection**:
   - o Click **Create** to establish the peering. Now, resources in both VPCs can communicate securely over private IPs.

Step 4: Configure VPC Firewall Rules

Firewalls are essential for controlling the flow of traffic in and out of your VPC. By default, Google Cloud allows certain traffic types (like SSH and RDP), but you can customize the rules.

1. **Create Firewall Rules**:
   - o In the **Google Cloud Console**, go to **VPC Network > Firewall rules**.
   - o Click + **Create Firewall Rule**.
   - o Name your rule (e.g., `allow-web-traffic`), and define the **source IP** (e.g., `0.0.0.0/0` for public access).
   - o Choose the **protocol** (e.g., TCP) and the **ports** (e.g., **80** for HTTP or **443** for HTTPS).
2. **Apply the Rule**:
   - o After configuring the firewall rule, click **Create**. This will allow HTTP traffic to reach your web servers in the VPC.

Step 5: Connecting On-Premises Infrastructure to Google Cloud

If you want to securely connect your on-premises infrastructure to your Google Cloud VPC, you can use **Cloud VPN** or **Interconnect**.

1. **Cloud VPN**:
   - o Use **Cloud VPN** to establish a secure, encrypted connection between your on-premises network and Google Cloud.

- o In the **Google Cloud Console**, navigate to **Hybrid Connectivity** > **VPN**.
- o Follow the steps to set up the VPN tunnel and configure the routing between your on-premises network and the VPC.

2. **Interconnect**:
   - o For high-throughput connections, consider **Dedicated Interconnect** or **Partner Interconnect** to establish a direct connection between your data center and Google Cloud's infrastructure.

Best Practices for Google Cloud VPC Networking

- **Use Subnets for Segmentation**: Divide your VPC into different subnets based on function (e.g., web servers, databases). This helps manage traffic flow and improves security.
- **Implement Least Privilege Access**: Use **IAM** roles and **firewall rules** to ensure that only authorized users and resources have access to your network.
- **Monitor VPC Traffic**: Use **Cloud Logging** and **Cloud Monitoring** to keep track of network traffic, detect issues, and ensure optimal performance.
- **Use Private IPs for Internal Communication**: For improved security, use **private IPs** for communication between Google Cloud resources. Use **public IPs** only when necessary (e.g., for external-facing web servers).
- **Automate Network Configuration**: Consider using **Terraform** or **Deployment Manager** to automate the creation and configuration of your VPC network, ensuring consistency across environments.

Case Study: Hosting a Multi-Tier Web Application with Google Cloud VPC

Scenario: **WebTech**, a software development company, wants to host a multi-tier web application with separate layers for the web server, application server, and database.

Steps Taken:

1. **VPC Design**:
   - WebTech creates a **VPC** with **three subnets**:
     - **Web Subnet** for the web server (public-facing).
     - **App Subnet** for the application server (private).
     - **DB Subnet** for the database (private).
2. **VM Deployment**:
   - WebTech deploys **Compute Engine instances** in each subnet, configuring **fire

wall rules** to allow traffic only between the layers (e.g., web server can talk to the app server, but not directly to the database).

3. **VPC Peering**:
   - They configure **VPC peering** between the production and staging environments to allow testing of changes in a secure, isolated environment.
4. **VPN Setup**:
   - WebTech uses **Cloud VPN** to securely connect their on-premises infrastructure (where their internal tools are hosted) to the Google Cloud VPC.
5. **Monitoring and Scaling**:
   - WebTech uses **Cloud Monitoring** and **Cloud Logging** to track the performance of their network and servers. They set up **autoscaling** for the app server to handle varying levels of traffic.

Google Cloud VPC is a powerful tool for designing secure, scalable, and efficient networks within Google Cloud. By understanding how to create and manage **VPC networks**, configure **subnets**, and implement **firewall rules**, you can ensure that your cloud resources are well-organized and protected. Additionally, integrating tools like **Cloud VPN** and **VPC peering** helps establish secure connections both internally and with on-premises infrastructure.

Part 3: Cloud Architecture Design and Management (Advanced Level)

Chapter 6: Cloud Architecture and Design Principles

Designing cloud systems that are efficient, reliable, scalable, and cost-effective is a critical skill for cloud architects and developers. This chapter explores fundamental design principles and techniques to help you build cloud-based applications that not only meet business requirements but also scale seamlessly as demand grows. We'll dive into various cloud design patterns, high-availability strategies, cost optimization techniques, and modern practices like automation and serverless architectures.

6.1 Designing for Scalability

Scalability is one of the most critical design considerations in cloud architecture. In the context of cloud computing, scalability refers to the ability of an application or system to handle increased demand by adding resources or adjusting capacity, without sacrificing performance or reliability. One of the key advantages of cloud platforms like **AWS**, **Azure**, and **Google Cloud** is their ability to scale resources quickly and efficiently.

What is Scalability?

Scalability refers to the capacity of a system to handle a growing amount of work, or its ability to accommodate growth. In cloud computing, scalability is achieved by adjusting resources—such as **compute power**, **memory**, **storage**, and **network bandwidth**—to meet the demands of an application.

Scalable systems are designed to:

- **Handle increased traffic** without degrading performance.
- **Scale automatically** based on demand, reducing manual intervention.

- **Optimize costs** by scaling resources only when necessary.

There are two primary types of scalability:

1. **Vertical Scaling (Scaling Up)**: Increasing the resources (CPU, memory, storage) on a single machine or server.
2. **Horizontal Scaling (Scaling Out)**: Adding more machines or instances to distribute the load.

Techniques for Building Scalable Architectures

1. Horizontal Scaling (Scaling Out)

Horizontal scaling is one of the most powerful and flexible methods of scaling. It involves adding more instances of a resource (such as virtual machines, containers, or databases) to distribute the load. This approach is essential for cloud-native applications as it offers greater flexibility, fault tolerance, and cost efficiency.

Key Steps for Horizontal Scaling:

- **Load Balancing**: Use a **load balancer** to distribute traffic evenly across multiple instances. Cloud services like **AWS Elastic Load Balancer (ELB)**, **Google Cloud Load Balancer**, and **Azure Load Balancer** provide scalable solutions to ensure that requests are routed to the least busy server.

  Example: Let's say you have a website hosted on **Google Cloud Compute Engine** instances. As traffic increases, you can scale out by adding more VM instances behind a **Google Cloud HTTP(S) Load Balancer** to distribute the incoming traffic.

```
gcloud compute instance-groups managed resize my-instance-
group --size=5
```

- **Auto-Scaling**: Many cloud providers offer **auto-scaling** services that automatically add or remove instances based on traffic or CPU usage. For example, **Google Cloud Autoscaler** and **AWS Auto**

Scaling dynamically adjust the number of instances in your infrastructure.

Example: In **AWS**, you can set up an Auto Scaling Group with policies that increase or decrease the number of EC2 instances based on **CPU utilization** or **network traffic**.

```
"ScalingPolicy": {
  "AdjustmentType": "ChangeInCapacity",
  "CoolDown": 300,
  "MetricAggregationType": "Average",
  "MinAdjustmentMagnitude": 1
}
```

2. Vertical Scaling (Scaling Up)

Vertical scaling involves adding more resources (e.g., CPU, RAM, disk) to an existing server. Although vertical scaling can be more straightforward than horizontal scaling, it has limitations, such as the physical limits of the hardware and potential single points of failure.

When to Use Vertical Scaling:

- When you need to temporarily handle a traffic spike.
- For database systems or applications that require high computing power (e.g., **in-memory databases**).
- For testing environments where scaling out might be unnecessary.

Example of Vertical Scaling in Google Cloud:

If your virtual machine is underperforming, you can resize it to a larger instance type with more CPU and memory.

1. **Resize the VM**:
   - Go to the **Google Cloud Console**, select your VM instance, and click **Edit**.
   - Under **Machine Type**, select a larger instance type (e.g., from **e2-medium** to **e2-standard-4**).
   - Click **Save** to apply the changes.

3. Microservices Architecture

In a traditional monolithic architecture, scaling is often difficult because all the components are tightly coupled. **Microservices architecture** breaks the application into smaller, independently deployable services, each focused on a specific business function (e.g., user management, payment processing, etc.).

Why Microservices Are Scalable:

- **Independent Scaling**: You can scale individual microservices based on their specific demands. For example, you might scale the **user service** more than the **payment service**.
- **Fault Isolation**: If one microservice fails, it doesn't affect the others, which improves the overall reliability of the system.

Example:

Imagine an e-commerce platform. Instead of a single large application, you deploy several independent services:

- **Product Service**: Handles product catalog and inventory.
- **Order Service**: Manages customer orders.
- **Payment Service**: Processes payments.

Each service can be scaled independently. If the **order service** experiences high traffic during sales events, only that service would scale up, while the **payment service** remains at normal capacity.

---

4. Caching and Data Replication

Caching is a technique that can significantly improve the scalability of your applications by reducing the load on databases and improving data access times.

Key Caching Strategies:

- **Content Delivery Networks (CDNs)**: Cloud providers like **AWS CloudFront**, **Google Cloud CDN**, and **Azure CDN** offer caching for static content like images, videos, and web pages at edge locations closer to end-users, which reduces latency and improves performance.

Example: You can cache static files such as images and CSS files at edge locations across the world using **Google Cloud CDN**. This way, users get faster access to the content without hitting your origin server.

- **In-memory Caching**: Use **Redis** or **Memcached** for caching frequently accessed data in memory, reducing the need for repetitive database queries and improving performance.

  Example: If you're building a news website, you can cache the top articles in **Redis** so that users don't need to query the database each time they visit the site.

---

5. Stateless Design

A **stateless architecture** is a design principle where each component of the system does not retain any client information between requests. This makes it easier to scale since any server instance can handle any request without requiring specific session information.

Why Stateless is Scalable:

- **Easier Load Balancing**: Since there is no state information, requests can be routed to any instance without concern for session data, making horizontal scaling much simpler.
- **Elasticity**: Stateless services can scale in and out quickly without complex synchronization of session states.

Example:

When implementing a **RESTful API**, ensure that the API endpoints do not store session data on the server. Instead, rely on **tokens** (e.g., **JWT**) to maintain session state on the client side.

Case Study: Designing a Scalable Web Application

Let's walk through a case study to apply the principles of scalability to a real-world scenario.

Scenario: Building a Scalable E-commerce Platform

E-Shop Inc. wants to build an e-commerce platform that can handle varying levels of traffic, especially during peak seasons like Black Friday.

Step 1: Design with Horizontal Scaling

- **Web Layer**: Use **AWS EC2 instances** behind an **Elastic Load Balancer** (ELB). As traffic increases, more EC2 instances will be spun up automatically through **Auto Scaling**.

Step 2: Implement Microservices Architecture

- **Product Microservice**: Manages the product catalog.
- **Order Microservice**: Handles customer orders.
- **Payment Microservice**: Integrates with payment gateways.

Each microservice is deployed in **Docker containers** and managed with **AWS ECS** (Elastic Container Service), allowing easy scaling of each service independently.

Step 3: Use Caching

- **Redis**: Implement **Redis** as an in-memory cache to store frequently accessed product information. This reduces database load during high traffic periods.
- **CDN**: Use **Amazon CloudFront** to cache images, product pages, and static content globally, reducing latency for users and offloading traffic from the backend servers.

Step 4: Auto-Scale and Load Balancing

- **Auto-Scaling**: Set up **auto-scaling groups** for EC2 instances and containers. If the CPU usage exceeds 75%, AWS will automatically add more instances.

- **Elastic Load Balancer** (ELB): The ELB ensures that traffic is balanced across multiple EC2 instances, preventing any single instance from being overwhelmed.

Step 5: Monitoring and Alerts

- Use **Amazon CloudWatch** to monitor application performance and set up alarms when CPU utilization, memory usage, or response time exceeds predefined thresholds.

Designing for scalability in cloud environments requires a combination of thoughtful architecture, flexible resource management, and continuous monitoring. By leveraging horizontal scaling, auto-scaling, stateless design, and microservices, you can ensure that your applications grow with your business and can handle unexpected surges in traffic. Additionally, caching, data replication, and CDN strategies help improve performance and reduce costs.

6.2 High Availability and Fault Tolerance

In the cloud, ensuring **high availability (HA)** and **fault tolerance (FT)** is critical for maintaining the continuous operation of your services. When designing cloud systems, you need to account for potential failures, whether they occur in a single server, an entire data center, or a region.

What is High Availability (HA) and Fault Tolerance (FT)?

- **High Availability (HA)**: HA is the ability of a system or application to remain operational and accessible even when some components fail. It is typically measured by uptime, with a goal of achieving as close to 100% availability as possible. HA ensures that your application continues to function even under heavy load or when hardware or software failures occur.

- **Fault Tolerance (FT)**: Fault tolerance refers to the system's ability to continue functioning properly in the event of a failure within its components. A fault-tolerant system can detect failures and quickly recover without affecting service quality.

Both HA and FT aim to minimize downtime, prevent data loss, and ensure continuous service availability.

Principles of High Availability and Fault Tolerance

Designing for **high availability** and **fault tolerance** involves understanding the potential points of failure in your infrastructure and implementing strategies to mitigate their impact. The following principles should guide your cloud architecture design:

1. **Redundancy**: Always build systems with redundancy. This means having backup components or systems that can take over when the primary system fails. This could include redundant servers, storage, and network paths.
2. **Failover Mechanisms**: A failover is a process that automatically switches to a backup system when the primary system fails. Implementing failover mechanisms ensures that services remain available even when parts of your infrastructure are down.
3. **Geographic Distribution**: Use multi-region or multi-availability zone (AZ) deployments to prevent regional or zone-level failures from affecting your services. Cloud providers like **AWS**, **Google Cloud**, and **Azure** offer multiple regions and availability zones to spread your infrastructure and improve resilience.
4. **Load Balancing**: Distribute traffic evenly across multiple instances of a service or application. This ensures that no single server is overwhelmed and that services can continue running even if one instance fails.
5. **Data Replication**: Replicate data across multiple locations to ensure that it remains accessible even if one copy of the data becomes unavailable. This is especially important for databases, object storage, and backup systems.

Techniques for Achieving High Availability and Fault Tolerance

1. Redundant and Distributed Infrastructure

Redundancy is the cornerstone of high availability and fault tolerance. By replicating critical components, you can ensure that a failure in one part of your system does not affect the entire application.

Cloud Availability Zones (AZs) and Regions

Cloud providers divide their infrastructure into **regions** and **availability zones (AZs)**. An **Availability Zone** is a physical data center in a region, and each region typically consists of several AZs. Designing your architecture to span multiple AZs within a region, or across multiple regions, ensures that your application remains available in the event of a failure in one zone or region.

Example:

- **AWS** offers **Multi-AZ deployments** for services like **Amazon RDS** and **Elastic Load Balancing**, allowing you to replicate your application across multiple AZs.
- **Google Cloud** offers **Global Load Balancer** and **Cloud SQL** replication across regions.

Best Practice:

Ensure that your application is distributed across **multiple AZs** within a region to mitigate the impact of a data center failure.

---

2. Load Balancing and Auto-Scaling

Load balancing distributes incoming traffic across multiple servers, ensuring that no single server becomes a bottleneck. When combined with **auto-scaling**, it helps maintain both availability and performance.

How It Works:

- A **load balancer** directs incoming traffic to the available instances of your application. If one instance becomes overloaded or fails, the load balancer can reroute traffic to healthy instances.
- **Auto-scaling** automatically adjusts the number of application instances based on demand. If traffic increases, more instances are added; if traffic decreases, unused instances are removed.

Example:

- In **AWS**, you can use **Elastic Load Balancing (ELB)** to distribute traffic to EC2 instances, and **Auto Scaling Groups** automatically scale the instances based on traffic.

```
{
  "AdjustmentType": "ChangeInCapacity",
  "MinAdjustmentMagnitude": 1,
  "ScalingAdjustment": 2
}
```

Best Practice:

Always configure **auto-scaling** with **load balancing** to ensure your service remains responsive and available during traffic spikes and decreases.

---

3. Data Replication and Backup

Data replication is another crucial technique for ensuring fault tolerance. By storing copies of your data in multiple locations, you can prevent data loss and maintain service continuity in the event of a failure.

Types of Data Replication:

- **Synchronous Replication**: Data is replicated in real-time between systems, ensuring that both copies of the data are always up-to-date. This is suitable for high-performance applications that need real-time data consistency.

- **Asynchronous Replication**: Data is replicated with a delay. This method is less resource-intensive and is used when near-real-time consistency is not a strict requirement.

Example:

- **Amazon S3** offers **Cross-Region Replication (CRR)** to replicate objects automatically across AWS regions for better fault tolerance and disaster recovery.
- **Google Cloud Storage** offers **Multi-Regional** storage that automatically replicates data across multiple locations within a region.

Best Practice:

- Use **Multi-Region Replication** for critical data to ensure that data remains accessible even if a region experiences downtime.

---

4. Health Monitoring and Self-Healing Systems

Having automated systems in place to monitor the health of your infrastructure is vital for maintaining high availability. Cloud providers offer tools to monitor the health of your application, virtual machines, storage, and network.

Health Checks and Auto-Restart:

- **Health Checks**: Use health checks to automatically detect when an instance is unhealthy and needs to be replaced or restarted. For example, **AWS EC2** instances can be monitored with **CloudWatch** health checks, and **Google Compute Engine** uses **HTTP health checks** for load balancers.
- **Auto-Restart**: Many cloud services provide the ability to automatically restart VMs or containers when they become unresponsive or crash.

- In **Azure**, you can configure **Health Probes** for load balancers to check the health of VMs. If a VM fails, traffic will automatically be redirected to healthy VMs.

Best Practice:

Use health checks and auto-healing mechanisms to ensure that failed instances are automatically replaced with new ones, minimizing downtime.

---

5. Multi-Region and Multi-Cloud Design

While most systems are designed to operate within a single region, critical systems may require **multi-region** or even **multi-cloud** architectures to ensure maximum availability. By distributing your infrastructure across multiple geographic locations or even different cloud providers, you can ensure that if one region or provider experiences issues, your system will remain operational.

Multi-Region Deployments:

Distribute your application across multiple regions to improve fault tolerance and reduce the risk of downtime. This is particularly important for global applications with users across different geographical locations.

Example:

- **AWS Global Accelerator** improves the availability and performance of global applications by routing traffic to the nearest healthy region.

Multi-Cloud Deployments:

Using multiple cloud providers (e.g., AWS, Azure, Google Cloud) can help mitigate the risk of a single cloud provider outage affecting your entire system. This approach requires advanced orchestration but provides the highest level of redundancy.

Case Study: High Availability and Fault Tolerance for an E-Commerce Platform

Let's consider an example where an **e-commerce platform** needs to ensure high availability and fault tolerance for its services during peak shopping seasons.

Step 1: Multi-AZ Deployment

- The platform is deployed across multiple **Availability Zones** within the same region using **AWS EC2** instances behind an **Elastic Load Balancer**.
- The platform's **RDS database** is deployed in a **Multi-AZ configuration** for automatic failover and redundancy.

Step 2: Auto-Scaling and Load Balancing

- The platform uses **AWS Auto Scaling Groups** to automatically add more EC2 instances as traffic spikes during sales events like Black Friday.
- **Amazon CloudFront** (CDN) is used to cache static content like images and CSS files to reduce load on the servers.

Step 3: Data Replication

- All product images and customer data are stored in **Amazon S3** with **Cross-Region Replication** enabled, ensuring that data is available in multiple regions.

Step 4: Monitoring and Health Checks

- **CloudWatch** monitors the health of EC2 instances and triggers an **Auto Scaling** event if a server becomes unhealthy.
- If a failure occurs in one AZ, **Amazon RDS** will failover to the standby instance in another AZ.

- In the event of a catastrophic failure, the platform has a **disaster recovery plan** to quickly spin up a new instance in a different region using pre-configured infrastructure as code (IaC) templates in **AWS CloudFormation**.

Designing for **High Availability** and **Fault Tolerance** is essential to ensuring that your cloud applications remain available, reliable, and resilient under all conditions. By utilizing techniques such as redundancy, load balancing, data replication, multi-region deployments, and continuous health monitoring, you can build systems that continue to operate even in the face of failures.

6.3 Cost Optimization Strategies

As businesses move to the cloud, managing and optimizing cloud costs becomes an essential part of the architecture design. Cloud services can quickly become expensive, especially if resources are not used efficiently. Fortunately, cloud platforms like **AWS**, **Google Cloud**, and **Azure** offer a wide range of tools and strategies to help organizations control and reduce costs.

Why Cost Optimization is Crucial

Cloud platforms offer incredible flexibility and scalability, but this can sometimes lead to inefficiency if resources are not carefully managed. Optimizing your cloud costs ensures that you:

- Avoid overspending by only paying for the resources you truly need.
- Take full advantage of cloud pricing models to reduce long-term operational expenses.

- Maintain financial control and visibility across multiple teams and departments.

To effectively optimize cloud costs, it's essential to focus on areas like **resource management**, **usage patterns**, **pricing models**, and **automation**.

Key Strategies for Cost Optimization

1. Right-Sizing Resources

One of the most effective ways to reduce cloud costs is by **right-sizing** resources. This involves adjusting the capacity of your cloud resources to match the actual demand, avoiding both over-provisioning and under-provisioning.

How Right-Sizing Works:

- **Under-provisioning** leads to performance issues, where your system might struggle to handle peak loads.
- **Over-provisioning** means you're paying for more resources than you need, which leads to unnecessary costs.

Best Practices for Right-Sizing:

1. **Monitor Resource Usage**: Use cloud monitoring tools to analyze the utilization of your instances, storage, and databases. Tools like **AWS CloudWatch**, **Google Cloud Monitoring**, and **Azure Monitor** provide metrics on CPU usage, memory, and disk I/O, helping you identify underutilized resources.

   Example: In **Google Cloud**, you can monitor the CPU usage of your VM instances to determine whether they need to be resized:

   ```
   gcloud compute instances describe instance-name --zone=zone
   ```

2. **Auto-Scaling**: Use **auto-scaling** to automatically adjust the number of instances based on real-time demand. This ensures that

168

resources are scaled up during peak periods and scaled down when not needed.

Example: **AWS EC2 Auto Scaling** automatically adjusts the number of EC2 instances based on traffic patterns:

```
{
  "AutoScalingGroupName": "my-auto-scaling-group",
  "LaunchConfigurationName": "my-launch-configuration",
  "MinSize": 1,
  "MaxSize": 5
}
```

3. **Select the Right Instance Types**: Choose instance types that best fit your workload. Cloud providers offer a variety of instance types, from general-purpose to compute-optimized and memory-optimized. Understanding your application's needs allows you to pick the right instance for the job.

---

2. Leverage Reserved and Spot Instances

Many cloud platforms offer **reserved instances** and **spot instances**, which provide significant savings compared to on-demand pricing.

Reserved Instances:

- **Reserved instances** allow you to commit to using a particular instance type in a specific region for a longer period (e.g., 1 or 3 years), in exchange for a discount of up to 75% off the on-demand rate.
- **Savings Plans** (AWS) are similar to reserved instances but offer more flexibility by applying to various instance types, regions, and operating systems.

Spot Instances:

- **Spot instances** allow you to bid on unused cloud capacity at a lower price than on-demand instances. These instances can be terminated by the cloud provider if they are needed for other tasks, so they are best suited for workloads that can tolerate interruptions, such as batch processing or non-critical applications.

Best Practices:

1. Use **reserved instances** for predictable workloads or services that require consistent performance, such as databases, web servers, or backend APIs.
2. Leverage **spot instances** for non-essential or stateless workloads that can handle interruptions, such as data processing tasks or background jobs.

Example: In **AWS**, you can purchase a reserved instance for **EC2**:

```
{
  "InstanceType": "t3.micro",
  "Region": "us-east-1",
  "Term": "3 years",
  "PaymentOption": "AllUpfront"
}
```

3. Utilize Serverless Architectures

Serverless computing is an excellent way to optimize cloud costs, particularly for workloads with unpredictable usage patterns.

Why Serverless?

- **Pay-as-you-go Pricing**: With serverless architectures, you only pay for the resources you use. If your functions aren't executing, you're not paying for idle time.
- **Automatic Scaling**: Serverless platforms automatically scale your application based on demand, without the need for manual intervention.
- **Reduced Operational Overhead**: Since you don't need to manage infrastructure, you can focus more on your application code and reduce operational costs.

1. **API Backends**: Use **AWS Lambda**, **Google Cloud Functions**, or **Azure Functions** to implement serverless APIs, where you only pay for the compute time your functions actually consume.
2. **Event-Driven Applications**: Serverless computing is great for event-driven workloads. For example, an application can trigger a serverless function when a file is uploaded to cloud storage or a database update occurs.

Example: Deploy a serverless function using **AWS Lambda**:

```
{
  "FunctionName": "MyServerlessFunction",
  "Runtime": "nodejs14.x",
  "Handler": "index.handler",
  "Role": "arn:aws:iam::123456789012:role/service-role/MyLambdaRole",
  "Timeout": 15,
  "MemorySize": 128
}
```

4. Optimize Storage Costs

Cloud storage services can be expensive if not managed properly, especially when you have large volumes of data. Implementing the right storage strategy is crucial for cost optimization.

Types of Cloud Storage:

1. **Standard Storage**: Used for frequently accessed data (e.g., images, videos, or active datasets).
2. **Nearline/Coldline/Archive Storage**: Used for infrequently accessed data or long-term storage (e.g., backups or archives).

Best Practices for Optimizing Storage:

1. **Choose the Right Storage Class**: Select storage classes based on access frequency. **Google Cloud Storage** offers different storage classes like **Standard**, **Nearline**, **Coldline**, and **Archive**.
2. **Data Lifecycle Management**: Set up **lifecycle policies** to automatically move data from one storage class to another based

on age or last access time. This helps reduce costs for infrequently accessed data.

Example: In **AWS S3**, you can create lifecycle policies to automatically transition objects to **Glacier** (an archival storage) after a specified period:

```
{
  "Rules": [
    {
      "ID": "MoveToGlacier",
      "Prefix": "logs/",
      "Status": "Enabled",
      "Transitions": [
        {
          "Days": 30,
          "StorageClass": "GLACIER"
        }
      ]
    }
  ]
}
```

3. **Data Deduplication**: Eliminate redundant data and store only one copy of critical files. Implementing data deduplication can help reduce storage consumption and costs.

---

5. Monitor and Analyze Usage

To truly optimize your cloud costs, it's important to continuously monitor and analyze your cloud usage and spending patterns. Cloud providers offer several tools to help you track and manage your expenses.

Cloud Cost Management Tools:

1. **AWS Cost Explorer**: Provides detailed insights into your usage and spending patterns. You can create custom reports and track cost trends over time.
2. **Google Cloud Billing Reports**: Offers detailed billing information and helps you monitor your cloud spending.
3. **Azure Cost Management and Billing**: Provides budgeting tools, cost alerts, and detailed cost breakdowns for your Azure resources.

Best Practices:

- Set up **budgets and alerts** to monitor your spending and receive notifications when costs exceed predefined thresholds.
- Regularly review and audit your cloud spending to identify areas of inefficiency and optimization.

Example: In **Google Cloud**, you can create a budget and set alerts based on specific cost thresholds:

```
gcloud beta billing budgets create --billing-account
YOUR_BILLING_ACCOUNT_ID --amount 500 --alert-threshold 0.8
```

Case Study: Cost Optimization for a SaaS Platform

Scenario: A Software-as-a-Service (SaaS) platform is facing high cloud costs due to unpredictable traffic spikes, underutilized instances, and inefficient data storage practices.

Step 1: Right-Size Resources

- The platform uses **AWS EC2 Auto Scaling** to automatically add or remove instances based on traffic demand. Unused EC2 instances are identified and resized to smaller, more cost-effective types.

Step 2: Move to Serverless

- The platform shifts some of its workload to **AWS Lambda** for processing background tasks and API requests, reducing the need to provision and manage EC2 instances.

Step 3: Optimize Storage

- The platform moves old logs and backups to **AWS Glacier** to reduce costs, while still retaining access to critical data for compliance purposes.

- For predictable traffic, the platform purchases **AWS Reserved Instances** for its database and backend services, saving up to 50% on EC2 costs.

Step 5: Monitor Usage and Costs

- The platform sets up **AWS Budgets** to monitor spending and receive alerts if the monthly cost exceeds a predefined threshold.

Cost optimization is a crucial aspect of cloud architecture that ensures your resources are used efficiently without overspending. By leveraging techniques like **right-sizing**, **reserved instances**, **serverless architectures**, and **storage optimization**, you can significantly reduce your cloud costs while maintaining performance and scalability.

Regularly monitoring your cloud usage and setting up automated cost management tools will help you stay on top of your expenses and prevent unexpected charges. Implementing these strategies ensures that your cloud infrastructure remains cost-effective, sustainable, and aligned with your business goals.

6.4 Automation and DevOps in the Cloud

In the modern cloud computing environment, **Automation** and **DevOps** are pivotal in ensuring the efficiency, scalability, and reliability of systems. The cloud's flexibility makes it an ideal environment for automating repetitive tasks, managing infrastructure as code, and creating a seamless integration and delivery pipeline for software. By adopting DevOps practices and automation, businesses can streamline operations, reduce human error, and deliver software updates faster and more reliably.

What is DevOps and Why is It Crucial in the Cloud?

DevOps is a cultural and technical movement that seeks to break down silos between development (Dev) and operations (Ops) teams to improve collaboration and efficiency in delivering software. The goal of DevOps is to automate and integrate the processes between software development and IT teams to enable continuous delivery with high software quality.

Core Benefits of DevOps in the Cloud:

- **Faster Time to Market**: DevOps enables **continuous integration** (CI) and **continuous delivery** (CD), ensuring faster and more reliable releases of software.
- **Increased Collaboration**: By integrating development and operations teams, DevOps enhances communication and collaboration, leading to quicker resolutions to issues.
- **Scalability and Flexibility**: Cloud platforms like AWS, Azure, and Google Cloud provide the infrastructure and tools needed to scale systems on demand, automate processes, and easily implement DevOps practices.

Key DevOps Practices in the Cloud

1. **Infrastructure as Code (IaC)**:
   - IaC is a practice where infrastructure is defined and provisioned using code, allowing teams to automate the setup, management, and scaling of infrastructure.
   - With IaC, your infrastructure is treated in the same way as application code—versioned, repeatable, and testable. This makes it possible to quickly and consistently replicate infrastructure setups across environments.

   Tools for IaC:

   - **Terraform**: A widely-used tool that allows you to define infrastructure using a high-level configuration language. Terraform is cloud-agnostic, meaning it works with all major cloud providers.
   - **AWS CloudFormation**: A service that enables you to define AWS resources using templates in JSON or YAML format.

- o **Google Cloud Deployment Manager**: Google Cloud's IaC tool to automate the setup of cloud resources.

Example: Here's a simple example of provisioning an EC2 instance in AWS using Terraform:

```
provider "aws" {
  region = "us-east-1"
}

resource "aws_instance" "my_ec2" {
  ami             = "ami-0c55b159cbfafe1f0"
  instance_type = "t2.micro"
}
```

2. **Continuous Integration (CI) and Continuous Delivery (CD)**:
   - o **CI/CD pipelines** automate the process of integrating code changes and deploying them to production. With CI, code changes are automatically tested and integrated into a shared repository, while CD ensures that the code is automatically deployed to staging or production environments after successful testing.

CI/CD Tools:

- o **Jenkins**: A popular open-source automation server that provides a vast array of plugins to support building, deploying, and automating software projects.
- o **GitLab CI/CD**: A robust DevOps tool integrated into the **GitLab** repository that supports all stages of CI/CD.
- o **AWS CodePipeline**: AWS's fully managed CI/CD service for automating the build, test, and deploy phases of application development.
- o **Google Cloud Build**: A Google Cloud service to automate your build, test, and deployment pipeline using cloud-native tools.

Example: A simple **GitLab CI/CD pipeline** YAML configuration:

```
stages:
  - build
  - test
```

```
    - deploy

build:
  stage: build
  script:
    - echo "Building the project..."

test:
  stage: test
  script:
    - echo "Running tests..."

deploy:
  stage: deploy
  script:
    - echo "Deploying to production..."
```

Automation in the Cloud: Tools and Best Practices

Automation in the cloud involves the use of tools to automate manual tasks, such as provisioning resources, monitoring system health, managing configurations, and scaling infrastructure. The cloud's flexibility and infrastructure-as-a-service (IaaS) offerings make it the ideal environment for implementing automated workflows.

1. Auto-Scaling and Load Balancing

- Cloud platforms offer **auto-scaling** to dynamically adjust the number of running instances based on demand. This ensures that you can handle traffic spikes without having to manually add or remove resources.
- **Load balancers** are used to distribute traffic across multiple servers to ensure no single server is overwhelmed and that traffic is routed to healthy instances.

Example: **AWS Auto Scaling** allows you to set up auto-scaling policies based on metrics like CPU utilization or network traffic.

```
{
  "AutoScalingGroupName": "my-auto-scaling-group",
  "DesiredCapacity": 3,
  "MaxSize": 6,
  "MinSize": 2
}
```

2. Continuous Monitoring and Alerts

- **CloudWatch (AWS), Stackdriver (Google Cloud)**, and **Azure Monitor** are cloud-native tools that provide monitoring capabilities for cloud resources and applications. These tools track performance metrics such as CPU usage, disk I/O, memory consumption, and network traffic.
- **Alerts** are crucial for detecting issues early and automating remediation processes.

Example: In **Google Cloud**, you can set up a **Stackdriver alert** for high CPU utilization:

```
gcloud alpha monitoring policies create --notification-
channels channels/[YOUR_CHANNEL] --notification-filters
metric.type="compute.googleapis.com/instance/disk/write_byt
es_count" comparison="COMPARISON_GT" threshold=10000
```

3. Configuration Management and Deployment Automation

- Configuration management tools help automate the management of configurations across multiple servers or environments.

Tools for Configuration Management:

- **Ansible**: A simple, agentless tool for configuration management, application deployment, and task automation.
- **Chef**: A robust automation platform that manages infrastructure through code.
- **Puppet**: An open-source tool for automating infrastructure and application delivery.

Example: Here's a simple **Ansible** playbook to install Apache on a server:

```
- name: Install Apache Web Server
  hosts: webservers
  become: yes
  tasks:
    - name: Ensure Apache is installed
      apt:
        name: apache2
        state: present
    - name: Start Apache service
      service:
```

```
        name: apache2
        state: started
        enabled: yes
```

4. Cost Management Automation

- Cloud platforms provide native tools for automating cost management, helping you to track, manage, and optimize your cloud spending.

Tools:

- **AWS Cost Explorer**: Helps visualize your AWS spending over time and allows setting up cost alerts.
- **Google Cloud Billing Reports**: Provides detailed cost and usage reports for Google Cloud resources.
- **Azure Cost Management**: Provides tools to track and manage your Azure costs and budgets.

Example: In **AWS**, you can automate cost management by setting up a **budget alert**:

```
{
  "Budget": {
    "BudgetType": "COST",
    "TimeUnit": "MONTHLY",
    "BudgetLimit": {
      "Amount": 1000,
      "Unit": "USD"
    }
  },
  "Notification": {
    "Subscribers": [
      {
        "SubscriptionType": "EMAIL",
        "Address": "admin@example.com"
      }
    ],
    "Thresholds": [
      {
        "ComparisonOperator": "GREATER_THAN",
        "Threshold": 80
      }
    ]
  }
}
```

Case Study: DevOps and Automation in a Cloud-Native SaaS Application

Scenario:

A Software-as-a-Service (SaaS) company, **WebApp Co.**, is looking to scale its infrastructure and streamline the deployment process to ensure faster time-to-market and higher reliability.

Step 1: Implementing Infrastructure as Code (IaC):

WebApp Co. uses **Terraform** to manage its cloud resources across **AWS**. They create a configuration to automate the provisioning of EC2 instances, load balancers, and RDS databases.

1. **Terraform Configuration** to launch an EC2 instance:

```
resource "aws_instance" "my_ec2" {
  ami             = "ami-0c55b159cbfafe1f0"
  instance_type = "t2.micro"
  tags = {
    Name = "WebApp-Instance"
  }
}
```

Step 2: Setting Up CI/CD Pipeline:

WebApp Co. uses **AWS CodePipeline** and **Jenkins** for continuous integration and delivery. Every time a developer pushes a change to the GitHub repository, the pipeline automatically runs tests and deploys the updated application to production.

1. **Jenkins Pipeline** for deploying code:

```
pipeline {
  agent any
  stages {
    stage('Build') {
      steps {
        sh 'npm install'
      }
    }
    stage('Test') {
      steps {
```

```
        sh 'npm test'
      }
    }
    stage('Deploy') {
      steps {
        sh 'aws ecs update-service --cluster my-cluster --
service my-service --force-new-deployment'
      }
    }
  }
}
```

Step 3: Auto-Scaling for Traffic Peaks:

WebApp Co. configures **AWS Auto Scaling** to automatically scale up the number of EC2 instances based on traffic demand during peak usage times.

1. **Auto Scaling Policy**:

```
{
  "AutoScalingGroupName": "my-auto-scaling-group",
  "DesiredCapacity": 3,
  "MinSize": 2,
  "MaxSize": 5,
  "HealthCheckType": "EC2"
}
```

Step 4: Cost Monitoring Automation:

WebApp Co. integrates **AWS Cost Explorer** into their DevOps pipeline to monitor usage and costs. Automated cost reports are generated weekly, and alerts are set up when spending exceeds predefined thresholds.

By adopting **Automation** and **DevOps** in the cloud, organizations can improve efficiency, speed up delivery times, and reduce human error. Whether through **Infrastructure as Code (IaC)**, **CI/CD pipelines**, **auto-scaling**, or **cost management automation**, these practices ensure that your cloud environment is agile, cost-effective, and scalable.

6.5 Building a Serverless Architecture

In recent years, **serverless architecture** has emerged as one of the most popular ways to build and deploy applications in the cloud. By abstracting away the need to manage servers, serverless computing allows developers to focus more on writing business logic and less on infrastructure management.

What is Serverless Architecture?

Serverless computing is a cloud-native development model that allows you to build and run applications without having to manage the infrastructure. While the term "serverless" may imply that there are no servers involved, this is not true. Rather, **serverless computing** abstracts away the underlying infrastructure and automatically manages the server resources for you.

Key characteristics of **serverless architectures** include:

1. **Event-driven**: Serverless applications are often triggered by specific events, such as HTTP requests, database changes, file uploads, etc.
2. **Automatic Scaling**: Serverless platforms scale automatically based on the number of incoming events or requests. You pay only for the compute resources used while your code is executing.
3. **Managed Infrastructure**: The cloud provider manages the servers, ensuring high availability, scaling, and performance without requiring manual intervention.

Key Benefits of Serverless Computing

1. **Cost-Effective**:
   - With serverless computing, you only pay for what you use. There are no charges for idle time since the infrastructure scales automatically based on the actual demand. This reduces unnecessary operational costs.

2. **Faster Time-to-Market**:
   o Serverless architectures allow teams to focus on writing and deploying business logic quickly. The absence of infrastructure management allows for faster development and quicker releases.
3. **Automatic Scaling**:
   o Serverless platforms automatically scale to handle any amount of load. Whether it's handling thousands or millions of requests per second, the platform takes care of the scaling without any intervention from the user.
4. **Reduced Operational Overhead**:
   o With serverless, there is no need to provision, maintain, or monitor servers. The cloud provider takes care of these tasks, freeing up the development team to focus on building and improving the application.
5. **Resiliency and Fault Tolerance**:
   o Serverless platforms are built on highly redundant and fault-tolerant infrastructure. This ensures high availability and automatic recovery in case of failures, leading to more reliable applications.

When to Use Serverless Architectures

While serverless architectures offer several advantages, they may not be suitable for all types of applications. Below are some use cases where serverless computing shines:

- **Event-driven applications**: Applications that respond to user events or triggers (e.g., file uploads, HTTP requests, or changes in a database).
- **Microservices**: Serverless is perfect for building small, independent services that perform specific tasks and can scale independently.
- **API Backends**: Serverless is ideal for building **RESTful APIs** where functions are triggered by HTTP requests.
- **Data processing**: Applications that process data asynchronously, such as image or video processing, log processing, or ETL jobs.

- **IoT applications**: When processing data from IoT devices, serverless functions can be triggered based on specific conditions or data inputs.

Building a Serverless Application: Core Concepts

A typical serverless application consists of the following core components:

1. **Function as a Service (FaaS)**: The core unit of a serverless architecture, where the actual code runs. This is often a single function that is triggered by an event (e.g., HTTP request, file upload).
2. **Event Source**: An event source is a cloud service or resource that triggers the execution of a function. Common event sources include HTTP endpoints (e.g., API Gateway), file uploads to cloud storage, changes in a database, or scheduled tasks (cron jobs).
3. **API Gateway**: A service that acts as a reverse proxy to route requests from clients to the appropriate serverless function.
4. **Storage**: Serverless applications often require persistent storage. This could be an object storage service (e.g., **Amazon S3**, **Google Cloud Storage**) or a database (e.g., **AWS DynamoDB**, **Google Firestore**).
5. **Monitoring and Logging**: Cloud providers offer integrated monitoring and logging tools to track the performance of your serverless application and help troubleshoot any issues.

Example: Building a Serverless API with AWS Lambda and API Gateway

To illustrate how a serverless architecture works in practice, let's build a simple **RESTful API** that accepts HTTP requests and returns a message. We'll use **AWS Lambda** for the function, **API Gateway** to route requests, and **AWS DynamoDB** to store data.

Step 1: Create an AWS Lambda Function

AWS Lambda is where the business logic of your serverless application resides. Lambda functions are triggered by various event sources, such as HTTP requests, changes to databases, or file uploads.

1. **Go to the AWS Lambda Console**:
   - Navigate to the **AWS Lambda Console** and click **Create Function**.
   - Choose the **Author from Scratch** option, give the function a name (e.g., `HelloWorldFunction`), and select the runtime (e.g., **Node.js 14.x**).
2. **Add Code to the Function**: In the function editor, add the following simple code that returns a greeting message:

```
exports.handler = async (event) => {
    return {
        statusCode: 200,
        body: JSON.stringify('Hello, world!'),
    };
};
```

This code returns a 200 HTTP status code along with a message when the function is triggered.

Step 2: Create an API Gateway Endpoint

API Gateway allows you to create a RESTful API that routes HTTP requests to your Lambda function.

1. **Create an API**:
   - Go to the **API Gateway Console**, select **Create API**, and choose **HTTP API**.
   - Name the API (e.g., `HelloWorldAPI`).
2. **Create a Route**:
   - Add a route for the GET method and link it to the Lambda function (`HelloWorldFunction`).
   - Select **Lambda Function** as the integration type and choose the Lambda function you created earlier.
3. **Deploy the API**:
   - Create a new stage (e.g., `prod`) and deploy your API. Once deployed, API Gateway will provide you with a public

endpoint URL that you can use to trigger your Lambda function.

Step 3: Test the Serverless API

Now that your Lambda function is integrated with API Gateway, you can test it by sending a GET request to the endpoint URL provided by API Gateway. You should receive the following response:

```
{
    "statusCode": 200,
    "body": "Hello, world!"
}
```

Step 4: Optional - Add Persistent Storage (DynamoDB)

If your application needs to store data, such as user requests or logs, you can integrate **AWS DynamoDB** with your Lambda function.

1. **Create a DynamoDB Table**:
   o Go to **DynamoDB Console** and create a table (e.g., `Requests`) with a **Partition Key** (e.g., `requestId`).
2. **Modify Lambda Function to Store Data**: Update the Lambda function to store the request details in DynamoDB:

```
const AWS = require('aws-sdk');
const dynamoDB = new AWS.DynamoDB.DocumentClient();

exports.handler = async (event) => {
    const requestId = new Date().toISOString();
    const params = {
        TableName: 'Requests',
        Item: {
            requestId: requestId,
            message: 'Hello, world!',
        },
    };

    // Store data in DynamoDB
    await dynamoDB.put(params).promise();

    return {
        statusCode: 200,
        body: JSON.stringify({ message: 'Hello, world!',
requestId: requestId }),
    };
```

```
};
```

3. **Test the API Again**: After making these changes, every time the API is called, a new record will be added to the DynamoDB table with the `requestId` and message.

Serverless Design Considerations

While serverless offers numerous advantages, there are several design considerations to keep in mind when building serverless applications:

1. **Cold Starts**: Serverless functions may experience a delay when they are invoked for the first time or after a period of inactivity. This is known as a **cold start**. Although cloud providers have optimized for this, it can still be a factor for performance-sensitive applications.
2. **State Management**: Serverless functions are typically stateless. If your application requires persistent state between function executions, consider using **external storage systems** (e.g., databases or distributed caches) to manage state.
3. **Timeouts and Limits**: Serverless platforms have **execution timeouts** and resource limits. Be sure to design your serverless functions to run within these limits. For instance, AWS Lambda has a maximum execution time of 15 minutes.
4. **Vendor Lock-in**: Serverless solutions are tightly coupled with specific cloud providers. While serverless architectures provide powerful benefits, they may lead to vendor lock-in due to the proprietary nature of the serverless functions and integrations with cloud-native services.

Case Study: Serverless Architecture for Image Processing

Scenario: A **media company** needs to process images uploaded by users. The process involves resizing, filtering, and storing images in a cloud storage bucket. They decide to use a serverless architecture to handle image uploads and processing.

Step 1: Event Trigger

- The company uses **AWS S3** as their object storage service. When a user uploads an image to a specific S3 bucket, an **S3 event** triggers the **AWS Lambda function**.

Step 2: Image Processing

- The Lambda function resizes and applies filters to the image using an image processing library such as **Sharp** (Node.js) or **Pillow** (Python). After processing, the image is stored in a different S3 bucket.

Step 3: Notification

- Once the image is processed, the Lambda function sends a notification via **Amazon SNS** to inform the user that their image is ready.

Serverless architecture is a powerful design model that offers significant advantages in terms of cost, scalability, and ease of use. By abstracting the infrastructure management and allowing you to focus purely on code, serverless computing accelerates application development, reduces operational overhead, and allows for seamless scaling. Whether you are building a RESTful API, processing events, or handling batch jobs, serverless platforms like **AWS Lambda**, **Google Cloud Functions**, and **Azure Functions** provide the flexibility and efficiency to design modern applications.

Chapter 7: Advanced Cloud Management

In the cloud, managing and maintaining infrastructure goes beyond simple provisioning and configuration. Once your cloud environment is up and running, ensuring that it remains healthy, secure, and resilient is crucial for long-term success. In this chapter, we'll explore advanced cloud management practices, focusing on tools and strategies for monitoring resources, ensuring security, designing disaster recovery plans, and automating systems.

By the end of this chapter, you'll have a thorough understanding of the critical components of advanced cloud management that ensure the performance, security, and reliability of your cloud infrastructure.

7.1 Managing and Monitoring Cloud Resources

In a cloud environment, effective management and monitoring of resources are vital to ensure that your infrastructure runs smoothly, is cost-effective, and provides high availability. Whether you're managing virtual machines, storage, databases, or networking resources, keeping track of their performance and health is a crucial part of maintaining a stable environment. Cloud providers like **AWS**, **Google Cloud**, and **Azure** offer a range of tools and services designed to help you monitor and manage your resources with ease.

What is Cloud Resource Management and Monitoring?

Cloud resource management refers to the process of provisioning, configuring, maintaining, and optimizing the usage of cloud resources such as compute instances, databases, storage, and networking. It also involves controlling access to these resources and ensuring they are operating optimally.

Cloud monitoring, on the other hand, involves tracking the performance, availability, and health of your cloud infrastructure. Monitoring helps you identify issues, bottlenecks, and opportunities for optimization. It provides insights into resource usage, allowing you to take proactive actions before issues escalate.

Key Strategies for Managing and Monitoring Cloud Resources

Effective management and monitoring of cloud resources require several key practices and strategies. Let's explore some of the most important techniques and tools available.

1. Real-Time Performance Monitoring

One of the fundamental aspects of cloud management is real-time monitoring of resource performance. Cloud environments are dynamic, and resource utilization can change quickly based on the application's workload. By continuously monitoring resources like **CPU usage**, **memory consumption**, **network traffic**, and **disk I/O**, you can detect performance bottlenecks and resolve issues before they affect end users.

Tools for Real-Time Monitoring

- **AWS CloudWatch**: A powerful monitoring service for AWS resources and applications, providing data on performance metrics such as CPU usage, disk space, and network activity for EC2 instances.
- **Google Cloud Monitoring**: Provides visibility into Google Cloud resources, enabling you to monitor everything from compute instances to cloud storage.
- **Azure Monitor**: Monitors the performance and health of your resources in Azure and integrates with other Azure services.

To monitor the **CPU utilization** of an EC2 instance in **AWS**, you can use **CloudWatch** to create alarms and trigger notifications if the CPU usage exceeds a certain threshold.

Creating a CloudWatch Alarm:

1. Go to the **CloudWatch Console**.
2. Click on **Alarms** > **Create Alarm**.
3. Choose the **EC2 Instance Metric** and select **CPUUtilization**.
4. Set the threshold for when the alarm should trigger (e.g., CPU utilization > 80% for 5 minutes).
5. Choose the notification method (e.g., an **SNS** topic for email alerts).

Command Example to Create an Alarm via AWS CLI:

```
aws cloudwatch put-metric-alarm --alarm-name
"HighCPUUtilization" --metric-name CPUUtilization --
namespace AWS/EC2 --statistic Average --period 300 --
threshold 80 --comparison-operator GreaterThanThreshold --
dimension Name=InstanceId,Value=i-1234567890abcdef0 --
evaluation-periods 2 --alarm-actions arn:aws:sns:us-east-
1:123456789012:MyTopic
```

2. Logging and Audit Trails

Logging provides a historical record of activities and events, helping you to troubleshoot, audit, and ensure compliance. Keeping track of who is doing what in your environment allows you to better secure your resources and understand your system's behavior.

Why Logging is Important

- **Security and Auditing**: Logs can help you track who accessed resources, what changes were made, and when they occurred.
- **Troubleshooting**: When things go wrong, logs allow you to quickly identify the root cause.

- **Compliance**: For industries that require strict compliance (e.g., finance, healthcare), logs can provide evidence of adherence to security protocols.

Tools for Logging

- **AWS CloudTrail**: Provides detailed logs of AWS API calls, allowing you to track user activities across your AWS environment.
- **Google Cloud Audit Logs**: Automatically records API calls made within your Google Cloud environment.
- **Azure Activity Log**: Provides insight into control plane events within your Azure resources, including resource creation, deletion, and configuration changes.

Example: AWS CloudTrail

To monitor API calls in **AWS** using **CloudTrail**, you can create a trail that records all management events (e.g., creating or deleting resources).

Creating a CloudTrail Trail:

1. Open the **CloudTrail Console**.
2. Choose **Create Trail** and provide a name.
3. Enable **Management Events** to log API calls and select a **S3 bucket** to store logs.
4. Configure logging for all regions.

Once set up, you can use the logs to track any changes made to resources or to troubleshoot any issues.

---

3. Resource Optimization and Cost Management

Managing cloud resources goes hand-in-hand with **cost optimization**. As cloud services operate on a pay-as-you-go model, it's important to ensure that you are using resources efficiently and avoiding unnecessary expenses. Monitoring resource usage allows you to identify underutilized resources and adjust them accordingly.

- **AWS Cost Explorer**: Allows you to visualize your AWS spending, helping you identify cost drivers and optimize resource usage.
- **Google Cloud Billing Reports**: Provides insights into your spending patterns on Google Cloud.
- **Azure Cost Management**: Helps track and manage Azure spending, as well as setting up budgets and alerts.

Example: AWS Cost Explorer

To monitor and reduce AWS costs, you can use **Cost Explorer** to analyze spending patterns and identify underutilized resources.

1. Go to the **AWS Cost Explorer** console.
2. Create a **cost and usage report** that groups services by the region or instance type.
3. Identify areas where resources are underutilized (e.g., unused EC2 instances or over-provisioned storage).

Once identified, you can either downsize or terminate unused instances to reduce costs.

---

4. Automating Resource Management

Automation is a key part of cloud management. Automating common tasks like scaling resources, provisioning infrastructure, and enforcing policies can help reduce manual intervention, improve operational efficiency, and reduce the risk of errors.

Tools for Automation

- **AWS CloudFormation**: Allows you to automate the provisioning and management of AWS resources using templates.
- **Google Cloud Deployment Manager**: Google Cloud's tool for automating the setup and management of resources.

- **Azure Resource Manager (ARM)**: Azure's native service for managing and automating resources.

Example: AWS CloudFormation

With **CloudFormation**, you can define your infrastructure as code and automate the deployment of resources.

Example CloudFormation Template (Provisioning EC2 Instance):

```
AWSTemplateFormatVersion: '2010-09-09'
Resources:
  MyEC2Instance:
    Type: 'AWS::EC2::Instance'
    Properties:
      InstanceType: t2.micro
      ImageId: ami-0c55b159cbfafe1f0
      KeyName: my-key-pair
```

Deploying the Template via AWS CLI:

```
aws cloudformation create-stack --stack-name MyStack --template-body file://template.yml
```

This CloudFormation template automatically provisions an EC2 instance when the stack is created.

---

5. Health Checks and Self-Healing Systems

In a cloud environment, systems should be designed to automatically recover from failures. **Health checks** are vital to detect and address issues before they impact users. Cloud platforms like **AWS**, **Google Cloud**, and **Azure** offer health check mechanisms that enable automatic failover, replacement of unhealthy instances, and traffic redirection.

Example of Health Check Implementation

In **AWS**, you can set up an **Elastic Load Balancer (ELB)** to automatically perform health checks on your EC2 instances. If an instance becomes unhealthy, the load balancer will stop routing traffic to it and replace it with a healthy instance.

1. **Set up ELB Health Checks**:
   - Go to the **EC2 Console**.
   - Select **Load Balancers** > **Health Checks**.
   - Configure health checks for your EC2 instances (e.g., HTTP, TCP).

Case Study: Managing and Monitoring a Scalable Web Application

Let's apply the concepts we've discussed to a real-world scenario. Assume you're managing a scalable web application running in **AWS**.

Step 1: Set Up CloudWatch for Monitoring

- Create a **CloudWatch Alarm** to monitor **CPU utilization** of your EC2 instances. If CPU usage exceeds 80%, trigger an alert to notify your operations team.

Step 2: Automate Scaling

- Set up **Auto Scaling** for your EC2 instances so that when traffic increases, new instances are automatically launched, and when traffic decreases, unnecessary instances are terminated.

Step 3: Implement CloudTrail for Auditing

- Use **CloudTrail** to record all API calls made in your environment, including changes to EC2 instances, security groups, and VPC settings. This provides a historical record of any changes that were made, allowing you to track down issues or identify unauthorized access.

- Regularly review your AWS spending using **Cost Explorer** to identify instances that are underutilized. For example, you might find that several t2.large EC2 instances are running at only 10% CPU usage, so you can resize them to smaller t2.micro instances to save costs.

Managing and monitoring cloud resources is essential to ensure that your cloud infrastructure remains cost-effective, high-performing, and secure. By leveraging cloud-native tools like **AWS CloudWatch**, **Google Cloud Monitoring**, and **Azure Monitor**, you can gain deep insights into your resource utilization and take proactive measures to optimize performance.

Implementing practices like real-time monitoring, logging, cost management, and automated scaling helps you manage your cloud resources efficiently. Moreover, setting up health checks, monitoring costs, and automating provisioning will allow you to maintain a robust and reliable cloud environment.

7.2 Cloud Security Best Practices

Cloud security is a multi-layered approach that aims to protect cloud-based systems, data, and applications from malicious attacks and unintentional breaches. With organizations increasingly moving their sensitive data and business operations to the cloud, securing these assets has never been more critical. A successful cloud security strategy involves protecting data, ensuring compliance, and maintaining the availability and integrity of services.

What Is Cloud Security?

Cloud security refers to the set of policies, controls, and technologies designed to protect cloud-based data, applications, and systems from security threats. It involves ensuring the confidentiality, integrity, and availability of data and services hosted in the cloud. The primary objectives of cloud security are:

1. **Data Confidentiality**: Ensuring that sensitive data is kept private and protected from unauthorized access.
2. **Data Integrity**: Ensuring that data is accurate, consistent, and protected from corruption or unauthorized modifications.
3. **Availability**: Ensuring that cloud services are always available, even in the event of an attack or technical failure.

Cloud security practices apply not only to cloud service providers but also to cloud consumers (the businesses and users who use the cloud services).

Key Cloud Security Best Practices

1. Identity and Access Management (IAM)

One of the most important aspects of cloud security is ensuring that only authorized users have access to cloud resources. Identity and Access Management (IAM) provides control over who can access which resources, and what actions they can perform on them.

Key Principles for IAM:

1. **Least Privilege**: Users should only have access to the resources they need to do their jobs and nothing more.
2. **Role-Based Access Control (RBAC)**: Assign users to roles based on their job functions and provide the least privilege access required for that role.
3. **Multi-Factor Authentication (MFA)**: Enforce MFA to add an extra layer of security by requiring users to authenticate with something they know (password) and something they have (e.g., a smartphone).

In **AWS**, you can create users and roles with specific permissions using IAM policies. Here's an example of creating a user with restricted permissions using **AWS CLI**:

1. **Create an IAM User**:

```
aws iam create-user --user-name readOnlyUser
```

2. **Attach Permissions to the User**: Attach a policy that only allows read-only access to **S3**.

```
aws iam attach-user-policy --user-name readOnlyUser --
policy-arn arn:aws:iam::aws:policy/AmazonS3ReadOnlyAccess
```

3. **Enable MFA for the User**: Enabling MFA increases the security by requiring the user to authenticate using both their password and a second factor (such as a mobile device).

```
aws iam enable-mfa-device --user-name readOnlyUser --
serial-number arn:aws:iam::123456789012:mfa/readOnlyUserMFA
--authentication-code1 123456 --authentication-code2 789012
```

---

2. Data Encryption

Data encryption is a cornerstone of cloud security. It ensures that data is protected both at rest (in storage) and in transit (when being transmitted over networks).

Encryption Best Practices:

1. **Encrypt Data at Rest**: Use cloud provider tools to encrypt data stored in cloud storage (e.g., databases, file systems).
2. **Encrypt Data in Transit**: Use protocols like **SSL/TLS** to secure data being transmitted across networks.
3. **Key Management**: Use services like **AWS KMS (Key Management Service)**, **Google Cloud KMS**, or **Azure Key Vault** to manage and rotate encryption keys securely.

Practical Example: Encrypting Data in AWS S3

To encrypt objects stored in an **S3 bucket** using **server-side encryption (SSE)**, you can enable encryption in the bucket's configuration:

1. **Enable SSE on S3 Bucket**:

```
aws s3api put-bucket-encryption --bucket my-bucket --
server-side-encryption-configuration
'{"Rules":[{"ApplyServerSideEncryptionByDefault":{"SSEAlgor
ithm":"AES256"}}]}'
```

This ensures that all objects uploaded to the bucket are encrypted using the AES-256 algorithm by default.

---

3. Network Security and Isolation

Cloud services provide multiple layers of security to ensure that your network is protected from unauthorized access and malicious actors.

Network Security Best Practices:

1. **Virtual Private Network (VPN)**: Use VPNs to securely connect on-premises systems to your cloud environment.
2. **Virtual Private Cloud (VPC)**: Isolate cloud resources in a private network (VPC) and control access with **Security Groups** and **Network ACLs**.
3. **Firewalls**: Configure firewalls to block unauthorized traffic and restrict access to your cloud resources.
4. **DDoS Protection**: Use built-in tools like **AWS Shield** or **Google Cloud Armor** to protect against Distributed Denial of Service (DDoS) attacks.

Practical Example: AWS VPC Security Group

In **AWS**, a **Security Group** acts as a virtual firewall for EC2 instances. Here's an example of how to configure a security group to only allow SSH access from a specific IP:

1. **Create a Security Group**:

```
aws ec2 create-security-group --group-name MySecurityGroup
--description "Allow SSH from trusted IP"
```

2. **Add Inbound Rule for SSH**: Allow SSH traffic only from your specific IP address (e.g., `192.168.1.1`):

```
aws ec2 authorize-security-group-ingress --group-name
MySecurityGroup --protocol tcp --port 22 --cidr
192.168.1.1/32
```

3. **Assign the Security Group to an EC2 Instance**:

```
aws ec2 modify-instance-attribute --instance-id i-
1234567890abcdef0 --groups sg-12345678
```

---

4. Regular Security Audits and Compliance

Ensuring that your cloud resources are secure requires continuous monitoring and regular security audits. Cloud providers offer several tools to help you maintain compliance with industry standards and security best practices.

Security Auditing Best Practices:

1. **Automate Security Audits**: Use cloud-native tools to run periodic security audits. For example, **AWS Inspector**, **Google Cloud Security Command Center**, and **Azure Security Center** help automate security checks.
2. **Compliance Reports**: Use cloud provider tools to generate compliance reports for industry standards like **PCI-DSS**, **HIPAA**, and **GDPR**.

Practical Example: Google Cloud Security Command Center

Google Cloud offers the **Security Command Center** to provide a comprehensive overview of your cloud security posture. You can use it to identify vulnerabilities and ensure compliance with security standards.

1. **Enable Security Command Center**:

```
gcloud services enable securitycenter.googleapis.com
```

2. **View Findings**: To view potential security issues in your environment, you can check the findings through the **Security Command Center**:

```
gcloud alpha securitycenter findings list --
organization=your-org-id
```

---

5. Monitoring and Incident Response

Real-time monitoring and a rapid response to security incidents are key to preventing or mitigating the impact of security breaches.

Incident Response Best Practices:

1. **Real-Time Monitoring**: Use cloud-native monitoring tools like **AWS CloudWatch**, **Google Cloud Operations Suite**, and **Azure Monitor** to track activity and detect abnormal behavior.
2. **Automated Incident Response**: Set up automated workflows for responding to incidents, such as terminating compromised instances or blocking malicious IP addresses.
3. **Security Information and Event Management (SIEM)**: Use SIEM solutions to aggregate logs, detect patterns, and respond to security threats.

Practical Example: AWS CloudWatch Logs and Alarms

In **AWS**, you can monitor CloudWatch logs for suspicious activity and set alarms to trigger automatic responses.

1. **Create a CloudWatch Alarm for Suspicious Activity**: For example, if you detect multiple failed login attempts, you can trigger an alarm:

```
aws cloudwatch put-metric-alarm --alarm-name
"FailedLoginAttempts" --metric-name "FailedLogins" --
namespace "AWS/EC2" --statistic "Sum" --period 60 --
threshold 5 --comparison-operator "GreaterThanThreshold" --
evaluation-periods 1 --alarm-actions arn:aws:sns:us-east-
1:123456789012:NotifyMe
```

2. **Automated Remediation**: You can trigger **AWS Lambda** functions to automatically mitigate the threat, such as blocking an IP address or isolating an instance.

Case Study: Securing a Cloud-based E-commerce Application

Scenario: An e-commerce company hosts a web application in **AWS** and needs to implement security best practices to protect customer data and prevent unauthorized access.

Step 1: IAM Policies

- The company configures **IAM roles** with fine-grained permissions, ensuring that only authorized personnel have access to sensitive data (e.g., payment information).

Step 2: Data Encryption

- All customer data in **Amazon S3** is encrypted using **server-side encryption (SSE)**, and all communications between the client and server are secured using **SSL/TLS**.

Step 3: Network Security

- The company uses **Security Groups** to restrict access to the EC2 instances, allowing only HTTP and HTTPS traffic and blocking all other ports.
- **VPC Peering** is used to securely connect on-premises infrastructure to AWS resources.

Step 4: Compliance and Auditing

- The company enables **AWS CloudTrail** to log all API calls and **AWS Config** to track configuration changes.
- Regular **PCI-DSS** compliance checks are run using **AWS Inspector**.

- **AWS CloudWatch** monitors the application's performance and security, and **AWS Lambda** is used to automatically isolate compromised instances.
- Alerts are set up to notify security teams if suspicious activity is detected.

Cloud security is a complex and multi-layered field that requires a proactive approach. Implementing best practices in **IAM, data encryption, network security, auditing**, and **incident response** is crucial for protecting your cloud infrastructure. By following these best practices and using cloud-native tools like **AWS CloudTrail, Google Cloud Security Command Center**, and **Azure Security Center**, you can ensure that your cloud environment remains secure and resilient against potential threats.

7.3 Disaster Recovery and Backup Solutions

Disaster recovery (DR) is an essential part of maintaining a resilient cloud infrastructure. In the face of disruptions—be they hardware failures, cyberattacks, or natural disasters—having a disaster recovery plan in place can make the difference between business continuity and catastrophic downtime. Similarly, **backup solutions** play a critical role in ensuring that your data remains protected and can be restored quickly if lost or corrupted.

What is Disaster Recovery (DR)?

Disaster Recovery (DR) refers to the strategies and processes in place to ensure that an organization's infrastructure and data can be quickly recovered after an unexpected event, such as a system failure, data breach, or natural disaster. DR plans aim to minimize downtime and data loss, ensuring that business operations can continue as quickly as possible.

Key components of a **Disaster Recovery** plan:

1. **Backup Strategies**: Ensuring that critical data is regularly backed up and available for recovery.
2. **Failover Mechanisms**: Automatically switching to a backup system or infrastructure when the primary system fails.
3. **Recovery Time Objective (RTO)**: The maximum acceptable downtime before operations need to be restored.
4. **Recovery Point Objective (RPO)**: The maximum acceptable amount of data loss, measured by the time between the last backup and the failure.

---

1. Disaster Recovery Strategies

Designing a DR strategy in the cloud involves understanding the **criticality** of your data and systems, setting appropriate **RTO** and **RPO** goals, and using the right tools to ensure availability and recovery.

Types of Disaster Recovery Models

1. **Backup and Restore**: This is the most basic form of DR. It involves regularly backing up your data and restoring it when needed. This model works best for applications that can afford significant downtime and where data loss is minimal.
2. **Pilot Light**: In this model, you keep a minimal version of your environment running at all times. In the event of a failure, you can quickly scale up the environment to meet the demand. This is a good middle-ground approach for businesses looking to minimize costs but still need a fast recovery.
3. **Warm Standby**: This model involves running a scaled-down version of your production environment in another location. If the primary environment fails, the standby environment can be scaled up to take over the workload.
4. **Hot Standby/Active-Active**: In an active-active setup, both the primary and backup environments are running simultaneously. Traffic is load-balanced across both environments, which helps

ensure that there is no downtime. This is the most expensive but the most reliable DR model.

2. Backup Solutions in the Cloud

Cloud providers offer robust backup services that can help protect your data, ensuring it can be restored quickly in case of disaster.

Best Practices for Cloud Backups

1. **Automate Backups**: Cloud services often provide automation tools to ensure that backups are taken regularly, reducing the risk of human error and ensuring that you don't miss critical backup windows.
2. **Use Multi-Region Backups**: Storing backups in a single region is risky, especially in case of a region-wide failure. Use **multi-region backup solutions** to ensure that your data is backed up across multiple geographical locations.
3. **Encrypt Backups**: Always encrypt your backups to protect sensitive data. Cloud providers offer encryption tools that automatically encrypt data at rest and in transit.
4. **Test Backup Restoration**: Regularly test your backup restoration process to ensure that you can recover your data when needed. It's important to verify that your backups are not only complete but also restorable.

Cloud Backup Solutions by Provider

AWS Backup

- **AWS Backup** is a fully managed backup service that automates and centralizes backup processes across AWS services like EC2, RDS, and DynamoDB.
- It offers automated backup scheduling, retention management, and recovery.

Example of creating a backup plan using AWS CLI:

```
aws backup create-backup-plan --backup-plan
'{"BackupPlanName": "MyBackupPlan", "Rules": [{"RuleName":
"DailyBackup", "ScheduleExpression": "cron(0 12 * * ? *)",
"TargetBackupVaultName": "MyBackupVault", "Lifecycle":
{"MoveToColdStorageAfterDays": 30}}]}'
```

Google Cloud Backup and DR

- **Google Cloud Storage** and **Google Cloud Filestore** offer cloud backup solutions. Google Cloud also integrates with third-party backup services such as **Veeam** and **CloudEndure** for DR.
- **Cloud Storage** can be used for low-cost, durable backup storage.

Example of enabling backup for Cloud SQL on Google Cloud:

```
gcloud sql backups create --instance=my-database
```

Azure Backup

- **Azure Backup** is a scalable solution that protects against data loss by enabling backup of on-premises and cloud workloads. It supports both file-based and application-based backups for Azure VMs and databases.

Example of backing up an Azure VM:

```
az backup protection enable-for-azurewm --resource-group
MyResourceGroup --vault-name MyBackupVault --vm MyVM --
policy-name DefaultPolicy
```

3. Designing Disaster Recovery (DR) Plans

A well-designed DR plan ensures that, in the event of a disaster, your application and infrastructure can be quickly restored. Here's how you can design an effective DR plan using the cloud.

Step 1: Determine Your RTO and RPO

- **RTO**: Define how quickly you need to restore your application and systems after an outage.

- **RPO**: Determine how much data loss is acceptable. If your application updates data frequently, you may want near-zero data loss, which will require more frequent backups.

Step 2: Select a DR Strategy

Based on your RTO and RPO, choose a disaster recovery model:

- **Backup and Restore**: For less critical workloads.
- **Pilot Light** or **Warm Standby**: For critical workloads where faster recovery is necessary.
- **Active-Active (Hot Standby)**: For mission-critical applications that cannot afford downtime.

Step 3: Choose DR Tools

- **Cloud-Native Services**: Use the built-in DR tools provided by your cloud provider (e.g., **AWS CloudFormation**, **Google Cloud Deployment Manager**, **Azure Site Recovery**).
- **Third-Party DR Services**: Consider third-party services like **Veeam** or **Zerto** for advanced DR capabilities.

Step 4: Implement and Test Your DR Plan

Once your plan is designed, implement it using the selected DR tools. Regularly test your DR plan to ensure that it works as expected. Test failover, failback, and recovery processes at least once every six months.

---

4. Automated Disaster Recovery and Backup Testing

Automation is a crucial part of cloud DR and backup strategies. Automating your DR and backup workflows ensures that backups are performed regularly, and recovery processes can be executed with minimal intervention.

- **AWS Lambda**: Use Lambda functions to automate backup and recovery tasks.
- **Google Cloud Functions**: Implement functions that automatically trigger backups or initiate failover processes.
- **Azure Logic Apps**: Use Azure Logic Apps to automate backup scheduling, notification alerts, and even failover processes.

Case Study: Cloud Disaster Recovery for an E-Commerce Platform

Scenario: **E-Shop**, an e-commerce company, is hosted on **AWS** and needs a disaster recovery solution for their critical systems, including product catalogs, order processing, and customer data.

Step 1: Determine RTO and RPO

- **RTO**: The business cannot afford more than **2 hours of downtime**.
- **RPO**: The company can tolerate **15 minutes of data loss**.

Step 2: Choose DR Strategy

- **Pilot Light**: They opt for a **Pilot Light** strategy for their application. They will keep a minimal version of their application running in **AWS Elastic Beanstalk** and replicate data to **S3**.
- **Backup and Restore**: The product catalog and customer data will be backed up daily to **Amazon S3** with versioning enabled.

Step 3: Implement DR Tools

- **AWS S3**: Used to store daily backups of product data.
- **AWS Lambda**: Lambda functions are used to automate the backup process every night and initiate the restore process in case of disaster.
- **Amazon RDS**: Daily snapshots are scheduled for the database.

- AWS CloudWatch monitors system health and triggers **CloudWatch Alarms** in case of a failure. Lambda functions are set to automatically scale up the minimal environment in the event of a disaster.
- Periodic **DR tests** are conducted by simulating the failure of an AWS Availability Zone to ensure fast failover.

Step 5: Recovery

- During a test recovery, AWS Lambda automatically restores the application in another Availability Zone, and the database is restored from the most recent snapshot.

Disaster recovery and backup solutions are vital components of any cloud infrastructure strategy. Cloud services offer a variety of tools that allow you to design robust DR plans, automate backup processes, and ensure data resilience. By selecting the appropriate DR model (e.g., backup and restore, pilot light, or active-active), using cloud-native backup tools, and automating recovery processes, you can build a resilient infrastructure capable of handling failures with minimal impact.

7.4 Automation with Cloud Services

Automation in cloud environments is a game-changer for improving operational efficiency, reducing human error, and accelerating deployment processes. By automating routine tasks—such as provisioning infrastructure, scaling resources, monitoring, and backup—you can create more reliable, scalable, and cost-effective cloud solutions.

What is Cloud Automation?

Cloud automation involves the use of tools, scripts, and services to automatically manage cloud infrastructure and applications. The goal is to eliminate manual intervention in tasks like resource provisioning, scaling, and managing the lifecycle of cloud services.

Key Benefits of Cloud Automation:

1. **Reduced Human Error**: Automation reduces the risk of mistakes made during manual configurations and repetitive tasks.
2. **Efficiency**: Tasks that would otherwise take a long time can be completed in minutes or seconds, saving time and improving productivity.
3. **Consistency**: Automation ensures that tasks are performed consistently, improving the reliability of your cloud infrastructure.
4. **Cost Optimization**: By automating resource provisioning and scaling, you can ensure that you're only using and paying for the resources you need.
5. **Scalability**: Automation allows you to scale infrastructure up or down in response to changes in demand without manual intervention.

Key Cloud Automation Practices

There are several core practices when it comes to automating cloud environments. Let's explore them in detail.

1. Infrastructure as Code (IaC)

Infrastructure as Code (IaC) allows you to define and provision your cloud infrastructure using configuration files, reducing the need for manual setup. IaC tools let you treat your infrastructure in the same way you treat application code—by versioning, testing, and deploying it.

Benefits of IaC:

- **Consistency**: IaC ensures that environments are replicated exactly every time.

- **Scalability**: Automate the creation and management of infrastructure across different environments (e.g., development, staging, production).
- **Versioning**: Changes to infrastructure are version-controlled and can be rolled back if needed.

Popular IaC Tools:

- **AWS CloudFormation**: Automates the provisioning of AWS resources using templates written in JSON or YAML.
- **Terraform**: A cloud-agnostic IaC tool that allows you to define infrastructure for multiple cloud providers.
- **Google Cloud Deployment Manager**: Google Cloud's native IaC tool for automating resource management.

Practical Example: AWS CloudFormation

Here's a simple **AWS CloudFormation** template to provision an EC2 instance:

```
AWSTemplateFormatVersion: '2010-09-09'
Resources:
  MyEC2Instance:
    Type: 'AWS::EC2::Instance'
    Properties:
      InstanceType: t2.micro
      ImageId: ami-0c55b159cbfafe1f0
      KeyName: my-key-pair
```

This CloudFormation template automatically provisions an EC2 instance with the specified properties.

To deploy this template:

```
aws cloudformation create-stack --stack-name MyStack --template-body file://template.yml
```

---

2. Continuous Integration and Continuous Delivery (CI/CD)

CI/CD automation pipelines are essential for automating the build, test, and deployment process for applications. By integrating **Continuous**

Integration (CI) and **Continuous Delivery (CD)**, you can ensure that updates are delivered quickly, securely, and reliably.

Benefits of CI/CD:

- **Faster Deployment**: Automate testing and deployment to ensure that code changes are rolled out quickly and safely.
- **Quality Assurance**: Ensure that each update passes automated tests before it is deployed to production.
- **Consistent Deployments**: Automate the entire deployment pipeline to reduce configuration drift and errors.

Popular CI/CD Tools:

- **AWS CodePipeline**: A fully managed CI/CD service for automating the build, test, and deployment of AWS applications.
- **Google Cloud Build**: A fully managed build service that allows you to create CI/CD pipelines for Google Cloud applications.
- **Azure DevOps**: A comprehensive CI/CD platform for automating deployments on Azure.

Practical Example: AWS CodePipeline

Here's a simple setup to automate a deployment process using **AWS CodePipeline**:

1. **Create a Source Stage**: Use **AWS CodeCommit** or **GitHub** to store your application code.
2. **Create a Build Stage**: Use **AWS CodeBuild** to compile and test the application.
3. **Create a Deploy Stage**: Use **AWS CodeDeploy** to automatically deploy the application to EC2 instances.

```
{
  "name": "MyPipeline",
  "roleArn": "arn:aws:iam::123456789012:role/service-
role/MyPipelineRole",
  "artifactStore": {
    "type": "S3",
    "location": "my-artifact-store"
  },
  "stages": [
    {
```

```
    "name": "Source",
    "actions": [
      {
        "name": "SourceAction",
        "actionTypeId": {
          "category": "Source",
          "owner": "AWS",
          "provider": "GitHub",
          "version": "1"
        },
        "outputArtifacts": [{"name": "SourceArtifact"}],
        "configuration": {
          "Owner": "my-username",
          "Repo": "my-repo",
          "Branch": "main",
          "OAuthToken": "my-oauth-token"
        }
      }
    ]
  },
  {
    "name": "Build",
    "actions": [
      {
        "name": "BuildAction",
        "actionTypeId": {
          "category": "Build",
          "owner": "AWS",
          "provider": "CodeBuild",
          "version": "1"
        },
        "inputArtifacts": [{"name": "SourceArtifact"}],
        "outputArtifacts": [{"name": "BuildArtifact"}],
        "configuration": {
          "ProjectName": "my-build-project"
        }
      }
    ]
  },
  {
    "name": "Deploy",
    "actions": [
      {
        "name": "DeployAction",
        "actionTypeId": {
          "category": "Deploy",
          "owner": "AWS",
          "provider": "CodeDeploy",
          "version": "1"
        },
```

```
        "inputArtifacts": [{"name": "BuildArtifact"}],
        "configuration": {
          "ApplicationName": "MyApp",
          "DeploymentGroupName": "MyDeploymentGroup"
        }
      }
    ]
  }
 ]
}
```

This pipeline automatically pulls code from **GitHub**, builds it using **CodeBuild**, and deploys it using **CodeDeploy**.

---

3. Automated Scaling and Resource Management

In cloud environments, scaling up or down resources based on demand is essential to maintaining performance and minimizing costs. **Auto-scaling** allows you to automatically adjust the number of resources available based on real-time metrics.

Benefits of Automated Scaling:

- **Cost Efficiency**: Automatically scale down resources during off-peak hours to reduce costs.
- **Performance Optimization**: Scale up resources during traffic spikes to ensure that your application remains responsive.
- **Operational Efficiency**: Automate resource provisioning and de-provisioning to reduce manual intervention.

Tools for Automated Scaling:

- **AWS Auto Scaling**: Automatically scales EC2 instances based on demand.
- **Google Cloud Autoscaler**: Automatically adjusts the number of VM instances based on CPU usage, HTTP traffic, or other metrics.
- **Azure Virtual Machine Scale Sets**: Automatically scale VM instances up or down based on load.

Here's how you can set up **AWS Auto Scaling** for EC2 instances:

1. **Create a Launch Configuration**: This defines the EC2 instance type, AMI, and other settings.

```
aws autoscaling create-launch-configuration --launch-
configuration-name MyLaunchConfig --image-id ami-12345678 -
-instance-type t2.micro
```

2. **Create an Auto Scaling Group**:

```
aws autoscaling create-auto-scaling-group --auto-scaling-
group-name MyAutoScalingGroup --launch-configuration-name
MyLaunchConfig --min-size 1 --max-size 5 --desired-capacity
3 --availability-zones us-east-1a us-east-1b
```

3. **Set Scaling Policies**: Automatically scale up or down based on metrics (e.g., CPU utilization).

```
aws autoscaling put-scaling-policy --auto-scaling-group-
name MyAutoScalingGroup --policy-name ScaleUpPolicy --
scaling-adjustment 1 --adjustment-type ChangeInCapacity --
cooldown 300
```

4. Automated Monitoring and Incident Response

Monitoring cloud environments is critical to ensure systems remain healthy and performant. **Automated monitoring** involves using cloud-native tools to track resource health and set alerts for anomalies, ensuring rapid response to incidents.

Benefits of Automated Monitoring:

- **Proactive Management**: Detect and resolve issues before they impact users.
- **Cost Control**: Monitor resource usage to prevent over-provisioning and minimize costs.
- **Security Monitoring**: Track unauthorized access or potential vulnerabilities.

Tools for Automated Monitoring:

- **AWS CloudWatch**: Provides a comprehensive view of AWS resources, including custom metrics and logs.
- **Google Cloud Monitoring**: Monitors Google Cloud resources and integrates with Google Cloud Logging for detailed tracking.
- **Azure Monitor**: Provides real-time monitoring for Azure resources, with integration for alerting and automation.

Practical Example: AWS CloudWatch Alarms

1. **Create a CloudWatch Alarm for CPU Utilization**:

```
aws cloudwatch put-metric-alarm --alarm-name
"HighCPUUtilization" --metric-name "CPUUtilization" --
namespace "AWS/EC2" --statistic "Average" --period 300 --
threshold 80 --comparison-operator "GreaterThanThreshold" -
-dimension Name=InstanceId,Value=i-1234567890abcdef0 --
evaluation-periods 2 --alarm-actions arn:aws:sns:us-east-
1:123456789012:NotifyMe
```

2. **Trigger an Action**: When the CPU utilization exceeds 80%, an email notification will be sent via **SNS**.

Case Study: Automating a Multi-Tier Web Application in AWS

Let's take a look at how automation can be applied to a **multi-tier web application** hosted in AWS, involving resource provisioning, CI/CD, and auto-scaling.

Step 1: Infrastructure Provisioning with CloudFormation

Use **AWS CloudFormation** to automatically provision EC2 instances, databases,

load balancers, and networking configurations.

Create a **CI/CD pipeline** using **CodePipeline**, automating the build, test, and deployment of application code.

Step 3: Auto-Scaling Configuration

Configure **Auto Scaling** for EC2 instances to adjust capacity based on incoming traffic patterns.

Step 4: Monitoring and Incident Response

Implement **CloudWatch** for monitoring application performance and set alarms to trigger automated scaling or notifications in case of failures.

Cloud automation plays a pivotal role in optimizing cloud resource management, improving operational efficiency, and reducing human errors. By leveraging **Infrastructure as Code (IaC)**, **CI/CD pipelines**, **automated scaling**, and **monitoring tools**, you can create a highly efficient, scalable, and resilient cloud infrastructure.

Part 4: Industry-Specific Cloud Solutions and Case Studies (Specialized Focus)

Chapter 8: Cloud Solutions for the Healthcare Industry

In recent years, the healthcare industry has experienced a significant shift towards cloud computing. The cloud offers solutions that not only streamline healthcare operations but also ensure the secure management of patient data while adhering to strict regulatory compliance standards. This chapter explores the role of cloud computing in the healthcare industry, with a focus on data management, compliance, and real-world adoption.

8.1 Cloud for Data Management and Compliance

The healthcare industry is one of the most data-intensive sectors in the world. From patient records and clinical trials to diagnostic images and billing systems, healthcare organizations generate massive volumes of sensitive data that must be stored, managed, and processed with the highest levels of security and compliance. With regulations like **HIPAA (Health Insurance Portability and Accountability Act)** in the U.S., GDPR (General Data Protection Regulation) in the EU, and other data protection laws, healthcare organizations must ensure that patient information is secure, accessible, and properly managed.

Cloud computing has revolutionized the way healthcare organizations manage data. Cloud providers offer scalable storage solutions, powerful computational resources, and a range of tools to support data privacy, security, and regulatory compliance.

---

1. The Role of the Cloud in Healthcare Data Management

The shift to the cloud provides healthcare organizations with several key advantages:

1. **Scalability**: Healthcare data is growing exponentially. The cloud offers virtually unlimited storage capacity, enabling healthcare organizations to scale up quickly as data volumes increase without the need for costly on-premises hardware upgrades.
2. **Collaboration**: Cloud-based healthcare systems allow for seamless sharing of patient data across different departments, healthcare providers, and specialists, enhancing collaborative care and improving decision-making.
3. **Cost-Effectiveness**: Cloud services operate on a pay-as-you-go model, meaning healthcare organizations can avoid upfront capital costs for infrastructure and only pay for what they actually use.
4. **Data Security**: With sensitive data like **Protected Health Information (PHI)**, maintaining security is crucial. Cloud providers offer robust data encryption, access controls, and compliance frameworks to ensure data protection.
5. **Flexibility and Availability**: Cloud-based systems provide 24/7 access to patient data, enabling healthcare providers to access information whenever and wherever it's needed—whether from a hospital, clinic, or remote location.

---

2. Managing Sensitive Data in the Cloud

In the cloud, managing sensitive healthcare data involves secure storage, efficient access management, and implementing privacy protections. Here's how cloud solutions address each of these aspects:

a. Data Storage and Organization

Cloud providers offer several storage solutions that are particularly suited to healthcare environments, where vast amounts of data need to be stored securely and accessed quickly.

1. **Object Storage**: Services like **Amazon S3**, **Google Cloud Storage**, and **Azure Blob Storage** are ideal for storing large volumes of unstructured data, such as medical images, documents, and diagnostic reports.
2. **Relational and NoSQL Databases**: For structured healthcare data, such as patient records, cloud databases like **Amazon RDS** (Relational Database Service), **Google Cloud SQL**, and **Azure**

SQL Database offer secure, scalable, and managed database solutions. Additionally, **NoSQL databases** like **Amazon DynamoDB** and **Google Firestore** are useful for handling semi-structured data.

3. **Data Lakes**: For big data analytics and storage, healthcare organizations can set up **data lakes** (e.g., **AWS Lake Formation**), where structured and unstructured data is stored in a central repository for easy access and processing.

b. Data Access Management

Ensuring that the right people have access to the right data at the right time is a critical part of cloud data management. This requires stringent **identity and access management (IAM)** policies to control user permissions and ensure that unauthorized users cannot access sensitive patient data.

1. **Role-Based Access Control (RBAC)**: Cloud providers implement **RBAC** to ensure that healthcare professionals and staff only have access to data that is relevant to their roles.
2. **Encryption**: Cloud solutions offer **end-to-end encryption** to protect data both at rest (stored data) and in transit (data being transmitted). Services like **AWS KMS** (Key Management Service), **Google Cloud KMS**, and **Azure Key Vault** allow organizations to manage encryption keys securely.
3. **Multi-Factor Authentication (MFA)**: Cloud platforms offer MFA to add an additional layer of security by requiring users to authenticate with multiple factors (e.g., password + mobile device) before gaining access to sensitive data.

---

3. Compliance with Healthcare Regulations

Healthcare organizations must meet strict compliance standards when managing patient data, especially regarding data privacy and security. In the U.S., **HIPAA** is the most well-known standard for handling PHI, while the **GDPR** applies to organizations operating in the EU or dealing with EU citizens' data. Cloud providers offer tools and frameworks that help healthcare organizations meet these requirements.

a. HIPAA Compliance in the Cloud

HIPAA sets guidelines for how healthcare providers and their business associates handle PHI. Cloud providers can support HIPAA compliance by providing tools and services that meet the required security standards.

Key HIPAA Requirements and Cloud Solutions:

1. **Data Encryption**: HIPAA requires that all PHI be encrypted, both in transit and at rest. Cloud providers such as **AWS**, **Google Cloud**, and **Azure** provide **server-side encryption** to ensure that sensitive data is protected.

   Example: Enabling **server-side encryption** in **Amazon S3**:

```
aws s3api put-bucket-encryption --bucket my-healthcare-
bucket --server-side-encryption-configuration
'{"Rules":[{"ApplyServerSideEncryptionByDefault":{"SSEAlgor
ithm":"AES256"}}]}'
```

2. **Business Associate Agreements (BAAs)**: Under HIPAA, any third-party service provider that handles PHI must sign a **Business Associate Agreement (BAA)**. Cloud providers offer these agreements as part of their service.

   Example: **AWS** offers a BAA that you can accept when you sign up for their services, ensuring compliance with HIPAA for data hosted on AWS.

3. **Access Control and Monitoring**: **AWS IAM**, **Azure Active Directory (AAD)**, and **Google Cloud IAM** provide role-based access control (RBAC), allowing healthcare organizations to limit access to PHI based on user roles and responsibilities. Additionally, **CloudTrail** (AWS) and **Google Cloud Audit Logs** provide continuous monitoring of who accessed data and what actions they performed.
4. **Backup and Disaster Recovery**: Cloud services offer automated backups and disaster recovery solutions to ensure that PHI is protected and recoverable in case of system failures or disasters.

GDPR governs how personal data is handled for residents of the European Union (EU). Healthcare organizations that deal with EU citizens' data must comply with GDPR's stringent rules regarding data privacy, including the right to access, correct, and erase personal data.

Key GDPR Requirements and Cloud Solutions:

1. **Data Processing Agreements (DPA)**: Healthcare organizations using cloud services must ensure that cloud providers offer a **Data Processing Agreement (DPA)**, which outlines how personal data will be handled and protected. Most cloud providers, such as AWS, Azure, and Google Cloud, provide a standard DPA.
2. **Data Access and Portability**: GDPR gives individuals the right to access their personal data and move it to other providers (data portability). Cloud providers help enable this by offering APIs to retrieve and export data easily.
3. **Data Retention and Deletion**: Under GDPR, data must be stored no longer than necessary. Cloud providers allow organizations to set **data retention policies** to automatically delete or anonymize data after a specified period.
4. **Encryption and Anonymization**: GDPR mandates that personal data be encrypted or anonymized when possible. Cloud services like **Google Cloud** and **AWS** offer built-in encryption and anonymization tools.

---

4. Practical Example: Setting Up a HIPAA-Compliant Cloud Environment

Let's take a look at how a healthcare organization might set up a **HIPAA-compliant cloud environment** on **AWS** to securely store and manage patient data.

Step 1: Create an Encrypted S3 Bucket for PHI

1. **Create an S3 Bucket** for storing PHI:

```
aws s3api create-bucket --bucket healthcare-data-bucket --
region us-west-2
```

2. **Enable server-side encryption (SSE)** to encrypt data at rest:

```
aws s3api put-bucket-encryption --bucket healthcare-data-
bucket --server-side-encryption-configuration
'{"Rules":[{"ApplyServerSideEncryptionByDefault":{"SSEAlgor
ithm":"AES256"}}]}'
```

3. **Set Bucket Policy** to restrict access to only authorized users:

```
{
  "Version": "2012-10-17",
  "Statement": [
    {
      "Effect": "Allow",
      "Principal": "*",
      "Action": "s3:GetObject",
      "Resource": "arn:aws:s3:::healthcare-data-bucket/*",
      "Condition": {
        "IpAddress": {
          "aws:SourceIp": "203.0.113.0/24"
        }
      }
    }
  ]
}
```

Step 2: Configure IAM for Fine-Grained Access Control

1. **Create an IAM Role** that grants access to the S3 bucket only for specific healthcare staff:

```
aws iam create-role --role-name HealthcareDataAccessRole --
assume-role-policy-document file://trust-policy.json
```

2. **Attach a policy** to this role to allow access to the S3 bucket:

```
aws iam put-role-policy --role-name
HealthcareDataAccessRole --policy-name
HealthcareDataAccessPolicy --policy-document file://access-
policy.json
```

Enable **AWS CloudTrail** to log all access and actions performed on the S3 bucket:

```
aws cloudtrail create-trail --name healthcare-data-trail --
s3-bucket-name healthcare-logs-bucket
aws cloudtrail start-logging --name healthcare-data-trail
```

The cloud offers healthcare organizations powerful tools for managing sensitive data, enhancing collaboration, and improving operational efficiency. By utilizing the security and compliance features provided by cloud providers like AWS, Azure, and Google Cloud, healthcare organizations can ensure that they are managing patient data securely and in compliance with regulations like HIPAA and GDPR.

8.2 Case Study: Cloud in Healthcare

Let's a real-world case study that illustrates the transformative power of cloud computing in the healthcare sector. This case study focuses on a fictional healthcare organization, **MedCare Health**, which migrated its data management, collaboration, and service delivery systems to the cloud. The goal of this transition was to streamline operations, ensure compliance with regulations like HIPAA, improve patient care, and reduce costs.

We will walk through the process step-by-step, from initial challenges to the successful implementation of cloud solutions, highlighting the specific benefits and outcomes for MedCare Health.

Background: The Challenges Before Cloud Adoption

MedCare Health is a large healthcare provider with multiple hospitals, clinics, and outpatient services. The organization faced several key challenges before adopting cloud computing:

1. **Data Fragmentation**: Patient data was stored in various systems across different locations. Medical records, diagnostic images, and billing information were often siloed, making it difficult for healthcare providers to access real-time, complete patient information.
2. **Legacy IT Infrastructure**: MedCare relied on on-premises servers to store and manage healthcare data. The infrastructure was expensive to maintain and lacked the scalability required to meet the growing volume of patient data.
3. **Compliance Challenges**: As a healthcare provider, MedCare had to ensure compliance with strict regulations like HIPAA, which mandates how healthcare data should be stored, transmitted, and accessed. The organization struggled to implement the necessary security and auditing measures on its legacy infrastructure.
4. **High Operational Costs**: The cost of maintaining on-premises infrastructure, including hardware, software, and IT staff, was draining the organization's resources. MedCare needed a more cost-effective solution to manage and store data.

Step 1: Identifying Cloud Solutions and Objectives

MedCare Health decided to move its operations to the cloud, with the primary goals being:

- **Streamline data management**: Centralize patient data and create a unified platform for medical records, images, and other data to improve accessibility and collaboration.
- **Ensure HIPAA compliance**: Use cloud-based services that provide built-in compliance tools for managing Protected Health Information (PHI).
- **Enhance scalability**: Scale resources up or down based on demand without the need for heavy capital investment in physical hardware.
- **Improve cost efficiency**: Move to a pay-as-you-go model to reduce infrastructure and operational costs.

The team evaluated different cloud service providers, including **Amazon Web Services (AWS)**, **Microsoft Azure**, and **Google Cloud**, and decided to move forward with **AWS** due to its comprehensive healthcare-focused tools, security features, and proven track record in compliance.

Step 2: Cloud Migration Strategy

The migration process was designed to be carried out in phases to minimize disruption to day-to-day operations. Here's an overview of how the migration process unfolded:

Phase 1: Data Centralization and Storage Migration

MedCare Health began by migrating its patient data, including **Electronic Health Records (EHR)**, **medical images**, and **billing information**, to the cloud.

1. **S3 for Medical Image Storage**: MedCare moved its medical image storage (such as **X-rays**, **MRIs**, and **CT scans**) to **Amazon S3** (Simple Storage Service). S3 provided highly durable, scalable, and secure storage for large image files.

   Implementation:

   - Data was first encrypted using **AES-256** encryption to comply with HIPAA's encryption requirements.
   - **Versioning** was enabled to ensure that previous versions of medical images could be restored if needed.
   - **Lifecycle policies** were set to move older images to **Amazon S3 Glacier** for cost-effective, long-term storage.

   S3 Command Example (for enabling versioning):

   ```
   aws s3api put-bucket-versioning --bucket medcare-images --
   versioning-configuration Status=Enabled
   ```

2. **Amazon RDS for EHR System**: MedCare migrated its Electronic Health Records (EHR) system to **Amazon RDS (Relational Database Service)**. The RDS database hosted patient information and other critical data, making it accessible in real-time to authorized healthcare providers.

Implementation:

- o **Multi-AZ deployments** were used to ensure high availability and fault tolerance of the database.
- o **Automated backups** were configured to meet the organization's disaster recovery objectives.

RDS Command Example (for creating a multi-AZ instance):

```
aws rds create-db-instance --db-instance-identifier
medcare-db --db-instance-class db.m5.large --engine mysql -
-allocated-storage 100 --multi-az --master-username admin -
-master-user-password mypassword --backup-retention-period
7
```

Phase 2: Enabling Collaboration and Communication

MedCare Health needed to improve collaboration among healthcare professionals. With data now stored centrally in the cloud, MedCare integrated **Amazon WorkDocs** for document collaboration and **Amazon Chime** for virtual consultations.

1. **Amazon WorkDocs** was used for securely sharing medical documents, patient reports, and other files among doctors, nurses, and administrative staff. The platform ensured that only authorized users could access sensitive patient data.

Implementation:

- o WorkDocs was configured with access controls to ensure that only healthcare professionals had access to specific patient records.
- o Real-time collaboration on patient notes and reports was enabled, reducing delays in treatment and decision-making.
2. **Amazon Chime** was used to facilitate **virtual consultations** between doctors and patients, especially for remote or follow-up visits. This helped improve patient care and reduced the need for in-person visits.

Implementation:

- o Secure video conferencing was set up with Amazon Chime to ensure compliance with HIPAA's communication requirements.
- o Authentication and access control were implemented to ensure that only authorized users could initiate or join consultations.

Phase 3: Ensuring Compliance and Security

Maintaining compliance with HIPAA was a top priority throughout the migration process. MedCare Health leveraged several AWS security tools and features to ensure the protection of **Protected Health Information (PHI)**.

1. **HIPAA-eligible Services**: AWS provides a range of **HIPAA-eligible services** that are compliant with HIPAA standards. These services were carefully selected and implemented for data processing, storage, and analysis.
2. **AWS Key Management Service (KMS)** was used to manage encryption keys for PHI. MedCare implemented **encryption at rest** and **in transit** for all patient data.
3. **CloudTrail and CloudWatch** were enabled for logging and monitoring access to sensitive data. This provided MedCare with an audit trail to comply with HIPAA's logging requirements.

   Example (for enabling **AWS CloudTrail** logging):

```
aws cloudtrail create-trail --name medcare-cloudtrail --s3-
bucket-name medcare-cloudtrail-logs
aws cloudtrail start-logging --name medcare-cloudtrail
```

4. **Identity and Access Management (IAM)** was used to define **role-based access controls (RBAC),** ensuring that healthcare staff had access to only the data they needed. Multi-factor authentication (MFA) was implemented to enhance security.

Step 3: Results and Benefits

After successfully migrating to the cloud, MedCare Health achieved several key benefits:

1. **Improved Data Accessibility**: Healthcare providers were now able to access patient data from anywhere, whether in the hospital, clinic, or remotely. This led to faster decision-making and reduced delays in treatment.
2. **Reduced Operational Costs**: By moving to the cloud, MedCare significantly reduced the need for physical hardware and the associated costs. The pay-as-you-go pricing model allowed the hospital to optimize its spending based on actual usage.
3. **Enhanced Collaboration**: Using **Amazon WorkDocs** and **Chime**, MedCare's medical professionals could collaborate in real-time, leading to more accurate diagnoses and improved patient care.
4. **Stronger Compliance and Security**: With built-in encryption, robust IAM controls, and continuous monitoring using **CloudTrail** and **CloudWatch**, MedCare ensured that all patient data was securely stored and transmitted in accordance with HIPAA regulations.
5. **Scalable Infrastructure**: During high-demand periods (such as flu season), MedCare could automatically scale its resources to handle increased workloads without manual intervention, ensuring smooth operations during peak times.

Visual Aid: Cloud Migration Architecture for Healthcare

Below is a simplified flow of MedCare Health's cloud migration architecture:

```
+------------------+        +-----------------+        +---
                   ---------------+
| On-Premises EHR  |        | Cloud Migration |        |
                   Cloud Services   |
| System           |------>| Process         |-----> |
                   (AWS S3, RDS,    |
+------------------+        +-----------------+        |
                   WorkDocs, Chime) |
        |                   +------------------+
```

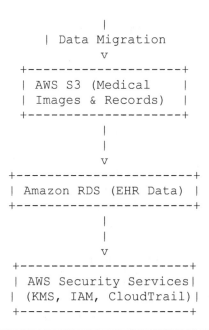

```
            |
            | Data Migration
            v
    +--------------------+
    | AWS S3 (Medical    |
    | Images & Records)  |
    +--------------------+
            |
            |
            v
    +-----------------------+
    | Amazon RDS (EHR Data) |
    +-----------------------+
            |
            |
            v
    +-----------------------+
    | AWS Security Services|
    | (KMS, IAM, CloudTrail)|
    +-----------------------+
```

The case of **MedCare Health** demonstrates how cloud computing can transform the healthcare industry by improving data management, enhancing collaboration, and ensuring compliance with regulations like HIPAA. By migrating to the cloud, MedCare was able to centralize patient data, improve access to medical information, and scale its infrastructure as needed—ultimately improving patient care while reducing operational costs.

Chapter 9: Cloud in the Financial Industry

The financial industry has always been at the forefront of adopting new technologies. With increasing demands for efficiency, security, and scalability, many financial institutions are turning to cloud computing to meet these challenges. The cloud offers a host of benefits, from cost savings and operational flexibility to enabling real-time data analysis and providing advanced security features.

In this chapter, we'll explore the role of cloud solutions in the financial industry, how banks and other financial institutions utilize the cloud, and dive into a real-world case study of cloud adoption in the finance sector. We will also address the challenges financial institutions face, particularly around security and regulatory compliance.

9.1 Financial Cloud Solutions

The financial services industry is one of the most regulated and data-sensitive sectors. As customer demands for faster, more personalized services increase, financial institutions face pressure to modernize their infrastructure while ensuring compliance, security, and scalability. Cloud computing offers the perfect solution, providing banks, insurance companies, investment firms, and other financial institutions with a robust platform to handle core banking, payment processing, data analysis, and more.

1. Core Banking in the Cloud

Core banking systems are the backbone of financial institutions, handling everything from account management to transaction processing. Traditionally, core banking systems were hosted on-premises infrastructure, which could be expensive to maintain and scale. However, with the rise of cloud computing, financial institutions are increasingly migrating core banking operations to the cloud.

Benefits of Cloud for Core Banking:

1. **Scalability**: As financial transactions grow, banks need systems that can scale quickly. Cloud platforms like **AWS**, **Google Cloud**, and **Microsoft Azure** offer flexible and elastic infrastructure that allows banks to scale up or down based on demand, especially during peak times such as holidays or year-end.
2. **Cost Efficiency**: Cloud adoption reduces the need for large capital expenditures in hardware and maintenance. Financial institutions can move to a **pay-as-you-go model**, where they pay only for the resources they use.
3. **Availability and Reliability**: Cloud providers offer **multi-region deployments** and **disaster recovery** options, ensuring high availability of critical systems. This is crucial in the financial industry, where downtime can lead to significant revenue losses and customer dissatisfaction.
4. **Faster Innovation**: With cloud infrastructure, banks can roll out new products and services faster. For example, launching a new mobile banking application or adding AI-driven customer support is easier in the cloud than on legacy systems.

Example: Core Banking on AWS

Let's take a look at how a financial institution might implement core banking on AWS using **Amazon RDS** (Relational Database Service) and **Amazon EC2** (Elastic Compute Cloud).

1. **Provisioning an RDS Instance**:
   o A bank can use **Amazon RDS** to manage their relational databases (such as MySQL or PostgreSQL) for storing customer accounts, transactions, and other financial data.

   Example of provisioning an RDS instance for core banking:

```
aws rds create-db-instance \
  --db-instance-identifier core-banking-db \
  --db-instance-class db.m5.large \
  --engine mysql \
  --allocated-storage 100 \
```

```
--master-username admin \
--master-user-password 'securepassword123' \
--multi-az \
--backup-retention-period 7
```

This command creates a highly available **MySQL** database instance, ensuring that the core banking data is stored securely with backup and failover capabilities.

2. **Running EC2 Instances for Processing**: Financial institutions often need powerful computing resources for transaction processing. **Amazon EC2** instances can run the necessary workloads for transaction processing and handle real-time data analysis.

Example of creating an EC2 instance:

```
aws ec2 run-instances \
  --image-id ami-0c55b159cbfafe1f0 \
  --count 1 \
  --instance-type t2.micro \
  --key-name banking-key \
  --security-group-ids sg-0123456789abcdef0
```

2. Cloud Solutions for Payment Processing

Payment processing is another core function for financial institutions, involving real-time transaction handling, fraud detection, and settlement. Cloud solutions offer the scalability, reliability, and security required to process thousands (or even millions) of payments daily.

Benefits of Cloud for Payment Processing:

1. **Real-Time Processing**: With cloud-based solutions, banks and financial institutions can process payments in real-time, improving customer satisfaction by ensuring that payments and transfers are completed quickly.
2. **Fraud Detection**: Cloud platforms provide advanced machine learning (ML) capabilities that help detect fraudulent transactions by analyzing large volumes of transaction data in real-time.
3. **PCI-DSS Compliance**: Cloud providers offer **PCI-DSS**-compliant services for payment data storage and processing. This is crucial

for banks and payment processors who must adhere to strict standards for handling payment card information.
4. **Global Reach**: Financial institutions can leverage the cloud's global infrastructure to offer payment processing services in multiple regions, with low latency and high availability.

Example: Payment Processing with Microsoft Azure

In Azure, financial institutions can leverage **Azure Payment Gateway** to handle payment transactions securely. Azure's **API Management** services allow easy integration with external payment networks, such as credit card networks and other financial institutions.

1. **Azure Payment Gateway Integration**: Azure integrates with payment gateways through **Azure API Management**, enabling financial institutions to securely route payment requests and manage transactions.
2. **Fraud Detection with Azure AI**: Using **Azure Machine Learning**, a bank can build predictive models to identify fraudulent transactions based on customer behavior, transaction patterns, and historical data.

---

3. Data Analysis and Business Intelligence in the Cloud

Cloud-based data analytics and business intelligence tools are transforming how financial institutions process and analyze data. Whether it's analyzing market trends, predicting customer behavior, or performing risk assessments, the cloud offers the computing power needed for advanced analytics.

Benefits of Cloud for Financial Data Analysis:

1. **Real-Time Analytics**: Cloud platforms allow for real-time data processing, which is crucial in a fast-paced financial environment where decisions need to be made quickly.
2. **Big Data Processing**: Financial institutions are often working with large volumes of transactional data. Cloud platforms like **AWS Redshift**, **Google BigQuery**, and **Azure Synapse Analytics** offer

managed data warehouses and tools for performing big data analytics.

3. **Predictive Analytics**: Financial organizations can use machine learning (ML) models in the cloud to predict future trends, such as loan defaults, stock market movements, and customer churn.

4. **Cost-Effective**: Cloud platforms provide the computational resources needed for data analytics without the need for investing in expensive on-premises hardware.

Example: AWS Redshift for Data Analysis

In this scenario, a financial institution wants to analyze customer transaction data stored in an **Amazon S3** data lake. They can use **Amazon Redshift** to query and analyze this data for insights into customer behavior and transaction trends.

1. **Setting Up Amazon Redshift**:
   o First, the institution provisions an Amazon Redshift cluster for performing analytics on large datasets.

   Example of creating a Redshift cluster:

```
aws redshift create-cluster \
  --cluster-identifier financial-analytics-cluster \
  --node-type dc2.large \
  --master-username admin \
  --master-user-password 'password123' \
  --database-name financial_db
```

2. **Querying Data from S3**:
   o After setting up the cluster, the financial institution can use SQL queries in **Amazon Redshift** to analyze customer transactions stored in **Amazon S3**.

   Example of querying data:

```
SELECT customer_id, SUM(transaction_amount)
FROM transactions
WHERE transaction_date BETWEEN '2023-01-01' AND '2023-12-31'
GROUP BY customer_id
HAVING SUM(transaction_amount) > 100000;
```

This query aggregates transactions for each customer in 2023 and identifies high-value customers for targeted marketing or further analysis.

4. Cloud Security and Compliance in the Financial Industry

Security and compliance are top priorities for financial institutions. Cloud providers have designed their infrastructure to meet the rigorous security requirements of the financial industry, including **PCI-DSS, SOC 2, ISO 27001**, and **GDPR**.

Cloud Security Benefits for Financial Institutions:

1. **Encryption**: Cloud platforms offer end-to-end encryption for data in transit and at rest, ensuring that financial data is protected from unauthorized access.
2. **Identity and Access Management (IAM)**: Cloud providers offer IAM tools that help financial institutions control who can access their systems and data, ensuring that only authorized personnel have access to sensitive information.
3. **Regulatory Compliance**: Major cloud providers offer built-in tools and services to help financial institutions comply with industry regulations, making it easier to pass audits and maintain certifications.

Example: Azure for Financial Data Security

Azure Security Center provides a comprehensive suite of tools for monitoring security and ensuring compliance across cloud services. Financial institutions can use **Azure Security Center** to track and manage vulnerabilities, implement security policies, and maintain continuous compliance with regulations like **PCI-DSS**.

Cloud computing has become a cornerstone of innovation in the financial industry, providing institutions with the scalability, flexibility, and security needed to meet evolving customer expectations and regulatory demands. By adopting cloud-based core banking solutions, payment processing systems, and data analytics platforms, financial institutions can improve efficiency, reduce costs, and gain insights that drive business growth.

9.2 Case Study: Cloud in Finance

The financial industry, known for handling vast amounts of sensitive data and operating under strict regulatory compliance standards, has been increasingly adopting cloud computing solutions. This transition is not without its challenges, particularly in terms of security, data privacy, and regulatory compliance. However, with the right approach, cloud computing can offer significant advantages in terms of scalability, efficiency, cost-effectiveness, and innovation.

Background: The Challenges Facing FinSecure Bank

FinSecure Bank, a mid-sized global bank, had a longstanding history of managing its IT infrastructure on-premises. However, as customer demands for digital services increased and the financial market became more competitive, the bank realized that its legacy systems were no longer meeting its needs. Some of the key challenges FinSecure faced included:

1. **Scalability Issues**: FinSecure's on-premises systems were unable to handle the increasing transaction volumes and data processing demands. The bank was frequently experiencing bottlenecks, especially during high-volume transaction periods such as holidays or end-of-quarter financial processing.
2. **Rising Operational Costs**: Maintaining and upgrading legacy infrastructure was becoming increasingly expensive. The bank needed to shift to a more cost-effective model to ensure its long-term sustainability.
3. **Security and Compliance**: As a financial institution, FinSecure Bank was bound by strict regulatory frameworks like **PCI-DSS** (Payment Card Industry Data Security Standard), **GDPR** (General Data Protection Regulation), and **SOX** (Sarbanes-Oxley Act).

Ensuring the confidentiality, integrity, and availability of data was a top priority.

4. **Innovation and Digital Transformation**: FinSecure Bank wanted to stay competitive in an increasingly digital world. Cloud computing offered an opportunity to rapidly deploy new services, such as mobile banking, AI-driven fraud detection, and real-time financial analytics, to enhance customer experience and operational efficiency.

Step 1: Cloud Adoption Strategy

To address these challenges, FinSecure Bank decided to migrate its core banking systems and infrastructure to the cloud. Their cloud adoption strategy was broken down into several key steps:

1. **Choosing the Right Cloud Provider**: After evaluating several options, FinSecure Bank decided to partner with **Amazon Web Services (AWS)** due to its robust offerings for the financial sector, including **AWS Financial Services** solutions, **high availability**, and **compliance with regulatory standards**.

2. **Establishing Security and Compliance Requirements**: FinSecure's IT team worked closely with the compliance department to ensure that all cloud-based solutions would meet or exceed the security and compliance standards required by industry regulations. They focused on ensuring the bank's data remained **secure**, **encrypted**, and **accessible** only to authorized personnel.

3. **Data Migration and Integration**: The bank decided to migrate its core banking system to the cloud, including customer accounts, transaction history, and other essential data. They also planned to integrate their existing on-premises systems with cloud-based services to minimize disruption during the migration process.

Step 2: Implementing Core Cloud Solutions

FinSecure Bank began implementing cloud solutions in stages to avoid system downtime and ensure seamless service to customers. Below is a breakdown of key cloud technologies they implemented.

1. Core Banking System Migration to AWS

The bank's **core banking system** was migrated to **Amazon RDS** (Relational Database Service), which provided a highly available, scalable, and secure relational database platform for storing customer accounts and transaction data.

- **High Availability**: The bank set up **Multi-AZ** deployments to ensure that their core banking database could failover automatically to a secondary database in the event of a failure, ensuring minimal downtime.
- **Automated Backups**: Automated backups were configured to comply with FinSecure's internal disaster recovery policies.

AWS RDS Command Example:

```
aws rds create-db-instance \
  --db-instance-identifier secure-core-banking-db \
  --db-instance-class db.m5.large \
  --engine mysql \
  --allocated-storage 100 \
  --master-username admin \
  --master-user-password 'strongpassword' \
  --multi-az \
  --backup-retention-period 7
```

This setup ensured that the core banking database was resilient, with automated backups and failover capabilities.

2. Payment Processing with AWS Payment Gateway

To handle online payment transactions securely, FinSecure integrated **AWS Payment Gateway** with their cloud infrastructure. This service allowed them to securely process payments in real-time, ensuring compliance with **PCI-DSS** requirements.

- **Transaction Data Encryption**: All transaction data was encrypted both **in transit** and **at rest** using **AWS KMS (Key Management Service)**.
- **Scalable Payment Processing**: AWS Elastic Load Balancing (ELB) was used to distribute incoming payment requests across

multiple application servers, ensuring scalability during high transaction periods.

Payment Gateway Configuration in AWS:

```
aws elb create-load-balancer \
  --load-balancer-name payment-gateway-lb \
  --listeners
"Protocol=HTTPS,LoadBalancerPort=443,InstanceProtocol=HTTP,
InstancePort=80" \
  --availability-zones us-east-1a us-east-1b
```

3. Real-Time Data Analysis with AWS Lambda and Redshift

To leverage real-time data for fraud detection and customer analytics, FinSecure Bank integrated **AWS Lambda** and **Amazon Redshift**.

- **AWS Lambda** was used to process transaction data in real-time, triggering fraud detection algorithms whenever a new transaction occurred.
- **Amazon Redshift**, a fully managed data warehouse, was used to analyze large datasets and generate insights into customer behavior, trends, and potential financial risks.

AWS Lambda Example:

```
aws lambda create-function \
  --function-name process-payment-transaction \
  --runtime python3.8 \
  --role arn:aws:iam::account-id:role/service-
role/LambdaRole \
  --handler lambda_function.lambda_handler \
  --zip-file fileb://function.zip
```

With this setup, FinSecure Bank was able to detect fraudulent transactions as they happened and take immediate action to mitigate risks.

4. Cloud Security and Compliance with AWS Services

To ensure that the bank's cloud infrastructure remained compliant with regulations such as **PCI-DSS**, **GDPR**, and **SOX**, FinSecure implemented several AWS security features:

- **Encryption**: All sensitive data was encrypted using **AWS KMS**, both in transit and at rest, ensuring data confidentiality.
- **Identity and Access Management (IAM)**: The bank set up **IAM policies** to control access to resources. Only authorized personnel could access sensitive data, and each user's actions were logged for auditing purposes.
- **CloudTrail**: AWS **CloudTrail** was enabled to provide a full audit trail of all actions taken on the bank's AWS infrastructure, ensuring compliance with industry standards.

IAM Role Example:

```
aws iam create-role \
  --role-name SecurePaymentProcessingRole \
  --assume-role-policy-document file://trust-policy.json
```

CloudTrail Command Example:

```
aws cloudtrail create-trail \
  --name finsecure-trail \
  --s3-bucket-name finsecure-logs \
  --include-global-service-events
```

Step 3: Results and Benefits

After migrating to the cloud, FinSecure Bank experienced several positive outcomes:

1. Increased Scalability and Reliability

- The bank was able to handle increased transaction volumes without worrying about scaling its infrastructure manually. **AWS Auto Scaling** allowed the bank to adjust its resources based on demand, ensuring a seamless customer experience even during peak hours.

2. Improved Security and Compliance

- By leveraging AWS's built-in security features like **IAM, KMS**, and **CloudTrail**, FinSecure was able to meet regulatory compliance requirements while ensuring that customer data was protected against unauthorized access or breaches.

3. Cost Efficiency

- The cloud enabled FinSecure to move to a **pay-as-you-go** pricing model, which meant they only paid for the computing power and storage they used. This led to a significant reduction in their IT infrastructure costs.

4. Faster Time to Market

- By migrating to the cloud, FinSecure was able to rapidly deploy new services like mobile banking, AI-driven fraud detection, and real-time transaction analytics, providing a competitive edge in the market.

5. Enhanced Customer Experience

- Real-time data processing and faster payment processing meant customers experienced quicker transaction confirmations and could access financial services with minimal delays.

Visual Aid: Cloud Architecture for FinSecure Bank

Below is a simplified diagram of the cloud architecture implemented by FinSecure Bank:

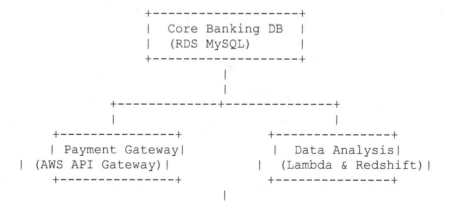

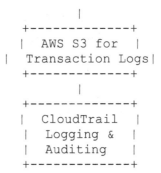

```
              |
 +--------------+
 |  AWS S3 for  |
 | Transaction Logs|
 +-------------+
              |
 +-------------+
 |  CloudTrail  |
 |  Logging &   |
 |  Auditing    |
 +-------------+
```

This architecture ensures high availability, scalability, and security while maintaining compliance with industry regulations.

This case study of **FinSecure Bank** demonstrates how cloud adoption can transform financial institutions by providing scalable, cost-effective, and secure solutions. By moving core banking, payment processing, and data analytics to the cloud, FinSecure was able to improve its operational efficiency, enhance customer experiences, and meet stringent compliance requirements.

Cloud computing offers financial institutions the flexibility to innovate rapidly, scale as needed, and secure sensitive data while staying competitive in a rapidly evolving industry. However, the adoption of cloud technology must be approached with a strong emphasis on security, compliance, and regulatory standards to mitigate risks and ensure the integrity of financial operations.

Chapter 10: Cloud Computing in Retail

The retail industry has undergone a massive transformation over the past decade, driven in large part by the adoption of cloud computing. Retail businesses, whether brick-and-mortar stores or online giants, now rely on cloud technologies to streamline operations, engage customers, and scale efficiently. From e-commerce platforms and inventory management systems to personalized customer service, cloud computing is at the heart of the modern retail experience.

In this chapter, we will explore how retail businesses leverage cloud technologies to optimize their e-commerce platforms, improve inventory management, and enhance customer engagement. Additionally, we will dive into a real-world case study to see how a retailer used the cloud to boost operational efficiency and enhance the overall customer experience.

10.1 E-commerce and Customer Engagement

The retail industry, particularly e-commerce, has evolved rapidly in the last decade, with cloud computing emerging as a transformative force. For retailers, leveraging cloud technologies has become crucial in building scalable, responsive, and engaging online platforms. By adopting the cloud, businesses can enhance their e-commerce operations, improve inventory management, and most importantly, offer personalized and seamless customer engagement experiences.

1. E-commerce Platforms in the Cloud

E-commerce platforms are the backbone of retail businesses that sell online. To meet the growing demands of customers, e-commerce platforms need to be fast, flexible, and scalable. The cloud offers several advantages in enabling these capabilities.

Advantages of Using Cloud for E-commerce:

1. **Scalability**: E-commerce platforms experience fluctuating traffic, especially during peak shopping seasons like Black Friday or Christmas. The cloud allows retailers to scale their resources up or down based on demand without any manual intervention.
2. **Cost Efficiency**: Cloud platforms operate on a pay-as-you-go model. This means businesses only pay for the resources they use, making cloud solutions more cost-effective compared to maintaining on-premises infrastructure.
3. **Security and Compliance**: Cloud service providers offer robust security features to protect sensitive data, such as **SSL/TLS encryption, firewalls**, and **multi-factor authentication (MFA)**, ensuring compliance with regulations such as **PCI-DSS** for payment processing.
4. **High Availability and Reliability**: Cloud infrastructure typically spans multiple data centers across regions. This geographic distribution ensures high availability and minimizes the risk of downtime, which is critical for e-commerce operations.
5. **Global Reach**: With cloud data centers located globally, businesses can ensure that their online stores provide fast load times and excellent user experiences to customers worldwide.

Example: Using AWS for E-commerce

AWS offers a comprehensive suite of tools to help retailers build and maintain their e-commerce platforms. These include:

- **Amazon EC2 (Elastic Compute Cloud)** for scalable compute capacity
- **Amazon RDS (Relational Database Service)** for managed database hosting
- **Amazon S3 (Simple Storage Service)** for storing product images and data
- **Amazon CloudFront** for content delivery (CDN)

Example of Setting Up a Scalable E-commerce Website on AWS:

1. **Launch EC2 Instances for the Website**: Start by setting up **Amazon EC2 instances** to run the e-commerce website backend.

```
aws ec2 run-instances \
  --image-id ami-xxxxxxxx \
  --count 2 \
  --instance-type t2.medium \
  --key-name my-key-pair \
  --security-group-ids sg-xxxxxxxx \
  --subnet-id subnet-xxxxxxxx
```

   In this example, we launch two EC2 instances, ensuring that the website can handle more traffic during high-demand periods.

2. **Set Up RDS for Database**: For storing product information, customer data, and transaction history, use **Amazon RDS**. The managed service ensures your database is highly available and automatically backed up.

```
aws rds create-db-instance \
  --db-instance-identifier ecommerce-db \
  --db-instance-class db.m5.large \
  --engine mysql \
  --allocated-storage 100 \
  --master-username admin \
  --master-user-password mypassword \
  --multi-az \
  --backup-retention-period 7
```

3. **Store Product Images on Amazon S3**: For efficient product image storage and retrieval, use **Amazon S3**. S3 is an object storage service that is highly scalable and cost-effective.
4. `aws s3 cp /local/image.jpg s3://ecommerce-bucket/product-images/`
5. **Distribute Content Globally with CloudFront**: **Amazon CloudFront** is a Content Delivery Network (CDN) that ensures fast delivery of your website's content, including images and videos, to users around the world.

```
aws cloudfront create-distribution \
  --origin-domain-name ecommerce-bucket.s3.amazonaws.com \
  --default-root-object index.html
```

With these AWS tools, you can create a scalable, secure, and cost-efficient e-commerce platform capable of handling fluctuating traffic and providing a seamless customer experience.

---

2. Enhancing Customer Engagement

Customer engagement is one of the most critical aspects of modern e-commerce. Cloud technologies offer several tools to help businesses create personalized experiences for their customers, improve customer support, and drive loyalty.

Key Strategies for Customer Engagement Using Cloud:

1. **Personalized Recommendations**: By using machine learning (ML) models, retailers can offer personalized product recommendations based on customer behavior, preferences, and browsing history.
   - **AWS Personalize** is a managed service that enables retailers to create individualized recommendations for customers by leveraging **machine learning**.
2. **Customer Support Automation**: Cloud platforms like **Google Cloud AI** and **AWS Lex** allow retailers to implement chatbots and virtual assistants to handle customer inquiries, provide product recommendations, and resolve issues in real-time.
3. **Targeted Marketing**: Cloud-based **Customer Relationship Management (CRM)** systems, such as **Salesforce** or **HubSpot**, allow retailers to segment their customers and send targeted marketing campaigns based on their purchase behavior and preferences.
4. **Omnichannel Engagement**: Cloud solutions enable retailers to engage with customers across multiple touchpoints—whether it's through the web, mobile app, email, or social media.

Example: Using AWS Personalize for Product Recommendations

With **AWS Personalize**, a retailer can deliver tailored product recommendations to users based on their browsing and purchasing history.

Steps to Integrate AWS Personalize:

1. **Create a Dataset Group**: Begin by creating a **dataset group** in AWS Personalize, which will store your data for personalized recommendations.

```
aws personalize create-dataset-group \
  --name ecommerce-dataset-group
```

2. **Import Historical Interaction Data**: The dataset group will contain interaction data such as product views, clicks, and purchases.

```
aws personalize create-dataset \
  --name ecommerce-interaction-dataset \
  --dataset-group-arn arn:aws:personalize:region:account-id:dataset-group/ecommerce-dataset-group \
  --schema arn:aws:personalize:region:account-id:schema/ecommerce-schema \
  --data-source s3://my-bucket/ecommerce-data.csv
```

3. **Train the Model**: AWS Personalize will automatically train a model using the historical data to generate recommendations.

```
aws personalize create-solution \
  --name ecommerce-solution \
  --dataset-group-arn arn:aws:personalize:region:account-id:dataset-group/ecommerce-dataset-group \
  --perform-auto-ml true
```

4. **Generate Recommendations**: Once the model is trained, retailers can use the trained model to generate personalized product recommendations for users.

```
aws personalize-runtime get-recommendations \
  --campaign-arn arn:aws:personalize:region:account-id:campaign/ecommerce-campaign \
  --user-id "user123"
```

With these steps, Retailer X can offer real-time personalized recommendations on their e-commerce platform, improving customer engagement and increasing conversion rates.

---

3. Inventory Management with Cloud Technologies

Cloud technologies are also transforming inventory management by providing retailers with real-time insights into stock levels, improving demand forecasting, and automating restocking processes.

Cloud-Based Inventory Management:

1. **Real-Time Stock Visibility**: Cloud-based inventory systems provide real-time visibility into stock levels, making it easier for retailers to track inventory across multiple locations and online channels.
2. **Automated Restocking**: By integrating **machine learning models** with inventory data, retailers can automate restocking decisions, reducing the risk of stockouts or overstocking.
3. **Integration with E-Commerce**: Cloud-based inventory systems can be seamlessly integrated with e-commerce platforms to ensure accurate stock levels are displayed on the website at all times.

Example: Using Google Cloud for Inventory Management

Google Cloud provides tools like **BigQuery** for analyzing inventory data and **Google Cloud Functions** for automating processes. For instance, Retailer X can analyze past sales data in **BigQuery** to predict future demand for a particular product.

BigQuery Example: Analyzing Sales Data to Forecast Demand:

```
SELECT product_id, SUM(quantity_sold) AS total_sales
FROM sales_data
WHERE sale_date BETWEEN '2023-01-01' AND '2023-12-31'
GROUP BY product_id
ORDER BY total_sales DESC
LIMIT 10;
```

This SQL query helps identify the top-selling products, which can inform inventory restocking and demand planning.

4. Case Study: Cloud in Retail - Retailer X's Success Story

Retailer X, a growing online fashion retailer, faced several operational challenges before adopting cloud technologies:

- **Manual inventory updates** led to inaccuracies in stock levels, resulting in stockouts or overstocking.
- **Slow website performance** during peak times resulted in poor customer experience and cart abandonment.
- **Limited personalization** for customers meant lost opportunities for upselling and cross-selling.

To address these challenges, Retailer X migrated its entire infrastructure to **AWS** and implemented cloud-based e-commerce solutions, personalized product recommendations, and automated inventory management.

Results:

- **Improved Website Performance**: The website's load times decreased by **25%**, and downtime was reduced to nearly zero, thanks to AWS's **Elastic Load Balancer** and **Auto Scaling**.
- **Increased Revenue**: Personalized recommendations powered by **AWS Personalize** led to a **30% increase** in average order value.
- **Operational Efficiency**: Real-time inventory management enabled by **AWS Lambda** and **Amazon RDS** reduced stockouts by **15%** and optimized the supply chain.

Cloud computing has revolutionized the retail industry, enabling businesses to scale efficiently, improve customer engagement, and optimize inventory management. By leveraging cloud-based services like **AWS EC2**, **AWS Personalize**, and **Google BigQuery**, retailers can deliver seamless shopping experiences, provide personalized recommendations, and streamline back-end operations.

10.2 Case Study: Cloud in Retail

Cloud computing has revolutionized the retail sector, enabling retailers to scale their businesses, improve operational efficiency, and enhance customer experience. In this case study, we'll explore how **Retailer X**, a growing e-commerce company specializing in fashion, leveraged cloud technologies to overcome operational challenges and enhance its competitiveness in the marketplace. This step-by-step guide will walk through the retailer's cloud adoption process, the tools and technologies used, and the tangible benefits realized from the transition.

Background: Retailer X's Initial Challenges

Retailer X had been operating successfully for several years, but with growth came new challenges. Despite its successes, the company was experiencing several inefficiencies that hindered further growth:

1. **Inventory Inaccuracies**: Retailer X operated both online and through physical retail locations. Managing inventory across these channels was difficult and led to stockouts, overstocking, and delays in fulfilling orders.
2. **Slow Website Performance**: During peak shopping seasons (e.g., Black Friday, end-of-season sales), the retailer's website would slow down, leading to poor customer experiences and cart abandonment.
3. **Limited Personalization**: Customer engagement was mostly generic. Retailer X lacked the ability to offer personalized product recommendations based on customer preferences and browsing behaviors.
4. **High Operational Costs**: Maintaining and scaling on-premises infrastructure was becoming increasingly expensive. The company needed a more cost-effective, flexible solution that would allow it to scale quickly and improve performance without overextending its budget.

Step 1: Identifying the Cloud Strategy

Retailer X's leadership decided to migrate to the cloud to address these challenges. Their goal was to:

- **Improve scalability** to handle high traffic during peak periods.

- **Enhance inventory management** with real-time stock visibility and forecasting.
- **Personalize the customer experience** using data-driven recommendations and targeted marketing.
- **Lower operational costs** by moving away from on-premises infrastructure.

After evaluating several cloud providers, Retailer X chose **Amazon Web Services (AWS)** because of its comprehensive offerings for e-commerce, scalability, and strong security and compliance features.

Step 2: Cloud Implementation and Tools Used

The migration process was carried out in stages to minimize disruption to ongoing operations. Below is an overview of the cloud solutions Retailer X implemented, focusing on core areas: e-commerce, inventory management, and customer engagement.

1. Migrating E-commerce Platform to the Cloud

Retailer X began by migrating their e-commerce platform to **AWS EC2** for compute resources. By doing so, they could ensure their platform could scale up or down according to demand without any downtime.

- **Elastic Load Balancing (ELB)** was used to distribute incoming traffic evenly across multiple EC2 instances, preventing any single instance from being overwhelmed.
- **AWS Auto Scaling** automatically adjusts the number of EC2 instances to meet traffic demands, ensuring high availability during peak shopping periods.

Example: Launching EC2 Instances for E-Commerce:

```
aws ec2 run-instances \
  --image-id ami-xxxxxxxx \
  --count 3 \
  --instance-type t2.medium \
  --key-name my-key-pair \
  --security-group-ids sg-xxxxxxxx \
  --subnet-id subnet-xxxxxxxx
```

This command starts three EC2 instances to handle high traffic, ensuring the e-commerce platform remains responsive even during high-traffic events.

2. Inventory Management with AWS

Retailer X used **Amazon RDS (Relational Database Service)** for storing and managing product data. By migrating their inventory data to the cloud, they could synchronize stock levels across their e-commerce platform and physical stores in real-time.

- **Amazon DynamoDB** was also implemented to store real-time transactional data, such as customer orders, while providing fast read and write access.
- **AWS Lambda** automated inventory updates. When a customer made a purchase, the inventory system automatically deducted the purchased quantity from stock, ensuring accurate stock levels.

Example: Setting Up RDS for Inventory:

```
aws rds create-db-instance \
  --db-instance-identifier ecommerce-inventory-db \
  --db-instance-class db.m5.large \
  --engine mysql \
  --allocated-storage 100 \
  --master-username admin \
  --master-user-password mypassword \
  --multi-az \
  --backup-retention-period 7
```

This command sets up a MySQL database for inventory management, ensuring that data is backed up and available even if a failure occurs.

3. Personalizing Customer Experience with AWS Personalize

Retailer X wanted to provide personalized product recommendations to increase sales and improve customer satisfaction. They implemented **AWS Personalize**, a machine learning service that enables real-time, personalized recommendations based on user behavior and preferences.

- **Customer Interaction Data**: Retailer X gathered historical data, including product views, purchases, and clicks, to train the recommendation model.
- **Real-Time Recommendations**: Using the trained model, Retailer X could offer personalized product suggestions on product pages, in email marketing campaigns, and on the homepage.

Example: Training a Recommendation Model with AWS Personalize:

1. **Create a Dataset**:

```
aws personalize create-dataset-group \
  --name ecommerce-dataset-group
```

2. **Import Interaction Data**:

```
aws personalize create-dataset \
  --name ecommerce-interaction-dataset \
  --dataset-group-arn arn:aws:personalize:region:account-
id:dataset-group/ecommerce-dataset-group \
  --schema arn:aws:personalize:region:account-
id:schema/ecommerce-schema \
  --data-source s3://my-bucket/ecommerce-data.csv
```

3. **Train the Model**:

```
aws personalize create-solution \
  --name ecommerce-solution \
  --dataset-group-arn arn:aws:personalize:region:account-
id:dataset-group/ecommerce-dataset-group \
  --perform-auto-ml true
```

This setup enables Retailer X to provide personalized recommendations to customers, driving higher engagement and sales.

4. Automated Marketing and Customer Engagement

Retailer X also implemented **Amazon SES (Simple Email Service)** and **AWS Pinpoint** for email marketing and targeted customer engagement. **Amazon SES** allowed them to send promotional emails at scale, while **AWS Pinpoint** provided customer segmentation and campaign analytics, enabling more effective targeting of high-value customers.

- **Segmentation**: Retailer X segmented their customer base based on purchasing behavior and used this data to send tailored promotions.
- **Real-Time Engagement**: Using **AWS Pinpoint**, the retailer could track user interactions with their marketing campaigns and adjust future campaigns based on user behavior.

Example: Sending Personalized Email Campaigns with Amazon SES:

```
aws ses send-email \
  --from "sales@retailerx.com" \
  --destination "ToAddresses=customer@domain.com" \
  --message "Subject={Data=Special Offer for
You},Body={Text={Data=Enjoy 20% off your next purchase at
Retailer X!}}"
```

This example sends a personalized email to a customer with a special offer, helping drive conversions and foster customer loyalty.

Step 3: Results and Benefits

After implementing these cloud technologies, Retailer X experienced significant improvements across various aspects of their operations:

1. Increased Website Performance

- **Reduced Load Time**: By using **AWS Elastic Load Balancer** and **Auto Scaling**, the retailer saw a **25% improvement** in website load times, even during high-traffic periods.
- **Reduced Downtime**: With **AWS Auto Scaling** and **RDS Multi-AZ deployments**, Retailer X minimized downtime and improved website reliability, ensuring a seamless shopping experience.

2. Enhanced Inventory Accuracy

- **Real-Time Updates**: The real-time inventory management system reduced stockouts by **15%** and overstocking by **10%**, ensuring products were available when customers wanted them.
- **Improved Forecasting**: By analyzing sales data in the cloud, Retailer X improved demand forecasting, leading to better stock planning and fewer missed sales opportunities.

3. Personalized Customer Experience

- **Increased Conversion Rates**: The personalized recommendations powered by **AWS Personalize** led to a **30% increase** in conversion rates.
- **Higher Average Order Value**: Personalized product suggestions helped increase **average order value (AOV)** by **20%** as customers added more items to their carts.

4. Cost Savings

- **Reduced Operational Costs**: By shifting to the cloud, Retailer X saved significantly on infrastructure and maintenance costs. The **pay-as-you-go** pricing model of AWS allowed the retailer to optimize costs and only pay for what they used, avoiding expensive upfront investments.

Visual Aid: Cloud Architecture for Retailer X

Below is a simplified diagram of Retailer X's cloud architecture:

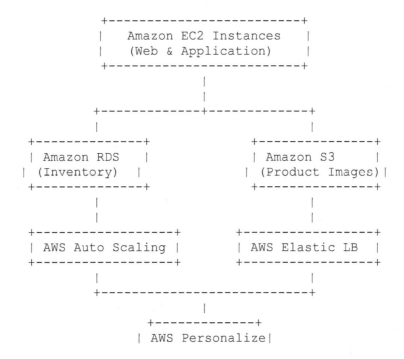

```
              +--------------------------+
              |    Amazon EC2 Instances  |
              |    (Web & Application)    |
              +--------------------------+
                           |
                           |
              +------------+------------+
              |                         |
    +--------------+            +---------------+
    | Amazon RDS   |            | Amazon S3     |
    | (Inventory)  |            | (Product Images)|
    +--------------+            +---------------+
           |                           |
           |                           |
    +------------------+        +-----------------+
    | AWS Auto Scaling |        | AWS Elastic LB  |
    +------------------+        +-----------------+
           |                           |
           +---------------------------+
                         |
              +-------------+
              | AWS Personalize|
```

```
    |  (Recommendations) |
    +--------------+
           |
    +--------------+
    |   Amazon SES  |
    | (Email Campaigns) |
    +--------------+
```

This case study of **Retailer X** illustrates the transformative power of cloud computing in the retail sector. By adopting **AWS EC2, RDS, S3, Auto Scaling**, and **AWS Personalize**, Retailer X was able to address key operational challenges, enhance customer engagement, and achieve tangible business results. Cloud technologies provided the scalability, flexibility, and cost-effectiveness needed to compete in the digital age while improving performance, customer experience, and inventory accuracy.

Part 5: The Future of Cloud Computing

Chapter 11: Emerging Cloud Trends

The cloud computing landscape is evolving rapidly, with new technologies and innovations constantly reshaping how businesses and individuals interact with data and applications. As organizations look to harness the full potential of cloud platforms, several emerging trends are poised to revolutionize the industry, making it more dynamic, efficient, and intelligent. In this chapter, we will explore three key emerging cloud trends: **Artificial Intelligence (AI) in the Cloud**, **Edge Computing**, and **5G's Impact on Cloud Services**.

11.1 The Role of Artificial Intelligence in Cloud

Artificial Intelligence (AI) has quickly become a powerful driver of innovation across industries, and cloud computing is one of the most effective platforms to scale AI solutions. By integrating AI and Machine Learning (ML) into cloud environments, businesses can enhance their operations, optimize workflows, and create intelligent applications that were previously unimaginable. This guide delves into how AI is integrated into cloud platforms, its benefits, practical applications, and how businesses can harness the power of AI to achieve their goals.

What is AI in the Cloud?

Artificial Intelligence in the cloud refers to the use of cloud-based services and infrastructure to deploy AI applications and models. These cloud-based AI solutions allow businesses to access powerful AI tools and capabilities without the need to manage physical hardware or infrastructure. Cloud providers like **Amazon Web Services (AWS)**, **Google Cloud**, and **Microsoft Azure** offer AI-as-a-Service, providing businesses with the ability to integrate machine learning models, natural language processing, predictive analytics, and more, directly into their applications.

AI in the cloud empowers businesses to build intelligent solutions that can:

- Analyze vast amounts of data in real-time
- Automate decision-making processes
- Provide personalized customer experiences
- Enable predictive maintenance and operations

How AI is Integrated into Cloud Platforms

Cloud platforms are becoming increasingly powerful in the realm of AI because they allow organizations to leverage the immense computational resources of the cloud to train, deploy, and scale AI models. Here's how cloud platforms make AI more accessible:

1. Pre-Built AI Services and APIs

Cloud providers offer a wide range of pre-built AI services that businesses can integrate directly into their applications without needing deep AI expertise. These services are designed to make AI accessible to all organizations, regardless of their technical capabilities.

Examples of Pre-Built AI Services:

- **Natural Language Processing (NLP)**: Services like **AWS Comprehend, Google Cloud Natural Language API**, and **Azure Text Analytics** allow businesses to analyze customer feedback, reviews, and social media posts to extract sentiment, key phrases, and entities.
- **Image Recognition**: **AWS Rekognition, Google Vision API**, and **Azure Computer Vision** allow businesses to build applications that can detect and classify images, recognize faces, and analyze videos for various purposes, from security to marketing.
- **Speech Recognition**: With **AWS Transcribe, Google Speech-to-Text**, and **Azure Speech Services**, businesses can convert speech

into text, making it easier to build voice-enabled applications, transcription tools, and customer service automation.

2. Custom AI and Machine Learning Models

In addition to pre-built services, cloud platforms also provide the tools and infrastructure necessary to build and train custom AI models. These platforms offer:

- **Managed Jupyter Notebooks** for model development
- **Scalable compute resources** to handle large datasets
- **Automated machine learning** (AutoML) features to simplify model creation

Cloud Services for Custom AI Models:

- **AWS SageMaker**: A fully managed service that provides everything needed to build, train, and deploy machine learning models at scale.
- **Google AI Platform**: A suite of tools for building custom machine learning models, including TensorFlow and PyTorch frameworks.
- **Azure Machine Learning**: A comprehensive platform for developing, training, and deploying AI models.

These tools allow businesses to work with their own data and create machine learning models that are fine-tuned for their specific needs, such as customer segmentation, predictive analytics, and fraud detection.

Key AI Capabilities in the Cloud

Let's break down some of the key AI capabilities that cloud platforms enable:

1. Predictive Analytics

Predictive analytics uses historical data, machine learning algorithms, and statistical models to predict future outcomes. In the cloud, businesses can use AI-powered predictive models to forecast sales, demand, and even customer behavior. By leveraging cloud-based AI tools, companies can gain insights into their operations, optimize inventory, and make informed decisions.

Example: A retail company could use AI to predict which products will be in high demand during the holiday season, optimizing stock levels and reducing waste.

2. Personalization and Recommendations

Cloud-based AI models allow businesses to deliver personalized experiences to their customers. By analyzing data on past behavior, preferences, and interactions, AI can suggest products, content, or services that are tailored to each individual customer.

Example: **Netflix** uses AI to recommend movies and TV shows based on the viewer's previous watching history. This personalized recommendation engine is built using machine learning models that run on cloud infrastructure.

3. Automation and Decision-Making

AI models in the cloud enable automation of complex tasks, such as customer service automation, fraud detection, and business process optimization. AI can analyze large datasets and make decisions in real-time, eliminating the need for human intervention in repetitive tasks.

Example: A bank could use AI to automatically flag suspicious transactions in real-time, improving fraud detection and reducing the need for manual oversight.

Practical Implementation of AI in the Cloud

Let's explore a practical example where **AWS SageMaker** is used to train a machine learning model for customer sentiment analysis. This example will show how businesses can leverage cloud-based AI tools to create intelligent applications.

Step 1: Setting Up AWS SageMaker

1. **Prepare the Dataset**: Store customer feedback (such as product reviews) in **Amazon S3**. This data will be used to train the sentiment analysis model.
2. **Launch a Jupyter Notebook Instance in SageMaker**: AWS SageMaker provides an environment for building and training machine learning models. You can use **Jupyter notebooks** to write your model code.

```
aws sagemaker create-notebook-instance \
  --notebook-instance-name sentiment-analysis-notebook \
  --instance-type ml.t2.medium \
  --role-arn arn:aws:iam::account-id:role/SageMakerRole
```

3. **Preprocess the Data**: Before training the model, preprocess the customer feedback data by tokenizing the text and transforming it into a suitable format for the model.

```
import pandas as pd
from sklearn.model_selection import train_test_split

# Load the customer feedback data
data = pd.read_csv('s3://my-bucket/customer_feedback.csv')

# Preprocess the text data
data['processed_text'] = data['feedback'].apply(lambda x:
x.lower())

# Split the data into training and testing sets
train_data, test_data = train_test_split(data,
test_size=0.2)
```

Step 2: Train the Model

1. **Create a Training Job** in SageMaker to train a sentiment analysis model on the processed data.

```
aws sagemaker create-training-job \
  --training-job-name sentiment-analysis-job \
  --algorithm-specification TrainingImage=amazon-sagemaker-
image,TrainingInputMode=File \
  --input-data-config file://training-data.json \
  --output-data-config file://output-data.json \
  --resource-config
InstanceCount=1,InstanceType=ml.m4.xlarge
```

2. **Train the Model**: SageMaker will train the model on your data, adjusting the weights of the model based on the feedback data.

Step 3: Deploy the Model for Real-Time Inference

Once the model is trained, deploy it as an endpoint in SageMaker to start making real-time predictions.

```
aws sagemaker create-endpoint \
  --endpoint-name sentiment-analysis-endpoint \
  --endpoint-config-name sentiment-analysis-config
```

Now, Retailer X can send customer feedback data to this endpoint to analyze sentiment (positive or negative).

Step 4: Make Predictions

Using the deployed model, send data to the endpoint to predict sentiment.

```python
import boto3

client = boto3.client('sagemaker-runtime')

response = client.invoke_endpoint(
    EndpointName='sentiment-analysis-endpoint',
    ContentType='application/json',
    Body='{"feedback": "I love this product!"}'
)

print(response['Body'].read().decode())
```

This will return the sentiment prediction for the customer feedback, helping Retailer X understand customer sentiment in real-time.

AI Use Cases in the Cloud

1. Healthcare: AI is being used to analyze medical data and assist in diagnostics. For example, AI models can detect patterns in medical images (such as MRIs or X-rays) to identify diseases early.

2. Retail: As mentioned, AI helps personalize customer recommendations and optimize inventory management, ensuring products are available when customers need them.

3. Finance: AI is used for fraud detection, risk analysis, and algorithmic trading. Machine learning models can analyze historical transaction data to predict fraudulent behavior and minimize financial risks.

Benefits of AI in the Cloud

- **Scalability**: The cloud provides the compute power needed to train large AI models, while also allowing businesses to scale their AI applications quickly as their data grows.
- **Cost-Effectiveness**: Cloud-based AI services eliminate the need for businesses to invest in expensive hardware and infrastructure. Instead, businesses only pay for the resources they use.
- **Access to Advanced Tools**: Cloud platforms offer access to advanced AI and ML tools that would be expensive and complex to set up on-premises.
- **Faster Innovation**: By leveraging pre-built AI services, businesses can quickly build and deploy AI solutions without needing specialized expertise.

AI in the cloud is enabling businesses to innovate faster, automate decision-making, and create personalized experiences for their customers. With AI-as-a-Service offerings and the ability to build custom AI models, cloud platforms make it easier for businesses to integrate intelligent applications into their operations. Whether it's enhancing customer service with chatbots, predicting trends with machine learning, or automating tasks to improve operational efficiency, AI is playing a central role in cloud computing's evolution.

11.2 Edge Computing and the Cloud

Edge computing is rapidly reshaping the way data is processed, stored, and analyzed. As businesses generate more data than ever before, particularly through IoT (Internet of Things) devices, there is a growing need for faster, more efficient processing. **Edge computing** addresses this need by bringing computation closer to the data source, rather than relying solely on centralized cloud servers. When paired with cloud computing, edge computing enables faster decision-making, reduced latency, and greater reliability, particularly in real-time applications.

What is Edge Computing?

At its core, **edge computing** involves processing data closer to where it is generated, such as on devices or local servers, rather than sending all data to centralized cloud data centers for processing. By handling data locally, edge computing reduces the amount of data that needs to be transmitted to the cloud, minimizing latency and bandwidth usage.

For example, think of a **smart thermostat** in a home. The thermostat generates data based on temperature readings and adjusts the environment accordingly. Rather than sending this data to a distant cloud server for processing and receiving commands back, the thermostat itself processes the data locally and makes decisions in real-time. However, the thermostat can still send relevant data (e.g., usage statistics) to the cloud for long-term storage, analysis, and insights.

Key Components of Edge Computing

1. **Edge Devices**: These are the physical devices or local servers that generate, collect, and process data. Examples include IoT devices, smart cameras, wearables, and sensors.
2. **Edge Gateways**: Gateways are intermediary devices that connect edge devices to the cloud. They aggregate data from multiple edge devices and perform preprocessing, filtering, and aggregation before sending it to the cloud.
3. **Edge Servers**: These are local servers or mini data centers located close to where data is generated. They perform more complex

computations than individual edge devices but are not as powerful as centralized cloud data centers.

4. **Cloud Integration**: While edge devices process data locally, they still rely on the cloud for storage, data analytics, and broader system management. Edge and cloud computing work together to provide both local processing and global-scale capabilities.

How Edge Computing Works with the Cloud

Edge computing does not replace cloud computing; rather, it complements it. The cloud provides centralized storage, powerful data analytics, and long-term processing capabilities, while edge computing brings data processing closer to the user, providing low-latency responses for time-sensitive tasks.

How the Integration Works:

1. **Local Processing with Edge Devices**: Data is processed locally on the edge device or edge server, reducing the need for sending large volumes of data to the cloud. This enables faster responses and improves reliability, especially in areas with limited connectivity.
2. **Aggregation at the Edge Gateway**: The edge gateway collects and aggregates data from multiple devices. It processes simple tasks locally, but if complex analysis is needed, it sends the relevant data to the cloud.
3. **Cloud for Analytics and Long-Term Storage**: The cloud handles long-term data storage, in-depth analytics, and machine learning tasks. While the edge devices handle immediate processing, the cloud can provide deeper insights by analyzing data from multiple sources over time.

Benefits of Edge Computing in Cloud Environments

The integration of edge computing with the cloud offers several advantages:

1. Reduced Latency

By processing data at the edge, the time it takes to respond to an event is significantly reduced. For real-time applications such as autonomous vehicles, industrial automation, and healthcare monitoring, low latency is crucial.

- **Example**: In **self-driving cars**, edge computing allows for real-time processing of sensor data (such as cameras and radar) to make decisions about steering, braking, and acceleration without relying on cloud latency.

2. Bandwidth Efficiency

Edge computing reduces the amount of data transmitted to the cloud, which lowers network congestion and decreases costs associated with data transfer.

- **Example**: In **smart homes**, sensors on smart devices collect data that is processed locally, with only the most relevant information sent to the cloud. This reduces bandwidth usage and prevents overwhelming the cloud with unnecessary data.

3. Enhanced Reliability

By processing data locally, edge computing ensures that devices can continue operating even when the internet connection to the cloud is disrupted. The edge device can perform tasks independently until the connection is restored.

- **Example**: In **healthcare**, edge devices like wearable health monitors can track a patient's vital signs in real-time, even without a constant connection to the cloud. Once the connection is restored, the data is uploaded for long-term analysis.

4. Scalability

Edge computing allows for scalable applications by distributing the load of data processing across many devices. As the number of connected devices grows, businesses can easily scale their operations by adding more edge devices without overwhelming the cloud infrastructure.

- **Example**: In **smart cities**, edge computing allows traffic lights, cameras, and sensors to process data locally, reducing the load on centralized cloud systems and allowing the city to scale more effectively.

Practical Implementation: Edge Computing with AWS IoT and Lambda

To demonstrate how edge computing can be integrated with the cloud, let's look at an example using **AWS IoT** and **AWS Lambda**.

Scenario: A company wants to monitor the temperature of refrigerators in remote stores. They deploy IoT temperature sensors that collect data and perform basic processing locally (edge). When an anomaly is detected (e.g., the temperature exceeds a certain threshold), the data is sent to the cloud for further analysis.

Step 1: Set Up AWS IoT for Device Communication

First, set up the **AWS IoT Core** service to connect IoT devices (temperature sensors) to the cloud.

1. **Create an IoT Thing**:
   - An IoT Thing represents the physical device in AWS IoT Core. Each temperature sensor is an IoT Thing.

```
aws iot create-thing --thing-name "fridge-sensor-01"
```

2. **Configure Device Certificates and Policies**:
   - Attach policies that define which resources the device can access.

```
aws iot create-keys-and-certificate --set-as-active \
  --certificate-pem-outfile "cert.pem" \
  --key-pair-outfile "key.pem"
```

3. **Connect Device to AWS IoT**:
   - o Use the generated certificate to establish a secure connection between the sensor and AWS IoT.

Step 2: Process Data Locally Using AWS IoT Greengrass

Next, use **AWS IoT Greengrass** to bring AWS cloud capabilities to edge devices. Greengrass enables local data processing, allowing the device to make decisions before sending data to the cloud.

1. **Install Greengrass Core** on the device:

```
aws greengrass create-group --name "fridge-monitoring-
group"
```

2. **Deploy Lambda Function** on the Edge:
   - o Write an AWS Lambda function to monitor the temperature locally. The function processes the sensor data and triggers an alert if the temperature exceeds the threshold.

```
import json

def lambda_handler(event, context):
    temperature = event['temperature']
    if temperature > 8:  # Threshold for alert
        print("ALERT: Refrigerator temperature too high!")
        # Send the data to the cloud for further processing
    return {
        'statusCode': 200,
        'body': json.dumps('Temperature Check Completed')
    }
```

Step 3: Sync with the Cloud for Long-Term Analysis

Once the local processing identifies an anomaly, the data is sent to the cloud for deeper analysis.

1. **Configure AWS IoT Rule** to trigger a Lambda function in the cloud:

```
aws iot create-topic-rule --rule-name "HighTempAlertRule" \
  --topic-rule-payload file://alert-rule.json
```

2. **Lambda Function in the Cloud**:

- The cloud function receives the temperature anomaly data and can log it for long-term analysis or send notifications.

Case Study: Edge Computing in Industrial IoT

Company: **Global Manufacturing Inc.**

Problem: Global Manufacturing Inc. operates a network of factories that produce machinery parts. The company faced challenges with **downtime** due to equipment failures and the **high cost** of transporting data to a central cloud server for analysis.

Solution: The company implemented **Edge Computing** to monitor factory equipment locally and predict failures before they occurred. By using IoT sensors to gather data from machines and **AWS IoT Greengrass** to process the data locally, the company was able to detect anomalies such as temperature fluctuations, vibration levels, and wear patterns in real-time.

1. **Edge Devices**: IoT sensors were placed on key machinery to collect operational data.
2. **Local Processing**: Using **AWS IoT Greengrass** and **AWS Lambda**, the data was processed at the edge. If a machine exceeded predefined thresholds (e.g., vibration levels indicating wear), an alert was triggered immediately.
3. **Cloud Sync**: Relevant data was sent to **Amazon S3** for long-term storage and analysis. Machine learning models ran in the cloud to predict maintenance needs and optimize production schedules.

Results:

- **Reduced Downtime**: Real-time anomaly detection reduced unexpected downtime by 25%.
- **Cost Savings**: By processing data locally, the company reduced the need for expensive data transfer to the cloud, saving on bandwidth costs.
- **Operational Efficiency**: The integration of edge computing and the cloud optimized machine maintenance schedules, leading to a more efficient production line.

Edge computing is a game-changer for industries that require low-latency, real-time data processing, particularly in scenarios involving large-scale IoT deployments. When combined with the cloud, edge computing enables businesses to process data locally for immediate decision-making while still leveraging the power of the cloud for analytics, storage, and global-scale operations.

Azure IoT Hub, and **Google Cloud IoT**, businesses can optimize operations, reduce costs, and improve responsiveness. As the number of connected devices continues to rise, the synergy between edge computing and cloud technologies will become increasingly essential for driving innovation and maintaining competitiveness in an increasingly digital world.

11.3 The Impact of 5G on Cloud Services

The introduction of **5G** technology is poised to revolutionize industries across the globe, particularly when it comes to cloud computing. 5G promises faster speeds, lower latency, and increased device connectivity, creating a new era of possibilities for cloud services. As 5G networks continue to roll out worldwide, businesses are beginning to realize the true potential of combining cloud computing with 5G technology. This combination has the power to accelerate digital transformation, optimize real-time applications, and drive new innovations in fields like autonomous vehicles, smart cities, healthcare, and beyond.

What is 5G and How Does it Impact Cloud Services?

5G refers to the fifth generation of mobile network technology. It is designed to provide faster internet speeds, lower latency, and support a higher density of connected devices compared to its predecessors (4G, 3G). The key features of 5G are:

- **Higher Speeds**: 5G can offer download speeds up to **10 Gbps**, which is up to 100 times faster than 4G.

- **Lower Latency**: Latency with 5G is reduced to **1 millisecond**, compared to **30-50 milliseconds** with 4G. This makes real-time communication and decision-making more efficient.
- **Increased Device Connectivity**: 5G supports a significantly higher number of devices per square kilometer (up to 1 million devices), making it ideal for IoT (Internet of Things) applications.

How 5G Integrates with Cloud Services:

5G enhances cloud services in several ways, enabling new use cases and improving the overall performance of cloud-based applications. Let's dive into the specific impacts:

1. Real-Time Data Processing and Low Latency Applications

One of the most significant advantages of 5G is its low latency, which dramatically reduces the time it takes for data to travel between the user's device and the cloud. In traditional cloud architectures, data is sent from edge devices to centralized data centers for processing. However, 5G's low-latency capabilities make it possible to process data in real-time at the edge, near the device, before sending it to the cloud for further analysis and storage.

How This Impacts Cloud Services:

- **Real-Time Decision Making**: 5G allows for the quick processing of data in cloud environments, making it easier for applications that require instant decision-making, such as **autonomous vehicles, smart manufacturing**, and **virtual reality (VR)** applications.
- **Increased Cloud Adoption for Real-Time Applications**: Industries such as healthcare and finance can benefit from 5G's speed and latency, enabling applications like **telemedicine** for real-time patient monitoring and **high-frequency trading** in the financial sector.

Example Use Case: Autonomous Vehicles

Autonomous vehicles rely on processing a significant amount of data in real-time, such as sensor data, traffic signals, and road conditions. With 5G's low latency, the vehicle can communicate with cloud services quickly, making real-time adjustments to its course, speed, and behavior. This data is processed both on the edge (e.g., vehicle sensors) and in the cloud (e.g., centralized processing for traffic data), resulting in faster, more accurate decisions.

---

2. Enhanced Cloud Gaming and Streaming

5G's high bandwidth and low latency make it ideal for **cloud gaming** and **video streaming** applications. Traditionally, cloud gaming services such as **Google Stadia** or **NVIDIA GeForce NOW** experience latency issues when streaming data-heavy games from cloud servers to end users, often resulting in delayed responses or poor user experiences. With 5G, cloud gaming can become more seamless.

How This Impacts Cloud Services:

- **Improved Streaming Quality**: 5G allows for faster data transmission, enabling **4K** or even **8K video streaming** with minimal buffering and lag.
- **Seamless User Experience**: With the reduced latency and high bandwidth that 5G provides, cloud-based gaming and streaming services can deliver a superior experience with minimal lag, supporting high-quality, real-time content delivery.

Example Use Case: **Cloud Gaming with 5G**

With 5G's ultra-low latency, players can enjoy immersive **cloud-based gaming** experiences without the need for powerful local hardware. Games are processed on cloud servers, and the visual output is streamed to the player's device in real-time. Whether it's a mobile phone, tablet, or laptop, 5G can deliver an experience almost identical to traditional gaming consoles or PCs, without the need for heavy local processing.

---

3. IoT and Smart Cities

5G enables the connectivity of millions of devices in a small area, which is crucial for **IoT (Internet of Things)** applications and the development of **smart cities**. With 5G, the ability to collect, transmit, and process vast amounts of data from IoT devices at high speeds and low latency becomes feasible.

How This Impacts Cloud Services:

- **Efficient Data Collection and Analysis**: In a smart city, 5G can connect millions of sensors, from traffic lights to environmental sensors. The cloud can handle the data aggregation, analysis, and storage, enabling smarter urban management.
- **Real-Time Monitoring**: 5G's real-time capabilities enable constant monitoring and feedback. For instance, in smart cities, real-time data from **traffic cameras**, **public transportation systems**, and **weather stations** can be processed and analyzed in the cloud, helping local governments optimize traffic flow, energy consumption, and emergency response times.

Example Use Case: **Smart Traffic Management with 5G**

In a smart city, **traffic cameras** and **sensors** embedded in the road can send data in real-time to the cloud, where AI and machine learning models process the information to optimize traffic flow. For instance, traffic lights can change based on real-time traffic patterns, improving city-wide traffic efficiency and reducing congestion.

---

4. The Role of Edge Computing and Cloud Synergy

Edge computing is crucial in the 5G era because it enables data processing closer to the source, reducing latency and allowing for faster decision-making. However, edge computing alone cannot handle large-scale data analysis or long-term storage. This is where cloud computing comes in.

5G enables better integration between **edge computing** and the **cloud**, creating a hybrid model where edge devices process data locally, and only critical or aggregated data is sent to the cloud for deeper analysis and storage.

How This Impacts Cloud Services:

- **Edge-to-Cloud Integration**: With 5G, more devices can perform local computations at the edge, reducing the load on centralized cloud data centers. Only important data or long-term storage requirements are sent to the cloud, optimizing bandwidth usage and reducing costs.
- **Hybrid Cloud and Edge Deployments**: Businesses can implement hybrid models, where real-time edge processing works in tandem with cloud services, providing both local processing power and global-scale analytics.

Example Use Case: **Industrial IoT (IIoT) in Manufacturing**

In **smart factories**, machines equipped with sensors collect data on temperature, pressure, and machine health. Edge computing devices process this data locally, immediately detecting anomalies and triggering corrective actions (e.g., shutting down a malfunctioning machine). Meanwhile, non-urgent data is sent to the cloud for deeper analysis, providing long-term insights into machine performance trends and predictive maintenance.

---

5. Improved Security and Privacy

With 5G, cloud services can implement more robust security and privacy measures. By processing data locally on edge devices, sensitive information can be kept closer to its source, reducing the risk of data interception during transmission. Furthermore, the increased bandwidth and low latency allow for better real-time monitoring and threat detection, enabling cloud providers to deploy security solutions that react faster to potential breaches.

- **Secure Data Transmission**: 5G enables better encryption and data integrity across cloud services, ensuring that data is securely transmitted to and from cloud servers.
- **Real-Time Security**: Cloud services can process data from multiple devices in real-time to detect unusual behavior, such as a sudden surge in traffic or unauthorized access attempts, allowing for faster responses to security threats.

Challenges and Considerations for Integrating 5G with Cloud Services

While the potential for 5G and cloud computing is vast, businesses must consider several factors when integrating these technologies:

1. **Infrastructure Costs**: Transitioning to 5G and integrating it with cloud services will require businesses to invest in new infrastructure, including edge devices, 5G antennas, and new cloud-based tools.
2. **Network Coverage**: The availability of 5G is still being rolled out in many regions. Businesses in areas without full 5G coverage may need to wait before realizing the full benefits.
3. **Security Concerns**: As more devices connect to the cloud via 5G, there is a higher risk of security breaches. Ensuring secure connections and encrypted data transmission will be essential to maintaining privacy and safety.
4. **Data Management**: With the vast amounts of data generated by 5G-connected devices, businesses will need to manage storage, processing, and real-time analytics effectively, ensuring that cloud services can handle the increased data load.

5G is set to revolutionize cloud services by enabling real-time, low-latency applications that were previously unimaginable. The integration of **edge computing** and **cloud computing** with 5G will unlock new opportunities across industries, from **autonomous vehicles** and **smart cities** to **cloud gaming** and **healthcare**. By embracing these

Chapter 12: Conclusion and Next Steps

As we wrap up our exploration of cloud computing, it's clear that the cloud is more than just a technological shift—it's a transformative force that's reshaping industries, creating new business models, and unlocking previously unimaginable opportunities. In this final chapter, we'll guide you through the essential next steps to help you take full advantage of the cloud's potential, both professionally and personally. Whether you're looking to build a career in cloud computing or keep up with the fast-paced world of cloud innovations, this chapter will provide you with practical advice and actionable insights to stay ahead.

12.1 Building a Cloud Career

Cloud computing has become one of the most sought-after skills in the tech industry. As businesses continue to adopt cloud services, the demand for professionals with cloud expertise has skyrocketed. Whether you're looking to enter the industry or further your career, this guide will provide you with detailed steps and expert advice on how to build a successful career in cloud computing.

We'll break down the essential skills you need, the certifications that will set you apart, and practical advice on navigating the ever-evolving cloud landscape. Whether you're eyeing a role as a **cloud architect**, **cloud engineer**, **cloud developer**, or **cloud security specialist**, this chapter will serve as a roadmap for getting started and excelling in the cloud space.

1. Understanding the Cloud Career Landscape

Cloud computing is vast and covers a range of roles, each requiring different skill sets. To embark on your cloud career, it's important to first understand the different paths you can take within the cloud domain.

Common Cloud Roles:

1. **Cloud Architect**: Cloud architects are responsible for designing and managing cloud infrastructure. This role involves defining the cloud architecture and ensuring it aligns with business needs. A cloud architect needs strong knowledge of cloud platforms (AWS, Azure, Google Cloud), networking, security, and cost management.
2. **Cloud Engineer**: Cloud engineers implement and manage the cloud infrastructure set by cloud architects. They ensure that cloud-based systems are running efficiently, automating deployment, and maintaining infrastructure. Cloud engineers typically need skills in **Infrastructure as Code (IaC)** tools like **Terraform** or **AWS CloudFormation**.
3. **Cloud Developer**: Cloud developers focus on building applications and services that run on the cloud. They use cloud APIs and tools to build scalable, efficient applications. Developers in the cloud often need to know languages such as **Python, Java,** or **Node.js** and be familiar with cloud platforms like **AWS Lambda** (serverless) or **Google App Engine** (PaaS).
4. **Cloud Security Specialist**: With more sensitive data stored in the cloud, businesses need professionals who specialize in securing cloud environments. Cloud security specialists work on **Identity and Access Management (IAM), encryption, firewalls**, and **compliance** standards like **PCI-DSS** or **GDPR**.
5. **DevOps Engineer**: DevOps engineers combine development and IT operations to automate and streamline processes for building, testing, and deploying applications. Cloud-based DevOps tools (such as **AWS CodePipeline** or **Jenkins**) are key to improving continuous integration/continuous deployment (CI/CD) pipelines.

Choosing the Right Role:

The first step to building a cloud career is to identify the role that most excites you. For example:

- If you enjoy designing systems and have a strong grasp of infrastructure, a **Cloud Architect** role might be the right fit.
- If you like coding and developing applications, a **Cloud Developer** role might align with your interests.

- If you're more inclined toward operational tasks and automation, consider **Cloud Engineering** or **DevOps**.
- If security and privacy are your passions, becoming a **Cloud Security Specialist** is a fantastic choice.

---

2. Acquiring Essential Cloud Skills

To stand out in the competitive cloud job market, it's essential to build a strong foundation in the core skills that cloud professionals need. These skills can vary depending on the role, but there are some common skills that will be beneficial across most cloud positions.

Technical Skills for Cloud Careers:

1. **Cloud Platforms**: You must be proficient in the main cloud platforms—**Amazon Web Services (AWS)**, **Microsoft Azure**, and **Google Cloud Platform (GCP)**. Familiarity with these services and their offerings (e.g., computing, storage, networking, security) is fundamental.
   - **AWS**: Widely used for infrastructure services and serverless computing.
   - **Azure**: Popular in enterprise settings, especially for integration with Microsoft services.
   - **Google Cloud**: Known for data analytics, AI/ML, and Kubernetes.

   Practical Tip: Start by getting hands-on experience with the free tiers of these platforms. For example, **AWS Free Tier** allows you to experiment with basic services like EC2, Lambda, and S3.

2. **Infrastructure as Code (IaC)**: Modern cloud applications rely heavily on automation, and **Infrastructure as Code (IaC)** tools like **Terraform**, **AWS CloudFormation**, or **Azure Resource Manager (ARM)** are essential for deploying and managing cloud resources automatically.
   - **Terraform** is a popular IaC tool that allows you to define cloud infrastructure using declarative configuration files.
   - **AWS CloudFormation** helps you model and provision AWS resources in a secure, automated manner.

Practical Tip: Create a small project using Terraform to automate the deployment of infrastructure in AWS, like launching EC2 instances or setting up an S3 bucket.

3. **Cloud Security and Compliance**: Security is critical in cloud environments, so you'll need to learn about encryption, identity management, IAM policies, secure access, and multi-factor authentication (MFA). Familiarity with industry standards such as **PCI-DSS**, **HIPAA**, and **GDPR** will also be beneficial.

   Practical Tip: Start by reading AWS's **Shared Responsibility Model** and learn how security is divided between the cloud provider and the customer.

4. **Containers and Kubernetes**: Cloud-native applications often use **containers** (like Docker) and **Kubernetes** for orchestration. As a cloud professional, learning about **Docker** for containerization and **Kubernetes** for container orchestration is crucial.

   Practical Tip: Set up a Kubernetes cluster using **Google Kubernetes Engine (GKE)** or **Amazon EKS**, and deploy simple applications on it.

5. **DevOps Tools**: Understanding DevOps principles and tools is highly recommended, as many cloud roles are integrated with CI/CD processes. Learn about tools like **Jenkins**, **CircleCI**, **GitLab CI**, and cloud-native CI/CD tools like **AWS CodePipeline**.

---

3. Earning Cloud Certifications

Certifications play an essential role in building a cloud career, especially when you're just starting. They validate your knowledge, provide structure to your learning path, and make your resume stand out. Here are some of the most popular cloud certifications:

- **AWS Certified Solutions Architect – Associate**: Ideal for cloud architects, this certification focuses on designing and deploying scalable systems on AWS.
- **AWS Certified Developer – Associate**: Aimed at developers, this certification covers building applications and deploying them in AWS.
- **AWS Certified Cloud Practitioner**: A foundational certification that covers basic cloud concepts and AWS services.

Azure Certifications:

- **Microsoft Certified: Azure Fundamentals**: This entry-level certification is perfect for beginners and covers the core Azure services.
- **Microsoft Certified: Azure Solutions Architect Expert**: For professionals looking to design and implement Azure solutions.
- **Microsoft Certified: Azure DevOps Engineer Expert**: For those interested in DevOps roles using Azure tools.

Google Cloud Certifications:

- **Google Cloud Associate Cloud Engineer**: An entry-level certification focused on deploying applications and managing cloud resources.
- **Google Cloud Professional Cloud Architect**: Ideal for professionals who want to design and manage cloud solutions on Google Cloud.

Practical Tip: Start with an entry-level certification, like AWS Certified Cloud Practitioner or Microsoft Certified: Azure Fundamentals, and work your way up. These certifications give you foundational knowledge and a structured path to advance your career.

---

4. Building a Cloud Portfolio

Once you've acquired the necessary skills and certifications, it's time to showcase your expertise. A strong portfolio is a great way to demonstrate your cloud skills to potential employers.

Steps to Build Your Cloud Portfolio:

1. **Create Cloud-Based Projects**: Build small applications and solutions that demonstrate your ability to work with cloud platforms. Some examples include:
   - Deploying a **web app** using **AWS Elastic Beanstalk** or **Google App Engine**.
   - Automating infrastructure deployment with **Terraform**.
   - Setting up a **CI/CD pipeline** on **AWS CodePipeline**.
2. **Contribute to Open-Source Projects**: Join open-source cloud projects on platforms like **GitHub**. Contributing to open-source projects not only improves your skills but also demonstrates your collaborative abilities.
3. **Write About Your Cloud Journey**: Share blog posts or articles about your learning process, cloud projects, and certifications. You can write about topics like setting up cloud infrastructure, managing cloud security, or deploying a machine learning model in the cloud.
4. **Host Your Projects on GitHub**: GitHub is the go-to place for showcasing coding and infrastructure projects. Upload your cloud projects and make them available for others to review.

---

5. Gaining Experience through Internships and Jobs

While certifications and a portfolio are essential, hands-on experience is critical for deepening your understanding of cloud computing. Consider internships, entry-level roles, or freelance opportunities to get real-world experience. Here are some steps you can take:

1. Apply for Internships: Many cloud providers and tech companies offer internships for aspiring cloud professionals. This is a great way to get experience with cloud platforms and learn from senior experts.

2. Look for Entry-Level Cloud Jobs: Positions like Cloud Support Engineer, Cloud Operations Associate, or Junior Cloud Developer are great starting points for gaining experience.

3. Freelance Cloud Projects: If you're looking to gain practical experience quickly, freelance work can offer opportunities to build cloud solutions for businesses. Websites like Upwork and Freelancer offer freelance cloud projects that can help you develop your skills while getting paid.

---

6. Networking and Staying Up-to-Date

The cloud industry is fast-paced, with new technologies, tools, and trends emerging all the time. To stay competitive, you must network with industry professionals and stay current with cloud innovations.

Ways to Network:

- **Cloud Conferences and Meetups**: Attend events like **AWS re:Invent**, **Microsoft Ignite**, or **Google Cloud Next**. These conferences are fantastic for learning about the latest cloud advancements and networking with cloud professionals.
- **Join Cloud Communities**: Participate in online communities such as **Reddit's cloud computing forums**, **LinkedIn groups**, or **cloud-specific Slack channels**.

Ways to Stay Current:

- **Follow Blogs and News**: Stay informed by reading cloud computing blogs, news sites, and vendor-specific announcements.
- **Engage in Continuous Learning**: Take online courses (like those offered by **Coursera**, **Pluralsight**, or **Udemy**) to stay updated on new tools and cloud practices.

Building a career in cloud computing offers incredible opportunities, and with the right approach, you can successfully enter this dynamic field. Start by choosing the right role, mastering essential skills, and earning certifications. Then, build a portfolio to demonstrate your expertise and gain real-world experience through internships or entry-level jobs. Stay engaged with the cloud community and continue learning to ensure you remain competitive in this fast-paced industry.

12.2 Keeping Up with Cloud Innovations

The cloud computing landscape is evolving at an unprecedented rate. As new services, technologies, and trends emerge, it can be challenging to stay up-to-date with the latest developments. However, keeping current is crucial not only to advance your career but also to stay competitive and leverage the most advanced tools in cloud computing.

1. Follow Key Cloud Industry News Sources

One of the best ways to stay updated on cloud innovations is to follow industry-leading blogs, news sources, and thought leaders. These sources will provide you with insights into new services, upcoming releases, industry trends, and expert opinions.

Recommended Blogs and Websites:

1. **AWS Blog**: AWS regularly publishes updates, new service announcements, tutorials, and case studies. It's an essential resource for anyone working with AWS.
   o **Link**: AWS Blog
2. **Google Cloud Blog**: Google Cloud shares technical articles, product updates, and solutions that focus on real-world cloud use cases.
   o **Link**: Google Cloud Blog
3. **Microsoft Azure Blog**: Microsoft Azure offers deep insights into their services, as well as new features, community-driven initiatives, and case studies.
   o **Link**: Microsoft Azure Blog
4. **The New Stack**: This site provides articles on cloud-native applications, Kubernetes, microservices, DevOps, and other cutting-edge technologies in the cloud ecosystem.

- o **Link**: The New Stack
5. **Cloud Academy Blog**: Cloud Academy offers not only training but also insightful articles and blogs on cloud computing, DevOps, and emerging cloud technologies.
   - o **Link**: Cloud Academy Blog

How to Stay Engaged with Blogs:

- **RSS Feeds**: Set up RSS feeds for the cloud blogs you follow to receive updates instantly.
- **Newsletters**: Subscribe to newsletters from major cloud providers. For instance, AWS and Google Cloud offer weekly or monthly newsletters with updates and announcements.

---

2. Attend Cloud Conferences and Events

Attending cloud-related conferences and events allows you to hear directly from experts, learn about cutting-edge technologies, and network with fellow cloud professionals. Conferences also provide the opportunity to gain hands-on experience through workshops and labs, which are invaluable for keeping your skills sharp.

Popular Cloud Conferences:

- **AWS re:Invent**: The annual event for AWS users where major announcements are made, and in-depth technical sessions are offered. It's one of the largest gatherings of cloud professionals in the world.
   - o **Link**: AWS re:Invent
- **Google Cloud Next**: Google's flagship conference, where they showcase new products and cloud strategies. It's ideal for anyone working with Google Cloud or interested in cloud-native technologies.
   - o **Link**: Google Cloud Next
- **Microsoft Ignite**: A premier Microsoft conference for IT professionals and developers. It covers a wide range of topics, from cloud infrastructure and security to AI and machine learning on Azure.
   - o **Link**: Microsoft Ignite

- **KubeCon + CloudNativeCon**: Focused on Kubernetes and cloud-native technologies, KubeCon is the go-to event for anyone working with containers, microservices, and orchestration platforms.
  - o **Link**: KubeCon + CloudNativeCon

How to Get the Most Out of Conferences:

- **Engage in Networking**: Connect with other attendees, speakers, and exhibitors. Share knowledge and get different perspectives on cloud technologies.
- **Hands-On Labs**: Most conferences offer workshops or hands-on labs where you can learn new tools and techniques. Participating in these sessions will help solidify your knowledge.
- **Take Notes and Follow Up**: After each session, take notes and revisit them later. Follow up with speakers and peers to deepen your understanding.

---

3. Join Cloud Communities and Forums

Cloud communities and forums provide an excellent opportunity to learn from peers, ask questions, and stay up-to-date with emerging technologies. Joining communities can help you expand your knowledge by seeing how other professionals approach cloud challenges and solutions.

Top Cloud Communities:

1. **Reddit's r/cloudcomputing**: A popular forum for cloud professionals to discuss the latest trends, ask for advice, and share experiences. It's an excellent source for real-time discussions on cloud developments.
   - o **Link**: r/cloudcomputing
2. **Stack Overflow**: A platform where cloud developers can post questions related to cloud programming, DevOps, automation, and deployment.
   - o **Link**: Stack Overflow
3. **LinkedIn Groups**: There are several LinkedIn groups dedicated to cloud computing, such as "Cloud Computing" or "Cloud

Architects." These groups share articles, news, job opportunities, and discussions related to the latest cloud innovations.

4. **Cloud Community Slack Channels**: Many cloud services, such as **AWS**, **Azure**, and **Google Cloud**, offer official Slack channels for networking and real-time discussions.

How to Stay Engaged:

- **Be Active**: Don't just lurk—actively participate in discussions, ask questions, and contribute your insights.
- **Follow Thought Leaders**: Many cloud professionals share updates and thoughts on the latest trends. Follow these thought leaders on platforms like **Twitter** and **LinkedIn** to gain insights into the cloud industry.

---

4. Enroll in Continuous Learning Platforms

As cloud technologies evolve, staying ahead of the curve requires continuous learning. Platforms like **Coursera**, **Udemy**, and **Pluralsight** offer up-to-date courses on cloud services, tools, and frameworks, often created by industry experts.

Popular Platforms for Continuous Learning:

1. **Cloud Academy**: Offers specialized cloud training courses for various cloud providers, including AWS, Azure, and Google Cloud. It also provides hands-on labs and certifications.
   - **Link**: Cloud Academy
2. **A Cloud Guru**: Known for its comprehensive cloud certifications and training courses, A Cloud Guru also has a community where you can interact with other learners and cloud professionals.
   - **Link**: A Cloud Guru
3. **Pluralsight**: Provides in-depth technical courses on cloud computing, including topics like DevOps, Kubernetes, and cloud-native application development.
   - **Link**: Pluralsight

- **Set Learning Goals**: Break down your learning into small, manageable milestones. For instance, focus on achieving certification in one cloud platform before branching out to others.
- **Experiment and Build Projects**: As you learn, build small cloud projects to apply what you're studying. This can be deploying a basic web app on AWS or using **Google Cloud's Firebase** for a mobile backend.

---

5. Leverage Vendor-Specific Resources

Each major cloud provider—AWS, Microsoft Azure, and Google Cloud—offers a wealth of resources to help users stay current with their products. These include documentation, free tutorials, and webinars on new services and features.

AWS:

- **AWS Training and Certification**: AWS provides free and paid training to help you learn about its cloud services and get certified.
    o **Link**: AWS Training
- **AWS Webinars**: AWS hosts regular webinars covering a wide range of topics, from machine learning to serverless architecture.
    o **Link**: AWS Webinars

Azure:

- **Microsoft Learn**: A free platform that offers learning paths for various Azure services and certifications.
    o **Link**: Microsoft Learn
- **Azure Friday**: A weekly video series that explores new Azure features and product deep dives.
    o **Link**: Azure Friday

- **Google Cloud Training**: Google Cloud offers free and paid learning resources, including courses on Kubernetes, machine learning, and cloud architecture.
    - **Link**: Google Cloud Training
- **Google Cloud Tech YouTube Channel**: Regular video updates on new features, services, and use cases for Google Cloud.
    - **Link**: Google Cloud Tech

---

6. Experiment with New Cloud Services and Tools

Staying up-to-date isn't just about reading articles and attending conferences—it's about getting your hands dirty with the latest cloud technologies. Cloud providers regularly release new services and tools, and experimenting with them is one of the best ways to learn and stay current.

How to Stay Engaged with New Tools:

- **Create Test Environments**: Use free tiers or sandbox environments provided by cloud platforms to experiment with new services (e.g., setting up **serverless architectures** or experimenting with **AI tools**).
- **Integrate New Features into Your Projects**: Whenever a new feature is announced, try to incorporate it into one of your existing projects. This could mean integrating a new AWS AI service into your app or deploying a new Kubernetes feature.
- **Join Beta Programs**: Many cloud providers offer early access to new features via beta programs. Participate in these to get hands-on experience with the latest tools before they become widely available.

Cloud computing is an ever-evolving field, and staying current with the latest innovations is crucial for success. By following the right resources, continuously learning, and engaging with the cloud community, you can ensure you stay ahead of the curve. Whether you're following blogs, attending conferences, taking online courses, or experimenting with new tools, your proactive approach to staying updated will help you leverage the latest cloud technologies to their fullest potential.

With 5G, edge computing, and AI-driven services continually transforming the cloud space, your career prospects and ability to innovate in cloud computing are only going to grow. Stay curious, stay connected, and keep building—this is just the beginning of what's possible with cloud computing.

Appendices

As we conclude this journey through the world of cloud computing, it's time to reflect on the key takeaways and provide additional resources that will help you continue your learning. The appendices will serve as a practical guide, offering quick references, essential tools, and valuable extra resources to make your cloud journey smoother and more efficient. Whether you're looking to dive deeper into specific topics, check out some helpful tools, or understand the next steps in your learning path, this section is here to help you out!

A1: Cloud Computing Glossary

Navigating the world of cloud computing can sometimes feel like learning a new language. Below, we've compiled a list of key terms and concepts that you'll encounter frequently. Understanding these terms will make it easier for you to digest advanced topics in cloud computing.

Key Cloud Terms:

- **IaaS (Infrastructure as a Service)**: A cloud service model where the provider supplies the infrastructure (e.g., servers, networking, storage) and the customer manages the operating system, applications, and data. **AWS EC2** is an example of IaaS.
- **PaaS (Platform as a Service)**: In PaaS, the cloud provider manages the infrastructure, runtime, and middleware, while the customer focuses on managing the applications. **Google App Engine** is a well-known example.
- **SaaS (Software as a Service)**: SaaS provides software applications that are delivered over the cloud. **Google Workspace (formerly G Suite)** and **Microsoft 365** are examples.
- **Hybrid Cloud**: A cloud environment that uses both on-premises infrastructure and public or private cloud services. It allows for data and applications to be shared between them.
- **Serverless Computing**: A cloud-computing model where the cloud provider runs the server and dynamically manages the allocation of resources. **AWS Lambda** is a prime example.

- **Containers**: Containers are a form of virtualization that allows developers to package applications and their dependencies together, ensuring that they run consistently across different computing environments. **Docker** is the most popular containerization platform.
- **Kubernetes**: A container orchestration platform that automates the deployment, scaling, and management of containerized applications.
- **Cloud Security**: Refers to the measures and controls used to protect data, applications, and services in the cloud. Key concepts include **IAM (Identity and Access Management)**, **encryption**, and **firewalls**.

A2: Useful Cloud Resources and Tools

Here's a curated list of useful tools, resources, and services that can help you gain deeper insights into cloud computing, build projects, and stay up-to-date with the latest cloud trends.

Cloud Providers Documentation and Learning Platforms:

1. **AWS Documentation**: The official AWS documentation covers everything from introductory topics to advanced tutorials. AWS also provides free training courses to get you started.
   - **Link**: AWS Documentation
2. **Azure Documentation**: The official Microsoft Azure documentation offers a deep dive into its services, tutorials, and guides.
   - **Link**: Azure Documentation
3. **Google Cloud Documentation**: Google Cloud's documentation is known for its clarity and step-by-step tutorials for developers.
   - **Link**: Google Cloud Documentation
4. **Cloud Academy**: A learning platform offering cloud-related courses, certifications, and hands-on labs for AWS, Azure, Google Cloud, and more.
   - **Link**: Cloud Academy
5. **A Cloud Guru**: A comprehensive cloud learning platform with courses, quizzes, and cloud labs for hands-on practice.
   - **Link**: A Cloud Guru

1. **Terraform**: A popular tool for Infrastructure as Code (IaC) that allows you to define cloud infrastructure using a configuration language.
   o **Link**: Terraform
2. **AWS CloudFormation**: AWS's own IaC tool for defining and provisioning infrastructure on AWS using templates.
   o **Link**: AWS CloudFormation
3. **Docker**: A tool for developing, shipping, and running applications in lightweight containers.
   o **Link**: Docker
4. **Kubernetes**: An open-source platform for managing containerized applications across clusters of machines.
   o **Link**: Kubernetes
5. **AWS Lambda**: A serverless computing service that lets you run code without provisioning or managing servers. Ideal for event-driven architecture.
   o **Link**: AWS Lambda
6. **Google Firebase**: A serverless platform for building and running mobile and web applications.
   o **Link**: Google Firebase

A3: Cloud Certifications Roadmap

Certifications are a great way to prove your cloud expertise. Below is a guide to help you decide which certifications align with your career goals.

Beginner Level:

- **AWS Certified Cloud Practitioner**: A foundational certification for beginners. It covers basic cloud concepts and AWS services.
  o **Link**: AWS Cloud Practitioner
- **Microsoft Certified: Azure Fundamentals**: For those new to cloud computing, it provides a high-level understanding of Azure services.
  o **Link**: Azure Fundamentals

- **Google Cloud Digital Leader**: An entry-level certification that covers the basic understanding of Google Cloud products and services.
  - o **Link**: Google Cloud Digital Leader

Intermediate Level:

- **AWS Certified Solutions Architect – Associate**: Ideal for cloud architects, this certification focuses on designing and deploying scalable and highly available systems.
  - o **Link**: AWS Solutions Architect Associate
- **Microsoft Certified: Azure Solutions Architect Expert**: For those who want to design and implement Azure solutions, including network and security.
  - o **Link**: Azure Solutions Architect Expert
- **Google Cloud Professional Cloud Architect**: Designed for professionals who want to design and manage scalable and secure solutions on Google Cloud.
  - o **Link**: Google Cloud Architect

Advanced Level:

- **AWS Certified DevOps Engineer – Professional**: Focuses on automating the processes of CI/CD, infrastructure management, and monitoring within AWS.
  - o **Link**: AWS DevOps Engineer
- **Microsoft Certified: Azure DevOps Engineer Expert**: Aimed at DevOps engineers who want to implement and manage CI/CD pipelines using Azure tools.
  - o **Link**: Azure DevOps Engineer Expert

A4: Common Cloud Architectures

Here are some common cloud architectures and patterns that cloud professionals should be familiar with:

1. Basic Web Application Architecture

Components:

- **Load Balancer**: Distributes incoming traffic across multiple web servers to ensure high availability and reliability.
- **Web Servers**: Handle HTTP requests and serve web pages.
- **Database**: Stores application data (e.g., MySQL, PostgreSQL).
- **Cache Layer**: Caching solutions (e.g., Redis) to store frequently accessed data for faster retrieval.

Diagram:

```
[User] --> [Load Balancer] --> [Web Servers] --> [Database]
```

2. Serverless Architecture

Components:

- **API Gateway**: Manages API requests, routes them to AWS Lambda functions.
- **AWS Lambda**: Runs code in response to events without needing to provision servers.
- **DynamoDB or S3**: Stores data generated by the serverless functions.
- **CloudWatch**: Monitors logs and metrics for serverless applications.

Diagram:

```
[User] --> [API Gateway] --> [AWS Lambda] --> [DynamoDB/S3]
```

A5: Cloud Career Resources

While certifications and hands-on experience are key to cloud careers, continuous learning and networking are just as important. Here are some resources to help you advance:

1. **LinkedIn Learning**: Offers a wide variety of cloud computing courses covering AWS, Azure, Google Cloud, DevOps, security, and more.

- o **Link**: LinkedIn Learning
2. **Cloud Academy**: Provides a rich library of cloud-related courses with practical labs and exercises.
   - o **Link**: Cloud Academy
3. **AWS Training and Certification**: The official AWS resource for learning paths, certifications, and self-paced training.
   - o **Link**: AWS Training
4. **Meetups and Cloud User Groups**: Find and attend meetups and user groups in your area for networking and learning opportunities. Websites like **Meetup.com** offer local cloud-related events.
5. **GitHub**: Explore open-source cloud projects to contribute to and learn from others in the community.
   - o **Link**: GitHub

The appendices provided in this chapter serve as essential tools and references to help you navigate the vast and ever-changing world of cloud computing. From understanding the key terms and tools, to discovering career resources and learning paths, these appendices will be your go-to guide as you embark on your cloud computing journey. The world of cloud is dynamic, and staying informed, engaged, and proactive is the best way to succeed in this exciting field!

www.ingramcontent.com/pod-product-compliance
Lightning Source LLC
LaVergne TN
LVHW082125070326
832902LV00041B/2562